MW01175121

A MONK FOR ALL SEASONS

Akhilananda
his life of love and service

A MONK FOR ALL SEASONS

Akhilananda
his life of love and service

"Arise, Awake..."
said Vivekananda

Elva Linnea Nelson

Llumina Press

ISBN: 978-1-59526-812-9 (PB)
       978-1-59526-813-6 (HC)

Printed in the United States of America by Llumina Press

Library of Congress Control Number: 2007903443

To those great ones who came here
the disciples
of the direct disciples of Ramakrishna
whom we all have known, revered and loved

TABLE OF CONTENTS

ILLUSTRATIONS

i

ACKNOWLEDGEMENTS

Grateful appreciation and many thanks to Swami Sarvagatananda, who suggested that I write about Swami Akhilananda, and to Swami Tyagananda for their helpful comments.

Many thanks to Dr. John Parks for sharing with me Swami Akhilananda's letters to him and his wife and for the letters of John Duane. We want to give thanks to those who kindly translated letters from Bengali into English: Swami Sarvatmananda, Dr. Chiranjab Sarkar, Dr. Sujit Purkayastha, Dr. Suprabhat Chatterjee, Maya De, and Bimal Lahiri. To Deborah Lowery many thanks for supplying information on the Internet.

Other devotees of Swami Akhilananda and friends have been very helpful. Carole Moreau for her information about Swami Akhilananda, many thanks. Also to Kinley Herboldsheimer and his daughter, Laurie, Dr. Frederick Shepard for their contributions. Many thanks to Jim and Jane Chadwick for supplying information on Swami Akhilananda in California, and to Pravrajika Brahmaprana for supplying letters of Swami Akhilananda to Mr. and Mrs. Louis. Others who have been very helpful: Chandi Sanyal, nephew of Swami Akhilananda, Libby Littlefield, the anonymous devotee, Jocelyn Todd, Joan Chadbourne, Asim Chaudhuri, and Ambalini Selvaraj. My thanks to Ron Elkin, the Computer Doctor for typing the manuscript and putting it on a CD.

Nor can we fully express our gratitude and appreciation to Dr. Stephen Walker and to the poet, Carla Panciera, for reading the manuscript so perceptively.

Many thanks to Dr. Shelley Brown for her suggestions.

Elva Linnea Nelson

FOREWORD

Swami Akhilananda was one of the foremost disciples of Swami Brahmananda and he was a very loving soul. Swami Akhilananda was a jewel. I never found a Swami like him. When I was asked to leave India and go to Boston to assist Swami Akhilananda, I came to know him as a great devotee of Brahmananda.

Swami Akhilananda influenced a lot of people. They liked him very much. He made a good contribution when he advocated meditation for spiritual and mental health. He knew many psychologists and many philosophers. He went to many of their meetings and attended inter-religious groups. His work was wonderful, in tune with other religions. He was open to all people and very kind and sympathetic. A very sweet soul.

Swami Sarvagatananda

PREFACE

You may not have known that Thoreau in writing *WALDEN,* his classic book on life in the woods, mentioned the sublimity of the *BHAGAVAD GITA.* For its time this was an astonishing statement. It signaled that something new was coming into our American life. In the midst of the 19th century, the Concord philosophers Emerson, Thoreau, Alcott and others were discussing the Vedic scriptures of India. Captivated, Emerson formulated the Oversoul which could be compared to Brahman of the Indian philosophers.

Through their writings a search had commenced perhaps unconsciously for a larger view of life. The Transcendental Movement had begun. But the Concord Philosophers were not alone. Walt Whitman's *LEAVES OF GRASS* had been published in 1855, a year after *WALDEN,* and it, too, bespoke of the transcendental. "In some ways this God of the first edition," wrote Malcolm Cowley in the 1959 reprint, "resembles Emerson's Oversoul, but he (Whitman) seems much closer to the Brahman of the *UPANISHADS...*"

You might think of these philosophers and poets as auspicious forerunners of an Indian monk, Swami Vivekananda, who, when he stepped into the spotlight at the Chicago Parliament of Religions in 1893 and addressed those gathered as "Sisters and Brothers of America" was acknowledged with minute-after-minute applause. His eloquence and the quality of his thoughts, his presence with light flashing in his eyes, captivated America. How Emerson and Thoreau would have welcomed him! He was the first monk of an Indian monastic Order to come to the Western world. To bring the timeless truths of Vedanta, the universal non-sectarian spiritual scriptures of India.

In the twentieth century he was followed by a cluster of exceptional monks such as Prabhavananda, Satprakashananda, Nikhilananda, Ashokananda and others who came from India in the 1920s and 1930s to teach Vedanta. Those monastics served respectively in Hollywood, St. Louis, New York City, and San Francisco. The Swami you will meet here is another exceptional monk, Swami Akhilananda, who founded the Vedanta Society of Providence and the Ramakrishna Vedanta Society of Boston. In trying to write about Swami Akhilananda for this book, how much can one say about a man who didn't talk about himself. As Swami Sarvagatananda, Akhilananda's successor, has said many times: "He was a silent worker." But his presence spoke for itself. What can one say about him whom Swami Gnaneswarananda (1893-1937), the leader of the Vivekananda Vedanta Society of Chicago, wrote that to know Swami Akhilananda was to love him and to love him was to love God.[1] At one of the annual banquets for Sri Ramakrishna in Boston in the 1950s, one woman recalls Dean Walter Muelder of Boston University School of Theology as saying to her that in looking at the face of Swami Akhilananda, one was looking into the face of God.[2]

Such words may seem exaggerated and hyperbolic to the sophisticated and to the skeptic. If one had to, how could one write about such a man? So when Swami Sarvagatananda approached me some years ago about writing a biography of Akhilananda, who had passed away in 1962, I didn't think I should do it. How much did I really know about Swami Akhilananda? Besides, I was reminded of what Swami Vivekananda had to say when he was asked to write about Sri Ramakrishna. That in trying to fashion a god, he would make a monkey.[3] How to make the holiness of a holy person real to those who have never experienced an illumined soul? The gifted orator that he was, Swami Vivekananda, who stole the show at the Parliament of Religions in Chicago in 1893, walked from one end of the stage to the other at the Madison Square Music Hall in New York City in 1896, in a fever of love trying to describe Ramakrishna, the god-man of modern India.[4]

I had known Swami Akhilananda since early 1949, having become acquainted with the GOSPEL OF SRI RAMAKRISHNA in February 1948. Perhaps Swami Sarvagatananda felt that since I had written a couple of little books, maybe I should write about Swami Akhilananda. Those books were "Vivekananda and his Swamis in Boston and vicinity", which came out in 1992; "Bhakti, the dedicated life of Helen Rubel", published 3 years later. Before these two publications I had worked on HUMAN BEING IN DEPTH; a scientific approach to religion, by Swami Ranganathananda, then the vice-president of the

viii

Ramakrishna Order. I had been inspired by reading a chapter of his *SCIENCE AND RELIGION*. Graciously he gave me permission to revise and edit it and add an additional chapter Consciousness Itself.

This new compilation became *HUMAN BEING IN DEPTH* and was published by the State University of New York in 1991. In 1996 I edited *THE LAMPLIGHTER*: Swami Sarvagatananda in the West; a book of tributes to him.

But in no way did these publications make me feel that I could write about Swami Akhilananda. Swami Sarvagatananda persisted, however, in suggesting that I do so. Then one day a devotee friend said: "If you don't do it, who will?" That made me to pause and then decide to try and write about this holy man.

We are not intending to make a cult figure out of the Swami. He would not approve of that nor would anyone else.

We want to present as much as possible of what Swami Akhilananda did and what he was. Unfortunately, as a result of research, we found that many letters were unavailable, some yearly diaries were missing, and that many friends and devotees had passed away. So that there are, regretfully, sins of omission in this book.

Throughout the research and the writing, it's been like chasing someone who is elusive. Swami Akhilananda has not been fully captured, but then, after all, he is not a butterfly to be pinned to a board. How to make real his "loving, magnetic and glowing personality?"[5] In 1954 when Swami Sarvagatananda was to leave India and come to Boston, Swami Vireswarananda, the president of the Ramakrishna Order, said of Swami Akhilananda, "He is a true monk."[6]

INTRODUCTION

Like the Indian monks, traveling 2400 years ago through the Hindu Kush mountains, bringing the teachings of Buddha, the Awakened One, to Afghanistan and then eastward along the Silk Route to China, so once again out of the heart of India in the late 19th century there began another journey of ochre-clad monks over different routes, by land and by sea, bringing teachings for a new age and for a new way of life. "I have a message to the West as Buddha had a message to the East,"[7] declared Swami Vivekananda before a large gathering of the Brooklyn Ethical Association on December 30, 1894. Coming from India the young 30 year old Vivekananda was the surprise of the Parliament of Religions at Chicago in 1893, where he was so much appreciated that he was acclaimed by thousands every time he spoke. He was the first monk to bring Vedanta, the eternal religion of India, to the Western world. He emphasized the teaching, "As many faiths, so many paths", and said that man in his essence was divine; that it was a sin to call a man a sinner.

If the message of Buddha is still spreading, so are the words of Swami Vivekananda. In 1897 when he returned to India he founded the Ramakrishna Order. Since then its monastic members have spread out all over the globe, bringing the teachings of Vedanta. Quietly, without media=hype, the monks have scattered the wisdom of the Upanishads, which are non-sectarian and impersoal, proclaiming that we are immortal and divine;and the *BHAGAVAD GITA*, which, over a hundred years ago was translated from the Sanscrit by Sir Edwin Arnold as *THE SONG CELESTIAL*. For the twentieth century and beyond we have Swami Ranganathananda's *UNIVERSAL MESSAGE OF THE BHAGAVAD GITA*, an exposition in the light of modern thought and modern needs. He introduces the Gita as "a book that is meant to be a help to realize the eternal spiritual reality within all men and women".[8] Then he adds that it is "the greatest book of practical Vedanta capable of helping us to create a society of fully developed human beings." [9]

Respect for other religions, curiosity about spirituality if not spiritual practices are there in those who have not been especially interested in religion. Even the popularity of Joseph Campbell's TV Series, the "Power of the Myth", where he says: "Myths are clues to the spiritual potentialities of the human life",[10] exemplifies this trend.

One monastic member who came to the United States in 1926 was Swami Akhilananda. Establishing a Vedanta Society in Providence, Rhode Island in 1928, this young monk became very well known and much respected. The same held true when, while still maintaining Providence, he founded the Ramakrishna Vedanta Society in Boston in 1941. In his ministry in Boston and Providence spanning 34 years, from 1928 to 1962, he was, as Dr. John H. Lavely, professor of philosophy at Boston University, has said:

..."not primarily interested in getting formal adherence or in advocating a doctrinal truth... He aimed completely to assist people to realize the goal of life - direct experience of Ultimate Reality or God - by a variety of spiritual disciplines and practices. He did not feel that this goal was the exclusive custody of any particular tradition. He was, therefore, hospitable to the religious dimension of all the great faiths."[11]

Akhilananda gained a reputation as a bridge builder between East and West. He did this through his several books and by attending many meetings of philosophers, psychologists and ministers. And by his participation in academic circles. His psychological approach to religion and spirituality was important and stimulating to many. Insightful and scientifically minded, Swami Akhilananda once said: "Our modern age of science is not out of harmony with religion. Religion is just as much a science as any other realm of knowledge."[12]

Beginning in the early 1940s he began to participate in the Conference on Science, Philosophy and Religion which was held frequently, mostly in New York. It was a diverse group of established savants, brilliant leaders, coming together for discussion. He became friends with Clarence H. Faust, who was Dean of the College, University of Chicago and who also was Vice-President of the Ford Foundation. Dean Faust writes:

"To impress or win the respect of such a group was not easy, especially for someone holding the Swami's views, which we Westerners tend to regard, at least to begin with, as unworthy of serious consideration. But the Swami soon did win the respect of the group.

xii

"His suggestions tended to be proposals for bridges across chasms that appeared to separate sharply opposed, even contradictory, views and opinions. ...This mode of discussion was sufficiently rare and so clearly valuable as practiced by the Swami that his respect for others won in turn the respect of a large majority of the group."[13]

As Gordon Allport wrote: "He is an architect bent on building a bridge between hemispheres."[14] This he did in writing *HINDU PSYCHOLOGY, ITS MEANING FOR THE WEST*, published by Harper and Brothers in 1946; and in 1949 appeared his *HINDU VIEW OF CHRIST*, about which Dean Walter Muelder of B. U. School of Theology wrote: "Swami Akhilananda unites East and West in a moving appreciation of Jesus Christ and his significance for the whole world."[15]

Swami Akhilananda was a pioneer in advocating spiritual practices for mental health. He attended meetings of psychotherapists and clinical psychologists, for his ministry brought him into contact with the troubled and the disturbed, many seriously. He mentions in his lectures: "Recently we have been going to visit a patient who is in the Boston. Psychopathic Hospital..." What wonderful sympathy he had for the problems of others. Under his loving direction minor problems melted away. He visited the son of one of his friends who was in a mental hospital in Framingham, where he met the psychiatrist who was treating him. As soon as I met the psychiatrist I thought to myself like this, 'Aha - now I would like to do something for him.' He threw a gloom around him. ... I invited him to have lunch with me one day. He came with his wife. The poor man has trouble, something that cannot be resolved..."[16]

Tirelessly he worked within the many psychological groups trying to bring about an understanding of the value of spiritual practices for the health of the human mind and psyche. He knew the difficulties and limitations the psychoanalysts had in treating people. He remarked in a sermon on November 27, 1949: "We were at a meeting of psychoanalysts and clinical psychologists and one man who wanted to bring out my answer - asked another of the psychologists about how many people were cured by psychoanalysis. And he answered about 60% of the people are not helped. About 25-30% are helped, and about 15% are cured... This answer was very discouraging."

One might say that the theme of his life was to love and serve. Whether it was that patient at the Boston Psychopathic Hospital, or the sick wife of one of his professor friends, or some alcoholic who had such good intentions, he was there. Swami not only labored for the spiritual aspirants who flocked to him, but for all with whom he came in contact. His was a warm healing presence. Nor was it confined to America. In March, 1950 he wrote a letter to Nalini Sarker, the finance minister of East Bengal; "I feel a very strong urge to go to India and to see you all, but my desire to be of service to some of you is also very strong." And in July, 1950s "I wish I were in India to be of some service to you."

As Dr. John Parks, a psychiatrist at the Kentucky Center of Psychosynthesis, Inc. and one of Swami Akhilananda's students who knew him well recalls:

"I first saw in Swami a personal example of unselfish love. I saw him work with many counselees - young and old - who were exceedingly difficult and trying. He was the personification of patience, love, forgiveness, faith, and a willingness to go to those in need, to unselfishly serve with no consideration of cost to himself."[17]

He brought to those who heard him, and also to a larger audience what was for many something new: meditation. "Meditate, meditate, meditate," he would urge in his sermons and talks. This was said years before the popularization of transcendental meditation. In his book, *MENTAL HEALTH AND HINDU PSYCHOLOGY,* he wrote: "Many clinical psychologists and other therapists wonder how the practice of concentration and meditation - the third form of prayer - can be helpful in conserving mental and physical energy and removing mental fatigue and tension."[18]

The Swami wanted to inspire individuals to develop their will power and increase their ability to become well-integrated human beings. As he wrote: "The practice of concentration and meditation also stabilizes the emotions and develops will power. These practices can have a tremendous effect and integrate his whole personality."[19] In his counseling he respected the differences in people. He felt that each mind had to be trained to suit its own temperament.[20]

The pragmatic practical purposes of meditation and concentration were not the only things that he had in mind. He wished and hoped that the minds of people would be lifted from the human plane to the divine plane. In a sermon of April 24, 1949. he said:

"I can tell you from my own humble experience that once a man has tasted even a little bit of love," and he is speaking of divine love, "he is satisfied forever - even a little bit of it. A man who has tasted love is willing to sacrifice everything. He forgets the world. The world - riches, power, position - the world means nothing to him. ...Real love conquers all the ills of life. ...In this highest type of love there is power - real power to conquer all."[21]

Swami Akhilananda had a radiant uplifting love which has been attested to by many. One who knew him well was Helen Rubel who met him in 1927. "The people must appreciate more and more," she wrote from India in 1940, "as they understand gradually all that you are giving them and doing for them. ...I hope that all come to understand spirituality better and better and get the happiness you want to give..."[22]

Holiness. We don't know what it is and what it can do.

Did Akhilananda expect his ideas to be widely accepted during his lifetime? On December 5, 1953 he had an interview with someone who felt that more people should hear about meditation. "Wait 25 years and you will see,"[23] he responded. We find it is now a common and widely accepted practice. So we now observe that his plea for spiritual practices for the betterment of mental health and other psychosomatic illnesses is also recognized. He might be considered a forerunner of early transpersonal psychology. You might say he was a hidden influence. And the need for the emotional training for children during their years of schooling as he saw it is now acknowledged.

He was a shepherd in what has been called a great ministry over the years in Boston. Dr. Amiya Chakravarty of Boston University remembers that he drew people of every level and condition who brought him their secret grief and torn confused lives.[24] In addition he attracted those of outstanding talent in the fields of science, education, and the medical sciences. "We worked together in the development of the Institute on Religion in an Age of Science,"[25] writes Ralph Burhoe, the longstanding editor of *Zygon*, a journal of religion and science. The Swami and Prof. James Houston Shrader of Eastern Nazarene College were frequent visitors at the home of Prof. Pitirim Sorokin in Winchester, MA where they planned the Research Society in Creative Altruism.[26]

Swami Akhilananda was a participant and founding member of such societies as Scientific Study of Religion, Research Society in Creative Altruism, and the American Foundation of Religion and Psychiatry, and a Charter member of the National Academy of Religion and Mental Health. He belonged, to the University Club of Boston, the American Academy for the Advancement of Science, the Institute of Pastoral Care, Fellowship of Reconciliation, American Philosophical Association, and numerous others . He made many appearances on the lecture platform before major university groups. He was a monk whose teachings and whose presence still touches many lives. He was a pioneer in bringing to the forefront the practice of meditation for restless Americans. In advocating its use for mental health. In bringing the therapeutic value of Hindu psychology to the attention psychiatrists and psychotherapists. As Swami Sarvagatananda has said of Swami Akhilananda: he was a master psychologist.

CHILDHOOD AND YOUTH

It wasn't the darkest of times in India when Nirode Chandra Sanyal, the future Swami Akhilananda, was born in 1894 on February 25th. India was beginning to dream of being independent and free of the British Empire. India was growing restive. Swami Vivekananda was to return in 1897 from the West where he had inspired the large audience at the Parliament of Religions in Chicago in 1893. Such had been his success that afterwards he lectured in Boston, New York, San Francisco, Detroit and other cities and even small towns. London was also to see and hear him. With his stirring lectures, dialogues and personal talks on the glory of India's spiritual culture lying buried beneath the almost despairing mentality of India's people, he wanted Indians to understand the magnificence of the Upanishads and to give up the religion of the "cooking pots and pans", the religion of don't touchism. It was a time when it was good to be alive and alert. Changes were in the offing.

Nirode Chandra Sanyal had his birth at the Netrakona residence of his grandfather, Rajkishore, in what was Bengal, but is now Bangladesh. Netrakona was a semi-urban town, surrounded by farming community. It was the local hub for cultural, musical and educational activities. His parents were Amar Chandra Sanyal and Rajbala Debi Sanyal (nee Bagchi). His father in 1892 joined the Civil Court at Netrakona as a junior Lawyer to his father, Rajkishore, a distinguished pleader of the Judges Court at Mymensingh.

A thoughtful man, Amar Chandra was politically minded from his early days. He actively took part in the Anti-Bengal Partition Movement in 1904. He joined the Non-Co-Operation Movement started by Mahatma Gandhi in 1921 and was falsely accused in a fraudulent case and sentenced to 3 months imprisonment.

There was such a protest against this by the people of Netrakona that the case was dropped. He attended the Calcutta session of the Indian National Congress in 1928. Amar Chandra was spoken of as the 'Gandhi' of Netrakona. He advised people to follow the path of non-violence.

Nirode's mother came from a learned Brahmin family, She was a straightforward lady of outstanding personality who shouldered many responsibilities of a joint-family household. When Nirode was about 11 or 12 years old, she passed away.[1] Many times in his talks Swami Akhilananda would mention about the irreplaceability of a mother's love.

It should then come as no surprise that being descended from a family of notable lawyers, the lectures of Swami Akhilananda were so well organized, and yet so spontaneous, and with his warm, friendly, charismatic personality, which he might have inherited from his mother, many people, no matter where they lived or their background, were interested in what he had to say.

The early years of Nirode's life are lost to us. What we gather from the reminiscences of his brother, Sudhansu Sanyal, and his cousin Shirish Chandra Sanyal, is that he was dearly loved. He had such an affectionate disposition that his family was charmed by his behavior. His cousin writes: "His essence of life was 'love'. He was born with the 'mantra' of love for everyone and love without any self-interest. No difficulties could divert him from his path, peace and love." His great heart was complemented by a gifted mind and a pleasing manner. He was firm in what he considered to be right. He would do what he considered to be just and was not deterred by any disapproving members of the family.[2] He looked out for his younger brother, Sudhansu, and used to tolerate his sometimes irrational demands, trying to keep him happy. Swami Akhilananda was a little unusual even as a boy.

In his early teens, and perhaps even before, Nirode's interest was the independence of India. His cousin, Shirish Chandra, writes that when Nirode was a school student, the nationalistic movement against the British rule spread throughout the region. The mood and condition of India before he was born has been well described by Jawaharlal Nehru in his book, *DISCOVERY OF INDIA*: "Bengal had the first full experience of British rule in India. That rule began with outright plunder, and a land revenue system which extracted the uttermost farthing not only from the living, but also dead cultivators. The English historians of India, Edward Thompson and G. T. Garrett, tell us 'a gold-lust unequalled since the hysteria that took hold of the Spaniards of Cortes' and Pizarro's age filled the English mind. Bengal in particular was not to know peace again until she had been bled white.'"[3]

With the British having consolidated their rule in India, there arose a cry for reform. The British had been in India over three hundred years. A number of notable Indians, including the Irish disciple of Swami Vivekananda, Sister Nivedita, tried to awaken the consciousness of the Indians to their cultural history. Vivekananda, in reply to an address of welcome in Calcutta in 1897, spoke words of fire and inspiration: "There cannot be friendship without equality, and there cannot be equality where one party is always the teacher and the other party sits always at his feet. If you want to become equal with the Englishman or the American, you will have to teach to the world for centuries to come....We have been ridiculed as an imaginative race, as men with a good deal of feeling. Let me tell you, my friends, intellect is great indeed, but it stops within certain bounds. It is through the heart, and the heart alone, that inspiration comes... Young men of Calcutta, arise, awake, for the time is propitious. Already everything is opening out before us. Be bold and fear not... Arise, awake, for your country needs this tremendous sacrifice. It is the young men that will do it."[4] Vivekananda had made a stir in Calcutta on his return from the West. "He was entertained by the princes in the city, and also by the most humble of people. Daily, large numbers, drawn from all ranks and callings, came... even great masters of philosophy and university professors were amazed at his genius. But his heart was with the educated unmarried youths. With them he was never tired of speaking. He was consumed with the desire to infuse his own spirit into them."[5]

A young man approached him who told of his difficulties in meditation: he couldn't find peace of mind. "Can you show me the way?" he asked Vivekananda. "Open the door of your room," said Vivekananda, "and look around instead of closing your eyes. There are hundreds of poor and helpless people in the neighborhood...them you have to serve to the best of your ability." He meant those who were sick, the starving, the ignorant. He concluded with: ..."if you want peace of mind, you have to serve others in this way as well as you can."[6] Vivekananda, a household name in Bengal. Nirode was only three to four years old at that time. It would not be until he was twelve that he first learned about Vivekananda from one of his disciples. A friend had brought him some of Vivekananda's letters. Nirode admired him very much.

The young people of Nirode's time were anxious to get rid of the foreign rule. The Indian National Congress had been started in 1885. The Bengalis, those who took to the law, were also political leaders.

The young people were restless. Shirish Chandral Sanyal, Nirode's cousin, writes that the revolutionary fever also affected Nirode and as a result he gradually lost interest in his studies during this time.[7]

His younger brother, Sudhansu explains:

"He became closely associated with secret revolutionary party leaders of the local Bandhab Samity headed by one courageous leader and lawyer friend of his father named Kailash Chandra Biswas. Due to Nirode's great quality of head and heart many young men of that place became associated with the social and secret political activities of the Samity.[8]

One of Nirode's friends, who was ardently opposed to the British and who was like Nirode a member of a secret organization was Satyen Chowdhury, who was five years older. They became close, both being courageous, talented, nationalistic, dignified and devoted to God. Satyen later became Swami Atmabodhananda. They discussed all manner of books, including Swami Vivekananda and the Gita. One of Nirode's favorites was "Anandamath" and "Debi Choud-hurani", by Bankim Chandra, a famous novelist who inspired many with his nationalistic writing. They used to visit cremation and burial grounds and the morgue at dead of night to test and develop their courage. They held secret meetings there.[9]

One of those meetings had its amusing ending. Swami Akhilananda recalls it:

"When I was a young boy - a school boy - I belonged to a group of boys who believed we should be bold. I was the youngest one of the group. In fact, I do not dare to tell you the age - I was so young. Somehow or other those boys trusted me even though I was so young. Well, they finally came to the conclusion that I was not bold enough. So one night a group of us had to go to the cremation ground. When we were there, we saw some people walking along one of the paths that led to the city. The cremation ground was outside of Calcutta. One of the boys lit a match. It was mischievous, of course. When the people saw the light in the cremation ground, they got frightened. One started to run and so all of them started to run. They did not stop to see whether the light came from a spook or a person.[10]

Nirode's father had a gun in his possession. One day it was found to be missing. The police were notified. The gun was never located. There was a rumor that Nirode had taken it. "He allegedly came to the house steathily at night, picked up the gun and passed it on to his fiercely nationalist friend 'Hemanta'," according to Nirode's cousin, Shirish.[11] Nirode was so young he was never under suspicion.When he was attending the high school at Netrakona, Nirode showed special aptitude for learning Sanskrit. He was then sent to another school for Sanskrit at his maternal uncle's place at Ramgopalpur. While there one of his maternal uncles fell ill with tuberculosis and later died. Nirode used to look after him single-handedly with great sincerity.[12] He would wait on him, freshen him, feed him, and try to cheer him up. But Vivekananda was on his mind.

In February 1911 the time had come when he would visit Belur Math, the headquarters and the monastery of the Ramakrishna Order, founded by Swami Vivekananda in 1897. Located on the Ganges a few miles north of Calcutta, here the monks were trained in meditation, spiritual practices, the scriptures of India as well as those of other cultures. Since Vivekananda called for the upliftment of the masses in India, the monks were also instructed to serve others with a spiritual outlook in the different fields of social service.The monks would establish centers of medical assistance, hospitals, schools and colleges, orphanages, and other monastic training centers. At that time Swami Brahmananda, who was looked upon as a giant in spirituality, was head of the Order.

Nirode had read the *GOSPEL OF SRI RAMAKRISHNA,* a book of inspiring conversations and parables with those who came to visit this spiritual leader at Dakshineswar near Calcutta. This would have been in the middle of 1908, when Nirode was in his fifteenth year. It had made him understand what would be his way of life. Such was the effect of reading Vivekananda and the *GOSPEL* that social and political activities had become of secondary value.[13] He had been thinking of visiting the monastery of the Order, but he knew his father would be concerned if he went there. He knew he would have to be a little tactful. He decided to wait a little. When he was 17 years old, an opportunity came in 1911 when he was in Calcutta. Accompanied by Satyen, they went to Balaram Bose's house. He was an ardent admirer of the monks, who were always welcome. As they approached the house, the first Swami Nirode saw was Premananda, a venerable direct disciple of Sri Ramakrishna, who was in Calcutta to organize the activities for the celebration of Ramakrishna's birthday.

Remembering the occasion, Swami Akhilananda has written:

"As we were approaching the home of Balaram Bose, we met the Swami on his way to make arrangements for the celebration. Immediately we prostrated before him and then my friend introduced me to him. He stood talking with us a few minutes and then took us back to the house so that he could be with us for some time...he asked me to go to the monastery for the birthday celebration of the Master. He also said; 'Maharaj (Swami Brahmananda) is there.' This visit was a memorable occasion in my life. He treated me as if he had known me for a long time. I intensely felt his love the first time we met."[14]

Entering the building, they learned that Maharaj was in the shrine room.

"It was a sight indescribable," recalls Swami Akhilananda, "Swami Brahmananda was fanning the altar as the worship was being completed. His appearance was gigantic and extremely attractive. His eyes were sparkling with divine bliss and were enchanting. After a while he came down to the compound and we all followed him and saluted him. He blessed everyone present. Then we all had dinner with him. Swami Premananda, 5wami Turiyananda, and other Swamis sat by him."[15]

As for the day of Ramakrishna's birthday celebration;

"I went to see Swami Brahmananda very early in the morning. It was almost impossible for me to stay away from him that day. When I met him and saluted him, he spoke a few pleasant words. As I think of the meeting of that day, I myself am amused for what I did. Every time a new group of people would arrive I went with them to salute Maharaj. He would smile with his sparkling eyes every time I went to him. This went on for hours. Finally, some great musicians came to play and sing spiritual songs. Everyone sat around Maharaj. It was indeed a great sight to see him in a god-intoxicated mood."[16]

Nirode shortly thereafter developed a serious illness and had to remain mostly in bed for about two years. He did not visit Belur Math until the later part of 1913. He would visit Swami Brahmananda at the home of Balaram Bose during the spring of 1913 although he was not well.[17]

Tuberculosis had been suspected, but was not verified. Medicines and diet were not helpful. It was decided to send Nirode to Calcutta. We hear from Shirish, his cousin:

"There he was put up at the Hostel where my elder brother was staying. He was taken to a very reputed physician named Dr. Nilratan Sarkar who subsequently arranged to have his tonsil operated. Although it was very painful, Nirode patiently bore with it throughout the operation. His forbearance was extraordinary. Dr. Sarkar then advised him to go for a change of climate to a place called 'Jamtara' in Santal District. Nirode stayed there for a few months with his father before going back to their home in Netrakona. Nirode was still not cured. Everyone began to lose hope about his recovery."[18]

After some time, it was discovered that he had tuberculosis. After long treatment by the local physicians at Netrakona, his father decided to send him to Calcutta to see if he could improve. He was taken by an uncle to a doctor (and was examined by) a very renowned physician, Dr. R. L. Dutta, who concluded Nirode was incurable and advised that they arrange for "Ganga Yatra" (last journey).[19]

However they heard of a sage in Allahabad who could treat incurable diseases with his own medicines. He was known by the popular name of Balaji Maharaj. Before going there Nirode visited Swami Brahmananda who suggested he visit a brother disciple, Swami Vijnanananda, as he was staying in that area. According to Nirode's cousin; "The sage accepted him with certain conditions: ... He was to take vegetarian diet, and while taking his medications he should go to the confluence of three rivers: Ganga, Yamuna, and Saraswati and take dips a hundred times everyday."[20] His medication was a black powder prepared by Balaji Maharaj.[21] Standing in the water of the rivers which covered his chest, the water cooled his body while the black powder burned away the pathology in his lungs. This minimized the degree of whatever discomfort he might have felt.

While he was there he visited Swami Vijnanananda with whom he had memorable conversations. The great monk, an engineer before renouncing the world, would greet Nirode with "Hello, Brother". In remembering those days, Akhilananda has said: "When I was ready to return to Calcutta, Swami Vijnanananda told me to ask Swami Brahmananda for something. I asked him: 'Why don't you give it to me?' He laughed and said, "No. you go to Maharaj. He is having spiritual realizations constantly; there cannot be any measure of his experiences.'"

Nirode having recovered and having gained weight returned to Calcutta after three months. As soon as possible he went to the monastery at Belur:

"Again I met Swami Premananda first and requested his permission to remain overnight. He took me at once to Swami Brahmananda, who was sitting alone facing the Ganges. As I saluted him, Swami Premananda reported that I would like to stay in the monastery all night. Swami Brahmananda at once gave permission. He said: 'Let the boy stay otherwise he will be hurt.' Then both of them smiled at me. Swami Premananda made arrangements for my bed. After dinner, as time for retirement came, he put me to bed like a mother. I found out later on that it was the bed of one of the disciples of Ramakrishna. I was allowed to stay in the same room with the older swamis.

"The next day was a memorable one in my life. In the morning I reported my last conversation with Swami Vijnanananda to Maharaj, He said: 'Why did not you ask Swami Vijnanananda to give it to you?' I replied: 'Yes, I asked him.' Then I reported what Swami Vijnanananda told me about him. Then Maharaj became very grave and remained silent for a little while. Finally he said: 'You have to do certain things for a few days to attain this. My child, you have to have initiation.' Of course, I immediately said: 'You give me what is needed.' He was extremely kind to give me the needful instructions and asked me to go to him for further instructions in a few months."

A few months later Nirode went to Benares to visit Swami Brahmananda. As he approached the monastery a little after four in the morning, he was amazed to see Swami Brahmananda and Swami Sankarananda, the secretary to Maharaj, both opening their doors almost at the same time. Swami Brahmananda was solicitious of Nirode and asked him to rest for a while. Then Brahmananda gave him beads, instructed him further and told him: "I used to initiate here before, but as Mother does not initiate in Benares, I stopped giving initiation here. My child, don't worry about it. I have taken your responsibility. I shall give you initiation as soon as I go back to Calcutta.'" Swami Brahmananda gave the future Swami great encouragement and assurance. The days that Nirode stayed there were spent mostly with Swami Brahmananda and Premananda. Akhilananda has written of that visit: "This period can never be forgotten because of Maharaj's tremendous spiritual atmosphere. When some young Swamis would sing devotional songs in his presence, he would be in a very high spiritual state. The very sight was not only uplifting, but transforming individuals."

After a few months Nirode again paid Swami Brahmananda a visit at Benares. "Swami Brahmananda expressed unforgettable motherly love," Swami Akhilananda recalled, "and showed extreme concern about my physical welfare. Again he gave tremendous encouragement for spiritual growth."

Nirode's absence from school because of his sickness delayed his high school graduation. During his illness he had continued to study at home feeling optimistic about his future. With his brother Sudhansu he appeared for the matriculation examination in 1915 at Jamtara and passed in the first division.

Not long afterwards Nirode returned to Calcutta shortly before his college entrance examinations. Brahmananda was at the monastery at Belur and Nirode would visit him in the early afternoon. One day Swami Brahmananda asked Nirode to come the next day for some intimate instruction. But Nirode hesitated as some interested parties would create trouble for him. But Brahmananda smiled and said: "Come, everything will be all right" The troublemakers stopped their mischief. Akhilananda wrote: "In an unexplainable way, Swami Brahmananda removed all obstacles from my path." Nirode would soon be going to college. His association with Swami Brahmananda would fill his life.

Swami Vivenkananda

Swami Brahmananda

2

COLLEGE DAYS

Attending the C.M.S. College in Calcutta Nirode would visit Belur Math frequently. He used to say of his association with Swami Brahmananda that those days could never be forgotten. One gets a glimpse of what some of them must have been like from the recollections of his cousin Shirish:

"During our Calcutta days it was at Nirode's urging and help that Sudhu, Sudhir Maharaj, my maternal uncle and I were able to visit Belur Math on most Sundays."[1] They would stay there the whole day spending hours sitting at the feet of the revered Swami Brahmananda and Swami Premananda. After taking prasad, they would return to Calcutta in the evening. For various birth anniversaries and such holy days as Durga puja and Kali puja, they would arrive at Belur early in the morning. Again they would spend all day there. Since it was not as crowded as it is now, it was not difficult to have a close association with the great Swamis. When Swami Brahmananda would visit Balaram Bose, a devoted follower of Ramakrishna, who lived in Bagbazar, a district in Calcutta, Nirode and others would also visit there and felt blessed to sit at his holy feet. Nirode would take it upon himself to find out about these visits at Balaram's.

His cousin recalls:

"While in Belur Math, the insightful Swami Brahmananda once said, 'Nirode's heart is full of divine love.' I happened to be present at that time. Nirode's main inspiration and source of strength was his devotion and deep reverence for his Guru. In return, he was blessed with his Guru's immense love, which allowed him to reach the highest pinnacle of spiritual life.... His pure life and heart full of universal love bear witness to this. ... that is why he was able to sacrifice himself so completely for the welfare of others without any consideration of his own health.[2]

While going to college in Calcutta, it was not long before Nirode met Sarada Devi, the Holy Mother, the consort of Sri Ramakrishna. Nirode and his friends used to visit her every Sunday when returning from the monastery. "I first saw her in 1912," Swami Akhilananda recalls, 'It was a great blessing to know her... a great blessing to see her. I used to see her every Sunday. For a few years she was away from Calcutta, but other than that I saw her every Sunday.'[3]

His relationship with Swami Premananda continued to be close:

...I went to the Monastery not only on Sundays but also on other holidays. One day Swami Brahmananda was sitting on the piazza. I was standing by him. He was in his usual mood. Swami Premananda came to the piazza. He looked at me and then at Swami Brahmananda, saying to him: "Why, Maharaj, do you make this boy come to the monastery so frequently?" Brahmananda looked at Nirode with a smile. "What do you mean that I am making him come and go? Any time he can come and go and stay. This is his place"' Then both Swamis laughed and Nirode was enchanted. "I was beside myself," was his response.

At the monastery, on the Ganges, early in the evening there would be a meditation, gathering together the young Swamis and devotees in the presence of Maharaj. There might be devotional music or maybe deep silence. Then all would sit in his presence and meditate. Swami Akhilananda writes:

"That period was indeed glorious and important. Very rarely would he talk unless someone asked questions. We had to go early in the morning or afternoon if we needed any spiritual instruction. We all felt a peculiar pull towards him as if our whole being was drawn to something very high and glorious... Maharaj would seldom talk about Ramakrishna, but Swami Premananda would often describe incidents of their life with Thakur. He also spoke very highly about Holy Mother, Sri Sri Swamiji (Vivekananda) and Maharaj to me. One day he said: 'The Master (Ramakrishna) was beyond human understanding. First understand Swamiji.' Similar ideas were often expressed like this."

One day Swami Brahmananda took Nirode to a small room in the monastery at Belur and said to him: "Finish your college, then you will join the Order."

Swami Akhilananda said that "he made this statement almost from the sky, though I always had an idea that I would join the Order and serve him - especially that I would cook for him. I never thought of doing anything else, what to speak of teaching or lecturing. These things were never in my mind, and they were unthinkable to me, even though in 1915 Swami Premananda asked me to study science and told me in a vigorous way: 'Go and study science, otherwise who will listen to you? Swamiji spoke in their language, so they listened to him. Go and study science.'"

Although Nirode thought he might be initiated in Benares in 1914, this took place on Sri Ramakrishna's birthday in 1916 when Swami Brahmananda initiated him. When the day arrived, Nirode went from the dormitory early in the morning bringing flowers to the monastery. He left the flowers in Brahmananda's room. Brahmananda then asked Nirode to take a bath in the Ganges and go to the shrine room.

"Of course," remembered Swami Akhilananda, "I went to take the bath, but he soon sent one young Swami for me as he had already gone to the main Temple. When I went running, I found him with the same gigantic appearance he had when I first saw him. He was walking on the veranda of the main shrine, waiting for me. 'Come, my child,' he said. I was beside myself and followed him. The door was closed behind us and we were together alone."

Being initiated is when an enlightened teacher or guru gives the student a prayer, or mantra, one or several words, along with an infusion of spiritual energy. It is usually a simple ceremony. The mantra is one's special prayer and should be repeated daily.

After the ceremony was over, Nirode did not know that he was to offer something to his guru. Brahmananda gave him a flower, which Nirode gave to Brahmananda as an offering.

Following the special worship for Sri Ramakrishna with flowers, incense, prayers and meditation, Swamis Brahmananda, Premananda and other monastic disciples had dinner with everyone. A few hundred people had come. Later in the afternoon, Swami Brahmananda suggested that Nirode should go back to the dormitory, which gave Nirode the feeling that Brahmananda was concerned about his health. In 1916 Swami Brahmananda accompanied by Premananda and several others visited eastern Bengal. When they returned to the monastery, Nirode went to see Brahmananda. He said to Nirode: "'Why did you not come with us? You would have enjoyed everything, including wonderful food!' Of course, I did not dream of going with him. Evidently it was in his mind that I should have gone on the trip."

14

Swami Akhilananda recalled more than once that when Maharaj was living in Balaram Bose's house, he went to visit him one morning. Swami Brahmananda was walking back and forth in the living room in deep thought. Swami Akhilananda was standing against a wall. Swami Brahmananda stood in front of him and said: "You eat everything that the doctors advise. You come from an orthodox family, but you can take a little holy water and eat everything." After a few minutes, Swami Brahmananda repeated, "Eat everything." He repeated it again several times.

HowNirode felt his love. Brahmananda would ask him to buy the best butter and cheese from a certain store while he was living in the dormitory. When Nirode was attending college and visiting the monastery there were many evenings when the Swamis and devotees would have devotional music after meditation. Some of the songs that were sung would cause Swami Brahmananda to enter into a high spiritual state. Swami Akhilananda says:

"One could not help feeling its effect. One evening I came a little late from the dormitory as the devotional songs were going on. Maharaj was in an exalted mood. As I saluted him, he touched my head. One can never forget its effect. As we were going away to the dormitory after this, he asked us: 'How was the night?' One of our young boys said, 'It was wonderful! We had deep meditation!' He answered back, 'Meditation? It was the father of meditation!' What he meant was, a superconscious state. As we were walking and taking the streetcar for the dormitory, we were all intoxicated."

This was not the only time that such an incident took place. Others were at Balaram Bose's house, Holy Mother's place and in the Monastery.

Maharaj between 1916 and 1919 spent a great deal of time either in Belur Math or in Calcutta. Particularly the years 1918 and 1919 he stayed in Calcutta for stretches of time. A number of boys of Nirode's age started to visit him frequently.

"A group was formed, almost unknowingly," Swami Akhlananda said, "and we all became intimate friends. As time went on, when Maharaj was in Calcutta I used to go almost every day in the afternoon and early evening. On one holy day I went to the monastery and served him while he was eating dinner with the other Swamis and devotees. I was fanning him and doing a little, but did not eat. He did not say anything

15

in the presence of others; but while he was washing his hands, he asked in a motherly way: 'Why did you not eat? This is the trouble with you.' I at once replied: 'Maharaj, I shall eat now.' I can never forget his loving and yet pained expression."

In Calcutta on one occasion the following was the dialogue between Maharaj, a serene mountain of a guru and the college student: "You are not to be seen nowadays," said the Swami. "OH, Maharaj, I came day before yesterday." The reply: "You and your day before yesterday!"

In India there are festivals and worship services looking upon God as a mother, a Divine Mother. Sometimes in the spring and in the autumn. On one of these occasions, one day after the special worship of the Divine Morher, Nirode visited the monastery in the early morning. A great disciple of Maharaj, Swami Ambikananda, had given him some offered food the previous night. Giving this to Maharaj, the great Brahmananda asked him to sing a song about the Divine Mother. Swami Ambikananda knelt in front of Maharaj, and with the singing, Maharaj entered into samadhi. Coming down from that state, Swami Brahmananda came to the compound of the monastery. Swami Akhilananda has said: "I could never forget those eyes, sparkling and shining with divine love. At the dinner time early that afternoon, he was nothing but Love itself."

Sometime during 1918 there was some trouble at the college Nirode attended. He took a leading part in it altho he never specified what that trouble was. He could not go to see Swami Brahmananda for four or five days. Maharaj decided to send a friend to see Nirode and ask him to visit him. When Nirode got the message, he felt guilty and decided to go immediately to see Brahmananda.

Nirode reported everything to him. "When he came to know that I was in touch with Sir Ashutosh Mukerji, Maharaj advised me to follow strictly the advice of this man, who was the head of Calcutta University," Akhilananda said. "During those troublesome days I used to go every night, not only to meditate in his presence but also to report developments to him, I also had to talk with Sir Ashutosh frequently." There was another occasion when Swami Brahmananda instructed Nirode about people and their behavior. In this case an institution of higher education was also involved. Sitting in the presence of Brahmananda with two other young monastics, "one of the younger Swamis came and asked me about a devotee who was creating considerable disturbance in our dormitory. I happened to be instrumental in getting the house started with the help of the University. Maharaj at once asked: 'What's the matter? What happened?' I briefly narrated the situation. He immediately asked: 'Why did you not ask me before you started this house with this other man?' I replied" 'Maharaj, I thought he was a devotee so everything would work out all right.' Then he exclaimed: "Keep quiet! I have seen many devotees."'

The great Swami talked regarding interpersonal relationships and activities. "He said: 'My child, you can do everything for the good of an individual but if you do one thing that does not suit him he will remember that and forget all your good deeds. He will criticize you. This is the world. But it is the reverse in the case of God. You may do everything wrong and do one good thing: He will remember that and use it for your good and transform you.'"

After talking about the nature of ordinary people, Swami Brahmananda said to Nirode: "But a holy man must never change his nature." Then he told the story of the holy man and the scorpion. It seems a holy man was sitting by the bank of a river. He looked up and saw a scorpion struggling for his life in the waters. The holy man picked him up and brought it to the shore. Immediately the scorpion stung him. Again the scorpion was seen struggling in the waters. Again the holy man picked him up and suffered an excruciating sting. After a while the scorpion was back in the waters for a third time. The holy man wondered what to do. "Then he thought to himself that it is the nature of the scorpion to sting and it is the nature of a holy man to render service to any suffering being. So he picked the scorpion up and was again stung; but he carried it far away from the river so that it would not get back into the water again.

"By this story Maharaj deeply impressed on me for life what is the real nature and spirit of a holy man. It seems that he saw the future of my life and gave instructions ahead of time. Many personal elements were there. As time went on, I found these words and other words were uttereed to teach me how to handle the future situations in my life."

There were occasions when Nirode would stay overnight at the Belur monastery. Swami Premananda would allow him to sleep in the same room with him. Since Swami Premananda was going to Eastern Bengal in the summer of 1917, Nirode felt that the Swami should also go to the place where his family were living. Nirode had a deep conviction that his presence there would not only bless the family but hundreds of others as well. He went to see Swami Premananda where the Swami was visiting just outside a small city and expressed his desire to him. Having gone by steamer and then having walked ten miles in the sun to the suburban area where Swami Premananda was staying, Nirode was very tired. When Swami Premananda saw him from a distance, he left the crowd, meeting him a little away from the group. This was very embarrassing to Nirode with the people staring at him, just a young boy.[4]

Swami Akhilananda's brother, Sudhansu Sanyal, writes:

"He accompanied Premananda Maharaj in his tour of North and East Bengal in May, 1917 and in compliance to his desire the Swami visited Mymensingh and Netrakona and very kindly resided at the Netrakona residence of his father for two/three days. Premananda Maharaj addressed largely attended public meetings at both these places and was widely appreciated by Hindus and Muslims alike. At both these places large numbers of Muslims came to pay their homage to this attractive and good-looking Hindu monk who was a benign personality."[5]

One departure was remembered by Swami Akhilananda: "Hundreds of men and women, Hindus and Muslims, young and old, rich and poor, were assembled. As he was leaving, the people were shedding tears as if he were leaving his nearest and dearest friends. This feeling was expressed by all whether Hindu or Muslim. One can never forget such an experience."[6]

As a result of these trips in eastern Bengal and the eating of food which was not pure, Swami Premananda became ill. Nirode was present when a Muslim schoolteacher went to see Swami Premananda while he was visiting some parts of eastern Bengal. The Muslim gentleman was friendly to Swami Premananda and wanted to eat with him. Fruits and sweets were brought, the gentleman eating them and offered his partly eaten food to Swami Premananda. Swami Akhilananda and what happened then:

"The Swami out of his extreme generosity ate it. In discussing this incident Maharaj said:'How could a man of his type stand this sort of thing? Thakur(Ramakrishna) used to say that Baburam's (Swami Premananda's) body is pure to the core, his whole being is purity itself. You people do not understand his nature and allow such things to happen. What a pity!"[7] After several months the sickness was beginning to take its toll. Nirode started to visit him in Calcutta where he was staying.

Swami Akhilananda's recollections:

"... somehow or other I felt that there might be very bad news, so I went to a friend's house a block from the place where Swami Premananda had been staying. The moment I entered, my friend asked me if I was coming from the funeral. I at once realized what had happened, and could not move for several hours. When I had recovered a little, I went to see Maharaj. Something amazing happened. He was alone in his room; there was only one young Swami in that part of the house. As I was saluting Maharaj, he uttered a very tender word. At once, all my agony vanished. He did not say anything about Swami Premananda. I remained in his presence for a couple of hours that night practically without any conversation."[8]

Nirode passed his B.A. examination with honors in philosophy in 1919 and was admitted to post-graduate course in philosophy at Calcutta University.[9]

However, after graduating from college, he, with borrowed money from his uncles, started a small business of supplying rice to the hostels in the area. He thought this would be a source of permanent income in the future when other family members would manage it.[10] But his business was to end, nor did he finish his post-graduate course. He wrote a long letter to his father seeking his permission to join the Ramakrishna Mission. His father, anticipating such consented.[11] Suddenly young Nirode went to Bhubaneswar where Swami Brahmananda was staying at the time. There he joined the Order in December, 1919.

Swami Premananda

3

BRAHMANANDA

We shouldn't need to ask: who was Swami Brahmananda? Aside from being the president of the Ramakrishna Order from 1900-1922, he was unmatched in being the 'mind-child' of Sri Ramakrishna (1836-1886). He was an answer to Ramakrishna's prayer.

One day Ramakrishna prayed to the Lord, the Divine Mother. "Mother, I want someone to be my constant companion. Bring me a boy who is pure-hearted and intensely devoted to you."[1] It wasn't long before his prayer was answered. Ramakrishna tells the story. "A few days before Rakhal (Swami Brahmananda) came to me the Mother placed a little boy on my lap and said: 'This is your son.' At first I was startled, 'My son?'" But the Divine Mother reassured Ramakrishna that Rakhal would not be a son in the ordinary sense. That he would be Ramakrishna's spiritual son who would embody the highest ideal of renunciation.[2] Ramakrishna's subtle superconscious perception had seen it all. Brahmananda would become the future monastic leader of the Ramakrishna Order. It is said that Ramakrishna brought Vivekananda for the world but Brahmananda (1863-1922) for himself. He came to Ramakrishna when he was only sixteen.

Then the question might arise - who was Ramakrishna? A man of God, who lived in a temple garden at Dakshineswar, outside of Calcutta, from his late teens until the end of his life. A seeker, wondering as many do, if God was really real, he undertook many spiritual disciplines. Unpretentiously he prayed, worshipped and meditated until one day, discouraged at not having received God's grace, he was ready to kill himself, but instead he became overwhelmed, his mind going beyond time and space, and he was heard to utter the word 'Mother'. Such was his first revelation bringing him unspeakable joy. God had become a reality to him.

He was to give that assurance of an abiding Reality to many, many people. Recalling his meeting with Ramakrishna when he first met him as a college student, Vivekananda wrote: "For the first time I found a man who dared to say that he saw God, that religion was a reality to be felt, to be sensed in an infinitely-more intense way than we can sense the world... I actually saw that religion could be given. One touch, one glance, can change a whole life."[3]

Ramakrishna had found the Unity behind the multiplicity of the world; he had transcended the boundaries of time, space and causation. He would discover the truth of the Rig-Veda, the ancient scriptures of the Hindus: "Truth is one, sages call it by various names." And he would say: "God is infinite, and infinite are the ways to reach Him."[4] Hundreds came to see Ramakrishna, a child of the Divine Mother. Many have told how he inspired all whom he met. He refashioned the minds and hearts of those who were desperately seeking. As Vivekananda said: "He gave words and encouragement even to the most degraded persons and lifted them up."[5] Even those who were considered worthless would find a change in their lives.

There are those who have tried to write about Ramakrishna. Romain Rolland, the French Nobel prize winner, was one. More recently Christopher Isherwood was another, who in his book, *RAMAKRISHNA AND HIS DISCIPLES* describes Ramakrishna as a phenomenon. Swami Bhajananda, however, in an editorial in <u>Prabuddha Bharata</u> in December 1986, calls attention to another point of view. He writes:

"… Sri Ramakrishna is not a past 'phenomenon' as Christopher Isherwood described him, but a continuing phenomenon."

He further states that Sri Ramakrishna was not merely a phenomenon, but more truly represented the Noumenon. "Indeed, it was as the revelation of the Noumenon that Sri Ramakrishna performed one of his important functions in the present age. What modern people need is an incontrovertible assurance of the existence of the Transcendent Reality and the possibility of realizing it. This assurance Sri Ramakrishna gave through his life."[6] Swami Brahmananda on more than one occasion said that Ramakrishna was the avatar for this age and was helping every sincere seeker. Once the Swami turned to Swami Saradananda and said: "Sri Ramakrishna is real. His divine incarnation is real."[7]

Ramakrishna came to enkindle spirituality everywhere. Whether one regards him as a phenomenon, the Noumenon, or as a sadhu,[8] as Vivekananda said, he is a towering Atlas of love and spirituality, having a wide open transcendent mind and greatness of heart. Everywhere in the world the religious systems had become stagnant and for many of the thoughtful, unbelievable. If we compare them to a pond, he removed by his spiritual striving and practices the scum on the surface so we could see the clear Truth in every one of them. "So many faiths, so many paths," he said. What would we know of God, the subtlest of the subtle and vast like the sky, except for such Beings. The enkindlers, the torch-bearers. As his great disciple, Swami Vivekananda said: "The human soul is potentially divine." Ramakrishna has laid down a challenge - Know Thy Self - which is a voyage of discovery to something beyond our body, mind, and senses.

He was questioned about all his spiritual disciplines: "What was the need for so many different kinds of practice? Immediately like a child, his tearful eyes quivered with emotion and he replied,'My boy, I did everything for all of you. Otherwise I personally had no need of them.'"[9] His spiritual practices reached across the divisions between religions. He had many, many rich and profound spiritual experiences. He was Spirituality Itself.

Ramakrishna had not confined himself in his religious search to the traditions of Hinduism or Vedanta. He became interested in Islam and followed the Islamic manner of religious living and spiritual practices. He did the same for Christianity. In each of these quests, Ramakrishna had the experience of Allah and Jesus. In regard to Buddhism, "Ramakrishna accepted the divinity of Buddha and used to point out the similarity of his teachings to those of the Upanishads..."[10] Vivekananda had an experience of Buddha when he was a boy.[11] Later, in the late 1890s, he spoke of Buddha: "He never drew a breath for himself," he exclaimed. "Above all, he never claimed worship. He said, 'Buddha is not a man, but a state. I have found the door. Enter, all of you.'" For Swami Vivekananda, Buddha was the greatest man who had ever lived.[12] Ramakrishna could overcome cultural differences. It was a universal approach that he brought to religion. Vivekananda once said that Ramakrishna's mission was to proclaim and make clear the fundamental unity underlying all religions.[13]

In the 1880s until his death in August, 1886, thousands came to see and hear Ramakrishna, whose presence when he was in ecstasy radiated light and whose smile was ineffable. "His mind, filled with knowledge and devotion, the depth of which cannot be fathomed, charmed the world with its sweet appeal."[14] And, "His personality used to exude so much gentle charm that anyone who saw him was captivated."[15] Ramakrishna was like a flower to whom the bees came of their own accord. He talked so many hours a day about God that finally in the middle of 1885 the physical strain brought on cancer of the throat. His disciples tried to prevent him from teaching. He said, "I do not care. I will give up twenty thousand such bodies to help one man."[16]

Out of the many who saw him, there were ardent followers from among which 16 or so became monastics. Swami Vivekananda, the foremost disciple, who came to the United States and Europe in the 1890s, brought the message of Ramakrishna.. It was his brother disciple, Swami Brahmananda, or Maharaj, who would become the first elected president of the Ramakrishna Order, which had its beginning at the time of Ramakrishna's death.

Swami Ashokananda, head of the San Francisco Vedanta Society recalls seeing those monastics when he was a young man:

"Until I saw the disciples of Sri Ramakrishna that day, I never thought there could be such resplendent beings. So free, so fearless, so peaceful, so joyful, so pure they were - as if there was nothing to compel them in the whole universe!"[17]

On first seeing Brahmananda, Swami Akhilananda describes it as an unforgettable sight: Brahmananda was in the shrine room fanning the Deity, his eyes sparkling with divine bliss.[18] He was majestic. Then in 1916 Swami Akhilananda, in his pre-monastic days, had another unforgettable experience:

"There was a time... when Maharaj was in samadhi. Only a few disciples and devotees knew about it. The door to his room was closed and, all that the others knew, was that they could not see him then. The door was closed until he, himself, a few hours later, opened the door and came out and walked down the stairs. We were just a young college boy then and we saw him when he came out of the room. His eyes - how bright they were - how they sparkled! You have never seen such eyes in the world! We knew that something had happened... I am telling you something very intimate now. How his eyes shone! And we were drawn to him. We felt his love intensely. We forgot the world even. The world did not exist for us then. You cannot understand this unless you experience it."[19]

All of Brahmananda's disciples revered him. As Sister Devamata, an American, who was in Madras when he visited in 1911, would write: "Everyone was so eager to please him, however, that his gentlest request had the carrying force of a command."[20] Ramakrishna had spoken of Brahmananda as so intelligent that he could rule a kingdom. He was Head of the Order for 22 years until his death in 1922. The work of the order expanded enormously in India under his guidance and 12 or more of his disciples came to teach in the West.

The love and reverence given to him by his disciples was also extended to him by his brother monks. When Swami Vivekananda returned to India after being in the West, he greeted Swami Brahmananda with "The son of a guru is to be regarded as the guru himself."[21] Once, as the monastic order was being gathered, Swami Vivekananda severely scolded Swami Brahmananda, who had shielded another and took the blame for another's mistake. When Vivekananda saw Brahmananda in tears, he rushed to embrace him and repeated over and over again: 'Brother, please forgive me. Our master loved you so much. He never said a harsh word to you."[22]

Holding Swami Brahmananda in great regard, Swami Saradananda who was the General Secretary, would not sit on the same cot with Brahmananda, even after a repeated request. Swami Saradananda would pick up the corner of the mattress and sit on the bare cot. It wasn't possible for him to feel worthy enough to sit on the same mattress as Maharaj.[23]

Another brother monk, Swami Turiyananda, while wandering in India with Swami Brahmananda, and who was trying to get some food for them to eat, burst out with: "Maharaj. You were very dear to our Master. How carefully he used to feed you with cream and butter! And what have I given you, and saying this he was choked with sorrow."[24] Turiyananda came to understand Brahmananda even more deeply. Swami Ashokananda writes:

"As a matter of fact, in time it became clear to the senior members of the Order that Maharaj was an actual representation of Sri Ramakrishna. One day it was revealed to Swami Turiyananda. He was walking towards Maharaj, who was seated in a chair, and found him to be Sri Ramakrishna himself. As he came nearer he continued to see Maharaj as the Master, and then he prostrated before him."[25]

Swami Shivananda, another brother monk, who became Head of the Order after Brahmananda's death, used to say: "Maharaj is gone. I have no desire to continue living. The Math belongs to Maharaj. He was its head, he was its charm, he was its wealth. Ha was everything to the Math. We are his servants..."[26]

What feeling Holy Mother had for Maharaj: She went once on a pilgrimage to Benares and one day gave a feast. Swamis Turiyananda, Saradananda, Subodhananda and other direct disciples were there. Holy Mother gave a cotton cloth to each of them, but she gave Swami Brahmananda a silk cloth. One Swami, Arupananda, who considered Holy Mother as his own mother, was very straightforward and had the boldness to ask her: "Why this kind of discrimination. All of them are disciples of Thakur. Why have you given ordinary cotton cloths to all of them but a silken one to Raja Maharaj?" Holy Mother simply replied, "Chhele je, chhele - he was their son, he was her own son, very-dear, very close to her."[27]

How close can be intimated from the following reminisce. One evening during a class Swami Akhilananda was speaking of Swami Vivekananda and Ramakrishna. He then said: "Sri Ramakrishna, Holy Mother, Swami Vivekananda, and Swami Brahmananda were Four-in-One. This has not happened since the birth of Sri Krishna."

Such a revelation brought a deep silence into the room. Swami had spoken with such conviction that no one asked a single question.[28]

Some, if not most of the great disciples of Sri Ramakrishna like Brahmananda, Vivekananda, Abhedananda, Akhandananda and others, had spent possibly several years in going on pilgrimages, not carrying any money, at times walking barefoot, and begging their food. Did it all serve a deeper purpose? One day when a new monk asked about doing austerities, Brahmananda replied: "We have done all that for you."[29]However, Swami Abhedananda, who had spent twenty years or more away from India, on his return from America, had remarked that the young monks had never gone out and begged their food. One day Brahmananda suggested that the monks should do just that. But he had such a tender regard for the young monastics. As they were about to leave, they were called to Brahmananda's presence.[30]Swami Jnanatmananda has written of that day. "When we presented ouselves before him, he told us with great affection, 'You are going for bhiksha (food gathered by begging), is it not so?' We replied,'Yes, Maharaj." At this he became more tender."[31] Then Brahmananda told that someone had given five rupees to the young monks so that they could buy rice and other things. Under a tree at the monastery, they could cook and eat their meal. "We did not have to go out for it even on a single day..." With a heart of a mother so it was that Swami Brahmananda trained them.[32] He had carried this burden of their austerities long ago.Swami Brahmananda was very particular about his monastics and about initiating devotees. One householder, then a boy, met Brahmananda around 1916 or 1917 when 10 or 11 years old. His father had taken him to meet Maharaj. After the boy made pranams to him, he noticed that Swami Brahmananda was scrutinizing him. Seeing the look in his eye, which were like X-ray eyes, the boy became frightened. He felt as if his body was transparent like glass. He recalls:

"It was as if his eyes understood everything about me, my body and mind, both within and without, leaving nothing unknown to him."[33]

When Swami Brahmananda at Belur Math said that Nirode (Swami Akhilananda) had a heart full of divine love, we can take it for granted that he knew him well.

Swami Aseshananda, who knew Swami Akhilananda when he was joining the Order in 1919, writes:"Akhilananda drew his inspiration that came from the lips of Swami Brahmananda. ... Faith in the Guru was the power behind all his activities which prompted him to undertake any responsibility, however difficult, and carry it out to its legitimate fulfillment. ... I believe it is due to the unwavering faith in his Guru, the spiritual teacher, that Akhilananda could achieve so much influence in the West."[34]

Sri Ramakrishna

Swami Vivekananda seated in the middle; from the left Swami Ramakrishnananda, Shivananda; seated below him, Swami Sadananda. To the right of Vivekananda, Swamis Turiyananda and Brahmananda.

Vivekananda in Meditation

4

BECOMING A MONK

Bhubaneswar, located in Orissa, a state in East India where the young Nirode began his monastic life, had captured Swami Brahmananda's heart when he first saw it. For it was an unusual sacred place with many beautiful ancient temples and an atmosphere of holiness. Swami Brahmananda, who was inspired and charmed by its beauty, by its silence and its peacefulness, opened a monastery there on October 31, 1919[1]. It was his wish and dream that the monastery would be used by the monks for exclusive spiritual practice and study[2]. It was often described as another Benares -- secret Benares, Swami Brahmananda would visit there often and stay for months at a time during the latter part of his life.

Nirode joined the Ramakrishna Order there in December, 1919. The night before he joined he had a conversation with Swami Shivananda, a disciple of Sri Ramakrishna. They spoke a few words. Swami Shivananda then said: "You know before we came here we thought that all we had to do is remain absorbed in samadhi, coming down once in a while to eat or something. But when we got here we saw it was altogether different... You are going to Maharaj. Good. But don't forget to work!"[3] In later years Swami Akhilananda used to reminisce that Swami Shivananda's words woke him up from his anticipation that he would be spending his time reading and studying. It was here and later in Madras with Swami Brahmananda that at times he would be meditating eight hours a day. This was a seminal period in his life that brought him great joy.

He recalls:

"Somebody once said to us, 'Ah, Swami, how hard it must have been for you to leave everything, your family, etc., to become a monk.' Rather it was a fulfillment. I dare say that 15% of those who joined the Ramakrishna Order in this generation did so because of the love of two personalities -- Swami Brahmananda -- my master, and Swami Premananda. The love of these two persons was all-consuming. You cannot imagine. It pulls you. So we did not feel any sacrifice in joining the Order. It was a fulfillment."[4]

On another occasion he said:

"A person who figures out things ahead of time cannot renounce. A person who thinks, 'Oh, where will I sleep, what will I eat, what kind of work will they give me to do?' Such a person does not renounce. I told my friend, 'I have been through it, I know.' You have to have a desperate -- yes -- almost a desperate feeling -- to drop everything like this (demonstrates)."[5]

"When I came to Bhubaneswar to live with Maharaj after joining the Order, he was extremely kind and generous to take me with him every day while walking during the mornings and evenings. This went on for several months. Often there would be no conversation. I would only follow him. ...One day Maharaj, a devotee, and I went out for a walk in the late afternoon. As we were returning to the Monastery, just about sunset time, we suddenly saw that a tiger was coming towards us. As I was behind Maharaj, I spontaneously came to his side. We all stopped and Maharaj was looking at the tiger. It also stopped running at a distance of a couple of hundred feet and looked at us for a minute or so, standing in a majestic way. Then it took a right turn and went away without doing anything to us... One cannot help being amazed how spiritual power can overcome ferocious tendencies."[6]

In Bhubaneswar, the young monks would come to Maharaj in the evening and sit in his presence. They would sit quietly, conversation not necessary. At that time, Maharaj would ask the young monks their opinions regarding the buying of food, building construction and many other details. He would listen patiently to their opinions. Swami Akhilananda said that he was amazed and he learned a great lesson from this: to see Maharaj giving consideration to opinions of even beginners. One day Maharaj told Nirode that one should notice everything. "No one can predict what experience will be used for the work of the Lord," said Swami Brahmananda. Then he told how the Benares Home of Service was established with just a few pennies. It grew into a gigantic institution serving the sick, destitute and aged. Swami Brahmananda deeply impressed on Nirode with how the way the Lord's work develops.

When Nirode was in Bhubaneswar, he used to sleep in the next room to Maharaj with another young Swami. He was surprised by how little Maharaj slept and his exalting life. Nirode used to sit for meditation in his presence, mostly in his room, towards the end of night.

Nirode was initiated into brahmacharya, a monastic vow of celibacy, in January, 1920 by his guru with the name Sharvachaitanya.[7]

Meanwhile he had been told by one young Swami that Maharaj had said just before his coming from Calcutta: "This boy is coming now, so the whole group will join the Order." Within a few months, all of his friends joined and later became important Swamis. Nirode's enthusiasm for monastic life was infectious. He had become a leader.

Remembering those days, Swami Akhilananda recalls that one day he was standing on the piazza with Maharaj, who said to an older devotee: "I am sending this boy to Madras so that he will learn to speak in English." While Nirode was in Bhubaneswar, he sometimes cooked for Maharaj. He was cooking at home before he joined the Order. His cousin Shirish Sanyal recalls: "During the Durga puja celebrations at home Mejda (later Swami Akhilananda) used to be in a jubilant mood. He used to cook on his own and feed everyone with delicious fish preparations. I never knew from where he learnt this art of cooking... When he joined Belur Math to serve the monks, he used to say that he would like to cook for them."[8]

In a very amusing way Brahmananda would say "Stay here and cook." Akhilananda writes: "But he always had in mind that he would send me to Madras. One day a letter came from Calcutta written by one of our young Swamis saying that Swami Saradananda, Secretary of the Order, wanted me to go to Calcutta to be instrumental in establishing an educational institution there. A wealthy man had offered a fund, and I had been connected with this offer. At the time I was just about to leave the University and join the Order. When this proposal came, Maharaj immediately decided to send me to Madras that very night without further delay. Of course I wanted to stay with him and serve him. He said: 'Do you think that the boys who are away from me and who are doing the Lord's work are not serving me?' I was at once silenced by such touching words." [9]One gentleman wanted Nirode to accompany Brahmananda when he went to Puri, a holy place. But the great Swami disagreed and said: "This boy is not owned by anyone now, so they are trying to pull him here and there. I want him to go immediately to Madras." One day Nirode asked him about dream experiences of incarnations and holy men. Brahmananda told him: "These are really true."[10]

At Madras he made friends with several who later would be Swamis in the West: Siddheswarananda, who would go to France, and Prabhavananda, Vishwananda, and Ashokananda, who went to the U. S. Swami Brahnananda gave some instructions to Yogesh, who would become Swami Ashokananda and that was to make a friend of Nirode. It so happened that Nirode met Yogesh at the railway station in Madras and the two young men became close friends.[11]

In Madras Nirode's activities included being manager of the office[12], preparing <u>payas</u> with Yogesh for special celebrations, the brunt of which would fall on Nirode, who would awake and get-up at 4 am, having gone to bed at 2 am[13]. He had other duties. He was chosen, being a brahmacharin, to perform the Durga puja, an autumnal worship service of the Divine Mother. He is remembered as being very nervous, consulting the senior Swamis on how to conduct himself during this time[14]. For the evening worship service of <u>arati</u> in the monastery, when hymns would be sung or chanted, only Swami Akhilananda and Swami Vishwananda would be playing on the harmonium. Since there were only a few monastics at that time, only the hymn <u>Om hrim</u> would be chanted.[15]

Not only did Nirode play the harmonium, he also was proficient on the tabla. His younger brother, Sudhansu has written that Nirode was fond of Indian classical music. He played on the tabla with the great musician and vocalist teacher, Girija Sankar Chakraborty, an uncle by relation who was very fond of Nirode because of his amiable nature[16]. After Swami Akhilananda and Swami Gnaneswarananda came to the U.S., Swami Akhilananda used to play the tabla whenever they visited each other, either in Providence or Chicago.

Swami Brahmananda was an observant and vigilant guru. One day he asked Nirode to go for a walk with him. Swami Akhilananda recorded the incident:

"Along the way we stood under a tree and he talked with me for about two hours. Many personal things were told. His special advice was on how to deal with people even though they may be unwise and harmful. He related many intimate incidents which cannot be discussed. There were the unfortunate conditions of many persons and how he handled them. He mentioned particular individuals who were living with him at the time. He said: 'Some (meaning the great Swamis) tell me to send these boys away because of their temperaments and tendencies.' He asked: 'Do you think it is better to live with Sanat and Sananda (saints) or with ordinary people?' Then he explained: 'Everyone can live with saints, but it requires something special to live with problem people.' I happen to know the situation and what forgiveness and love were shown by him to those boys. He also said: 'If I begin picking wool from a blanket, there will be nothing left.' This day was a memorable one..."

At another time two or three persons with their tricky ways gave a great deal of pain to Nirode. Swami Akhilananda recalled: "I came to Maharaj with a great deal of heartache. As soon as he saw me, his loving look made me actually weep. He himself was terribly pained, so just to take away my heartaches he asked me to rub his head. It was a unique experience. All my heartaches were wiped away just as it happened when Swami Premananda passed away. My inside was radically changed."

Swami Brahmananda then took Nirode for a walk, consoling him, giving him detailed instructions on how to talk with one of the persons. "He actually taught me the words I was to express, and I had to repeat them to him so that I would not make any mistake. The amazing thing was, even though they had been brutally cruel, yet I was supposed to apologize." On the way back to the Monastery, Nirode met this person. He was just about to say in an apologetic fashion the things Maharaj had asked him to say, when the gentleman, realizing his guilt, feeling very embarrassed, embraced Nirode, not allowing him to finish the sentence. "Forget all this," he said, "forget all this. Ah, how deeply Maharaj loves you. He talked with me about you," and he embraced Nirode.

"Everyone who came in contact with him (Brahmananda), whether they were his disciples or not, always felt his intense love," said Swami Akhilananda. "Many persons young or old felt it." One day in October 1921 Swami Brahmananda inquired of Nirode whether he had had his ordination. "My child, did you have your ordination?" "No, Maharaj...." Nirode said, who had been sitting quietly. "All right, make arrangements and go talk with Swami Shivananda and Swami Sharvananda. 'I was beside myself,' recalls Swami Akhilananda. "All the preliminary preparations and ceremonies were performed during the day, and Swami Prabhavananda and I were ordained very early in the following morning."[17] Swami Akhilananda has said that the receiving of the final vows, sannyas, was one of the greatest incidents in his life.

Swami Akhilananda'a training as a monk was, according to the present plan where a monk spends nine years in monastic training, a little unique. Technically he had been a monk for about two years when he was given sannyasa. But, not to be overlooked were the years when he was studying in Calcutta and went to see Swami Brahmananda every day, and prior to that all the instructions he had received from Brahmananda. Brahmananda, the "spiritual son" of Sri Ramakrishna, was in the words of Swami Vivekananda "the greatest treasure house of spirituality".[18] In other words, Swami Brahmananda knew his monks. Swami Akhilananda has remembered an unforgettable occurrence which took place at an informal gathering of several Swamis and novices sitting on the floor of the Monastery. Swami Shivananda, and the nephew of Ramakrishna as well as Swami Brahmananda were present. Someone expressed a few words about going to the Himalayas for spiritual practices. During the conversation that ensued Swami Brahmananda spoke up. Swami Akhilananda said: "But one thing cannot be forgotten. He (Brahmananda) said: 'Go for tapasya (spiritual practices) and you will see.' Then he added, looking at Swami Shivananda: 'Those who went for tapasya in Himalayas were ruined.' After a minute he added: 'Excepting a few.' This statement has a deep significance as we know the history of many persons." The watchful guru, Brahmananda. Another memorable event for the young Swami was the dedication of the Mission's Students Home in Madras in May, 1921. "Very graciously and lovingly Swami Brahmananda sent me ahead of time," said Swami Akhilananda, "to make needful preparations for the worship. Later on, Maharaj went with other Swamis and devotees in a procession... to the new educational institution. ...As the procession moved towards the building I went forward a few hundred yards to meet them. I had an unexplainable experience at that time just as I approached Maharaj. The amazing thing is all persons present felt something extremely unusual as if they lost themselves and were lifted to a higher plane."

Swami Shivananda later explained that Swami Brahmananda had the power to lift a number of people to a higher plane. When the Divine Mother was worshipped with Brahmananda present, all experienced unspeakable joy and upliftment on the final day.[19]

In Madras Swami Akhilananda would go for walks sometimes with a brother monastic like Swami Prabhavananda. Swami Akhilananda remembers a very meaningful incident. "One day my Master took me for a walk - only it was not for a walk. It was the last real conversation that I had with him in my life. It was as if he saw the future - not-as-if, he did. And one thing he told me, 'Tell the truth, but not the unpleasant.' And many times when I remembered those words I was saved from very disagreeable circumstances. To tell the truth is necessary. God does not come to a man who indulge in lies. You can take it for granted that a truly spiritual person does not indulge in lies."[20]

Looking back, Swami Akhilananda recalls: "It seems now in retrospect that Maharaj saw the whole of my future and gave me intimate instructions on how to handle problems of people and the different personalities. I could never dream that I was meant for work in America; nor could I imagine the problems I was to face in India and America. In that connection he said: 'Sri Ramakrishna used to say, 'Endure, endure, endure. The man who endures survives. The man who does not is ruined.' When he told me of many of his own personal experiences with people it was very inspiring and touching.

"One day I went to his room and sat in his presence very near to him. He began to tell me about my first intimate visit with him in Calcutta during my sickness. It was amazing to note that he even remembered what little offerings I took to him and many touching words were spoken."[21]: On November 19, 1921 Swami Brahmananda left Madras for Belur Math in Calcutta. While there he had a visit from an English lady. In his reminiscences Swami Akhilananda remembered her visit to Madras. One day she came to the monastery in a very disturbed mental state. Swami Akhilananda spoke with her and advised her to go to Calcutta to see Swami Brahmananda. Later she told Swami Akhilananda that as she approached Maharaj with her heartaches and knelt before him, he blessed her. Immediately she had an exalting spiritual realization which removed all her heartaches and gave her positive unbelievable joy and peace. Her whole life was changed. When Swami Akhilananda met her in London in 1934, she again described her experience and its effect on her entire life.[22]

In Calcutta, Swami Brahmananda had been staying at the home of a great devotee, Balaram Bose, off and on. Some time after the celebra-

36

tion of Sri Ramakrishna's birthday, he fell ill. First it was cholera, followed by diabetes, which became serious. He was having exalting spiritual experiences, but nothing could stop the disease. He would speak of his experiences and those present, his disciples and devotees, knew his time was coming. He passed away on April 10, 1922 without ever going into a coma.[23]

"'Do not grieve'", he said in his final days. "'I shall be with you always.' Those were his last words to his disciples.... More than forty years have passed since that day and every disciple can bear witness to the fact that Maharaj still lives, protects, and guides him onward toward the goal."[24] We can well imagine how Swami Akhilananda felt. Maharaj was the center of his life. Years later when Swami Prabhavananda invited him to California, he asked Swami Akhilananda to speak about Swami Brahmananda. Prabhavananda recalls: "I remember one occasion when he visited here. We got together with other monastic members and asked him to speak about Maharaj. While he spoke he was sobbing and weeping. His love was so great."[25]

Swami Akhilananda was associated with the Madras Monastery until 1925. During 1923-24 he was the warden at Sri Minakshe college.[26] For a time he was a visiting professor at Annamali University.[27] He also participated in flood relief work in the Cauvery in South India. He and another monk organized the operation. Swami Rudrananda, who was inspired to join the monastery, encouraged by Swami Akhilananda, described how Swami Akhilananda and another Swami were looking for somebody to help them immediately in the flood relief activities. Rudrananda relates: "A vast area was covered by flood for three weeks. Many districts were under water for miles together; hundreds of thousands of cottages and small houses, even brick-built houses, fell down. ...Thousands were homeless. There was no food for them. ...I at once offered my service to them. Swami Akhilananda was the leader of one district with one or more Swamis. ... Swami was very nice to me, very loving and very dear; and his thoroughness of work in the relief activities was so enchanting. We continued for about eleven months. ... during this time the contact was so intimate that I could study what this monastic life was and how the service aspect of Swami Vivekananda's teaching was so elevating to the mind."[28]

Swami Akhilananda himself would describe the flood relief work and helping those faced with famine in South India. How he and the two boys would swim day after day, forging rivers swollen with water, accompanied by crocodiles and snakes. Bringing what was needed to the people, the villagers at night would offer him a small bowl of rice. He would confide to some of his American friends that he could never forget the two young boys who swam along with him, oblivious of any danger. None of them felt any fear.[29]

The strain of flood relief work was damaging his health. He became ill with jaundice. Staying at the Madras monastery, he had planned to go to Belur Math with Swami Ashokananda for a visit. On the morning they were to get the train, Swami Akhilananda was too sick. Swami Ashokananda decided to stay with his brother monk and help him. Swami Akhilananda became very ill, dangerously so. Recovering he had to learn to walk again, the first day or two, with only a single step. Later, when he felt a little better, he and Swami Ashokananda went to the mountains of Kodaikanal, traveling by train, a journey of a few hundred miles south of Madras.

No sooner had they arrived then Swami Ashokananda, chilled while sleeping the first night, became ill with chronic stomach trouble. He was unable to eat. Swami Akhilananda, ailing a little, had to take care of him. They went to a doctor who prescribed meat for Ashokananda's condition. Where to get it? For a sannyasin to eat meat! Swami Akhilananda said he would get it at a European hotel, never mind the scandal of monks eating meat. "I shall go," said Swami Akhilananda. But Swami Ashokananda said no. Thinking it over, they knew of a man in the area who was a devotee of Ramakrishna. He helped them and the two monks picked up the meat, which was lamb, at his home. At their first meal, Swami Ashokananda was cured of his stomach problem. They stayed in this place for a month and then returned to Madras. Later they went to Belur Math.[30]

It seems that Swami Akhilananda was not completely over his jaundice. He went to where Swami Shivananda was. Remembering those days, Swami Akhilananda's brother Sudhansu writes that the Mission authorities decided to send him back to Netrakona to his family for rest and treatment. In no time at all Swami Akhilananda regained his health and returned to Belur Math. His family had given him special care, delighted to have his company for some time.[31]

This may not have been the first time that Swami Akhilananda probably had been ill while he was in Madras. At another time he and Swami Ashokananda went on a tour of South India in order to get subscriptions for the monthly magazine, <u>Vedanta Kesari.</u> In doing so, they had an enjoyable time.[32]

In the early part of 1926 at the time of the first Convention of the Ramakrishna Order, Swami Akhilananda was privileged to perform a special assignment. He never mentioned what it was, but he did write that it was a unique sight to see Swami Shivananda, Swami Akhandananda, and Swami Saradananda together; ..."to see their relationship, their love and appreciation for one another." He states that these three spiritual giants were the inspiring force behind this great gathering. "It was amazing to us to see how the three great persons could spend their time deeply absorbed in God, inspiring us in meditation and other devotional exercises, and, at the-same time, carry on the so-called Convention activities."[33]

Soon Swami Akhilananda was to leave India. At Belur one day Swami Shivananda, the president of the Order, had Akhilananda sit by his side and said: "How would you like to go to a foreign country?", and laughed. Swami Akhilananda also laughed. He did not take it too seriously. But Swami Shivananda became serious and told the Swami he would be going to America. Swami Akhilananda folded his hands together and said, "Yes, Maharaj."[34] Swami Paramananda, who had a Vedanta Center in Boston and an ashrama in California, had come to India thinking to bring back an assistant to help him.[35] It would be Swami Akhilananda. Another monk, Swami Dayananda, who would be going to San Francisco; a Mrs. French, Swamis Akhilananda and Paramananda along with his widowed niece, Gayatri Devi, would travel by a Pacific Liner from Calcutta via Rangoon, Penang, Singapore, Hong-Kong, and Yokahama.[36] The General Secretary, Swami Saradananda, came with other friends to the boat to see them off.

He offered some advice to Swami Akhilananda. "You are going there. Some people will praise you to the sky, others will condemn you like anything. Take both equally."[37] That great Swami had been in this country, the U. S., in the late 1890s.

The counsel that Swami Akhilananda had received from both Swami Brahmananda and Swami Saradananda was what he had in mind when he wrote to the President of the Order, Swami Vireswarananda, in a letter of July 28, 1950. He said: "...if I learned anything from the example of these great Swamis (Sri Maharaj and Swami Saradanandaji Maharaj) I learned this: that patience, endurance, forgiveness and sympathy ought to be basic principles of our handling of interpersonal relationships."

A group picture including Swami Akhilananda (warden), left, and
Swami Pavitrananda, right, at the Sri Minakshi College Home Chidambaram,
Malayalee Section, (1923-24)

Swami Akhilananda in California, 1926

5

AMERICA THE BEAUTIFUL

D ocking at San Francisco on June 13, 1926, the party of Swami Paramananda stopped at the Vedanta Society in San Francisco where Swami Dayananda would be assisting Swami Praka-shananda. Swami Paramananda's group then traveled to the Ananda Ashrama where Swami Akhilananda would give his first lecture in the U. S. The ashrama, purchased in 1923 and located about 16 miles from Los Angeles with a distant view of the blue Pacific Ocean, was some 500 feet above the valley of La Crescenta. Named the Temple of the Universal Spirit by Swami Paramananda, the ashrama in time became a cluster of buildings with many workers and large gatherings. The Swami Paramananda had wanted it to be a place where a group of people could find expression in music, art, the crafts, and industrial arts, not limited to religion, though that would be the heart of it.[1]

The young Akhilananda was about to experience an America rolling in affluence, awash in a tide of new mores. It was the age of the flapper and jazz music. Prohibition had been enacted, but nothing was prohibited. Speculation in the stock market was increasing, and, buried like a seed in all the financial euphoria, was the great Stock Market Crash of 1929. As Calvin Coolidge had said, "The business of America is business."[2]

Did Swami Akhilaninda, only 32, suffer cultural shock? The answer can only be surmised, but probably with "admirable equanimity."[3] At the Ananda Ashrama, it was not long before he would give Sunday services and start a weekly class. His first lecture, of which we do not have the date, began with: "It fills my heart with joy to rise in response to the hearty and warm welcome which you have so kindly given to me. I take this opportunity to express my gratitude to you all and to those who sent their loving greetings to us at Honolulu..."[4] Then he told a story about a conversation between Swami Shivananda and his brother monk, Brahmananda, the head of the Ramakrishna Order, that there should be no distinction or differentiation in regard to devotees.

In this matter "Maharaj became very serious and responded: 'Certainly not. We cannot make any distinction in the kingdom of the Lord. Devotees are born even in the furthest corner of the world. People are coming from the most unexpected places.' Then he told about some devotees in a most touching way. They did not even read the life of the Master still they love him deeply and they know none but him. The devotees are the same everywhere."

The young Swami concluded with: "I take it a rare privilege to be in your midst. And I think I am blessed to be allowed to serve you in America. It is true that I was meant for one of the newly established centers in India. Everything was settled and I was about to start for Gujrat... But the Lord decides my fate otherwise and brought me here. I am sure the Lord will grant us all strength to work in His name. Let us all serve Him in this land and be blessed." His expression "the Lord decides my fate" would be characteristic of him throughout his life. God's will, he felt, was expressed in circumstances and in interpersonal relationships, interactions between all the various factors. If something good or fortunate happened to one, it was always "God's will," "the grace of God", and "His grace".

Summoned by Swami Paramananda, Swami Akhilananda arrived in Boston in November, 1926[5] and went to the Vedanta Society at #1 Queensberry Street, a twenty-room house in the Fenway which had been enlarged in 1921, including an increased seating capacity in the chapel.[6] It wasn't long before the followers of Swami Paramananda objected to Swami Akhilananda's traditional and scholarly presentation. His approach to teaching was so different than Paramananda's spontaneous spirituality. It was Akhilananda's nature to be scholarly and he attracted eminent scholars throughout his life. What should be remembered is his utmost devotion to his guru, to the training he had under the direction of the great disciples of Sri Ramakrishna. This had determined, in his eyes, what the behavior of a monk should be. They had set the example.

While Swami Akhilananda was becoming better acquainted with American life, Swami Shivananda, the head of the Order, would write encouraging words to him. In a letter of 12 May 1927:

"With Almighty's grace your work has been outstanding and it will continue to excel. He is looking over you that is for sure. Never lose that faith."

And on June 23, 1927: "His thoughts are inside you. He is with you. Regarding His thought, you have to blend that with the thought and language of the soil over there and then deliver -- it will be a sure success. There may be some minor problems in the beginning but all of you are educated and smart, you will be able to figure out the problem and if you can do that, you will succeed. Don't be afraid. That endless power is behind you -- always remember Him and go ahead -- with His grace, all adversities and all hurdles will go away."

Another letter of Swami Shivananda on August 3, 1927:

"With His grace may your capabilities become multidimensional and comprehensive -- that is my prayer."

At the end of the summer of 1927, those critical of Akhilananda in Boston summoned Swami Paramananda from California. A cluster of factors, including behavior by some, which in India might have been considered impudence,[7] created a situation that terminated his association with the Boston Center. When on September 21, 1927, Swami Akhilananda was to leave the Boston Center, he was emaciated and sick.[8] Mr. and Mrs. Leonard Worcester, who had been attending the lectures, found him in this condition. They brought him to their home in Cambridge, fed him, clothed him and got a doctor. They contacted Swami Bodhananda in New York City at the Vedanta Society. There the young Swami went when he felt a little better to improve his health. It appears that there may have been a reoccurrence of his tuberculosis. On October 7, 1927, Swami Paramananda wrote to him while he was staying in New York: "I hope that you are feeling well and that you feel happy for the change you have made."

Returning to the Worcester's sometime the end of March, 1928,[9] we find from a letter of Helen Rubel that Swami Akhilananda gave a few lectures in the Worcester home in 1928.[10] No public announcements of these lectures have been found in the Cambridge newspapers. He also considered having a Center in Cambridge. At first Swami Shivananda looked on this new Center in Cambridge favorably. In his letter of 2 November, 1927: "There is no harm in having a new center in Cambridge. Of course, please do so only after consulting him and getting his concurrence." However this proposal was later felt to be inappropriate and a letter of Swami Shivananda confirms this: "We have decided that both of you stay in different places..."[11] At one point in May 1928 Akhilananda and Swami Gnaneswarananda of Chicago met with Swami Paramananda to discuss amalgamating Swami Akhilananda's group in Cambridge with the Boston Center, but Swami Paramananda declined.[12]

The following month Akhilananda contacted Swami Shivananda disclosing that he had received sufficient funds to open a new Center, but it must be in an Eastern city.[13] In July 1928 Swami Prabhavananda wrote to his brother monk: "By the grace of Sri Sri Thakur, what you have been wishing for has now been confirmed through instructions from the Math." Swami Shivananda had sent a cable: "We agree (with) Nirode's proposal opening center Eastern States..." and Prabhavananda continues: "Now you can start a Center without further worry, wherever convenient..."[14]

In 1959, referring to this period of his life, Swami Akhilananda, in an interview with a devotee, told of how he prayed and meditated, meditated and prayed, and how everything turned out wonderful.[15] And so it did.

It did for several reasons. It has been said that Swami Akhilananda had the power to adjust, to be flexible. He was in the world, but not of the world. He could adapt to the way we wore our clothes, to the way we eat our food. He was not remote or aloof; he was warm and engaged and happy, always with a smiling face. He always shook hands. It helped to make people feel at home. He moved easily between Indian ways and American ways, at times eating Indian food, at others, American. Everyone felt that he was one of us. Everyone felt that he was a holy man. His success was due to identifying with the people here. Those who accepted Ramakrishna and Vivekananda did not think of him as foreign, but as countryless, raceless, Vedanta being universal.[16] But most of all he loved the people.

Slightly over 30 years later in March, 1960, Prof. Edwin Booth of B. U. School of Theology, appeared on WHDH-TV in a program We Believe. This in part is what he had to say about Swami Akhilananda:

"It is interesting always to know him. He is a marvelous person. He does not live according to the customs of the East, for he speaks peace to us of the West, so he lives according to our customs. He has a good home, he wears our Western clothes, he drives a big good Western automobile. But everywhere he goes, his smiling face, his quiet word, his gentle hand, is a blessing of peace to all of us. I was ill once, quite seriously, a few years ago. He stepped into my hospital room on several occasions, and quietly, out of the ancient East, I heard his words: 'Peace, peace, peace.' Well, it is marvelous to know that the religions communicate to each other through living individuals, warm and gentle, quiet and patient." [17]

6

PROVIDENCE, PART ONE

Auspiciously, the eastern city chosen by Swami Akhilananda where he would establish a Vedanta Society was named Providence. The capital of Rhode Island, situated on a waterway, with Brown University on one of its hills, Providence was founded in the mid-17th century by Roger Williams (1603?-83). He was a man who believed in democracy with a long record of opposition to those who were privileged and engaged in self-seeking pursuits. He had been harassed and persecuted in Massachusetts for his religious beliefs. Roger Williams had a "lifelong advocacy of religious freedom."[1] Providence became a haven for religious outsiders.

The Vedanta movement can be said to have really begun with the success of Swami Vivekananda at the Parliament of Religions, held in Chicago in 1893. Newspapers all over the country reported on the Parliament. Vivekananda became a leading figure. As we say nowadays, he stole the show. News of him trickled everywhere, and even small towns in Indiana and Ohio invited him to speak in 1894.[2]

"The Parliament," writes Carl Jackson, Professor of History and Dean of the College of Liberal Arts at the University of Texas, "... opened doors for all the Asian delegates, yet Vivekananda alone succeeded in transplanting a new religion to the American shores in the years immediately after 1893... the Swami almost single-handedly created the Ramakrishna movement in America."[3]

The Society in Providence would be the fifth to be established in the United States. Vivekananda in 1896 founded the Vedanta Society of New York (some would say it was in 1894)[4], and another in San Francisco in 1900, followed by Los Angeles, the latter for a time suspended. Swami Paramananda opened a Vedanta Center in Boston in 1909.

Eager to begin his work in Providence, the young and energetic Swami Akhilananda announced a series of lectures to be held in September 1928 at the Biltmore Hotel, located in a busy downtown section. The <u>Providence Journal</u> printed the following:

Series of Free Lectures
by Swami Akhilananda
of India
at the Biltmore Hotel, Mezzanine floor
Sunday, September 9th, 8:00 pm
PSYCHOLOGY OF RELIGION

Tuesday, September 11, 8:00 pm
WAS CHRIST A YOGI?

Thursday, September 13th, 8:00 pm
HEALING AND PREVENTIVE METHODS
(of the great Disease)

The fledgling society was helped in various ways by two devotees whom the Swami knew in Boston. Miss Helen Rubel, who later was called Bhakti, young, cultured, and very devoted, and Mrs. Anna Worcester, a matronly mother, now separated from her husband, helped him financially, mostly from the funds of Miss Rubel. They assisted Swami Akhilananda with the services. If they didn't live immediately in Providence, they would soon.

A placard about the lectures was placed in a window at the Biltmore Hotel. One day a young man walked by and saw the sign. He attended the meeting. When the lecture was over, he was asked to pass the offering basket. His name was Italo Pellini. He would become in time the treasurer of the Society, which he served for over 60 years. He and several others, including Bertha and Edith Hawkhead, Mrs. Anna Worcester and Helen Rubel became a nucleus of the Society.

The response to the lectures by the public was immediate. Charlotte Morrison, who later became Mrs. Pellini, recalls: "After the first three lectures, rented quarters were obtained at 241 Weybosset Street, and regular services and classes were begun on December 9, 1928."[5] Swami's warm-hearted friendliness and intellectual acumen attracted many.

The Providence Journal for December 8, 1928 had a headline: "City Will have Vedanta Center ... Swami Akhilananda has over 100 devotees following early lectures."

The story, in part, follows: "Providence is to have a Vedanta Center, where devotees of the Upanishads, the Vedas, the Bhagavad Gita and other Hindu scriptures may sit under the tutorship of Swami Akhilananda and wrest their meaning for such spiritual inspiration as may be needed in this industrial age.

"From modest beginnings at the Hotel Biltmore, Swami Akhilananda has attracted more than 100 devotees and quarters will be opened tomorrow evening at 8, at room 320, 241 Weybosset Street, opposite Loew's State Theatre."

The news report continues with a description of dualism, qualified monism, and monism, the latter in which we are one with God. "... Swami Akhilananda will endeavor to harmonize these three conceptions of God as Sri Ramakrishna, the great master of Vivekananda, held that all these three distinct conceptions are true and valid, and are experienced by devotees in the course of their spiritual evolution. These are but different stages in our spiritual experience, he claims.

"'We can all reach to the highest realization of oneness by practically following the teachings of any of the great teachers of the world, that is Christ, Krishna, Buddha, and so forth,' said the Swami. 'This is possible from whatever standpoint we may start, be it dualistic, qualified monistic or monistic.'"

So it can be seen that Swami Akhilananda did not hesitate to plunge into the depths of Vedanta and Hindu philosophy for enlightening the American public.

In February, 1929, the birthday anniversary of Swami Vivekananda was observed at the Vedanta Society. The Providence Journal reported that there were three speakers: Swami Gnaneswarananda of New York, Swami Akhilananda, and Frederick A. Wilmot, religious editor of the Providence Journal. "Vivekananda bitterly opposed the fossilized caste system of India," the article stated, and also "child marriage and other social evils." He taught that all world teachers like Christ, Buddha, Krishna... and others contributed towards an ultimate religion.[6]

It was not long before the Swami faced a challenge. His views on science and religion were more thoroughly aired when the Providence Journal published on April 13, 1929, his rejoinder to the concepts of Prof. Harry Barnes of Smith College and Bishop McConnell, President of the Federal Council of Churches of Christ in America. The Barnes and McConnell piece had appeared in the March issue of <u>Current History.</u>

The lead headline: "Swami Discusses Science-Religion," with the following sub-heading: "Says Scientist must be met on Own Ground." The account begins: 'The scientist must be met on his own grounds -- not ridiculed by the custodians of religion,' declared Swami Akhilananda, a Vedantist leader of this city, referring to the articles pro and con on 'Our Conception of God: Should it be Revised?'"

The Swami continued: "Some leaders condemn Dr. Barnes for his frank discussion of religious matters, and it is to the credit of Bishop McGonnell that he gives patient consideration to the former's arguments...

"The fight between religious and secular knowledge has been going on ever since the dawn of civilization. Religionists have refused to accept evidence and arguments based on secular knowledge; to question anything religious evoked a categorical refusal to answer or a curse."

In this lengthy article, the Swami brought points to bear about the unscientific attitude of the scientists and the limited conceptions of God of the religionists.

The second article, appeared in the <u>Providence Journal</u> for April 27, 1929, with the headline: "Christ Defended by Hindu Leader" marks the continuation of the discussion with a Socratic method of question and answer. "Swami, tell me, if it is true, as Dr. Barnes claims, that there is no sin except, as a manifestation of adolescent emotional development, and no God outside the material universe -- the pantheism of Spinoza being most acceptable to scientists, as Einstein admitted this week -- what becomes of the personal God and the Christ of Christians?"

"That is a very direct question. We shall answer it. Dr. Barnes denies the existence of a personal God and Bishop McConnell by limiting God's personality to the attributes of self -consciousness and self-determination makes Him to that extent impersonal. God must have all the attributes of personality if He is personal."

"Did not Einstein say that he believed in Spinoza's God-Pantheism, that is, that God pervades everything? What is wrong with that idea?" Swami - "God must be absolute and infinite. Spinoza thought that God was everywhere. Let us see what that means. A tree has roots, trunk, branches, leaves -- they are all parts of a tree, but no one part of the tree can be defined as the tree. There is a separation there, and that very separation would make a God so conceived as finite, not infinite."

"Is God impersonal?"

Swami - "Yes, God is impersonal, but the human mind is so arranged that we must assign attributes to God, that is, we make Him personal. Some ordinary minds even have to give Him name and form, because they cannot think of anything which is not existing in time and space, in other words, anything which cannot be experienced through the senses. ...."

"But you remember I asked you to clear up what Dr. Barnes said about there being no sin and no extra-cosmic God, and therefore no need for a Savior like Christ?"

Swami - "I was just coming to that, Jesus, Buddha, Krishna and other great incarnations of God are the practical demonstrations of the Impersonal God being conceived as personal. In Jesus we can thoroughly understand the necessity of a Personal God based upon impersonal existence. Whether man is originally pure or impure does not matter. That is, Dr. Barnes's statement regarding sin has no point. In the present state man is in ignorance and unconscious of his divine nature.

"If it were not for Jesus, and -- if you will allow me, those other great teachers I have mentioned, living as human beings, how would we become conscious of our divine heritage? Apart from other considerations, even in this sense Jesus's existence is absolutely necessary for us. Without Him we could not have any idea of God and the method of realizing Him."

"… Am I right in understanding that Dr. Barnes and his confreres seem prepared to accept a religion which will make man happy in this world?*"

Swami - "Professor Barnes does not give us any plan of happiness that does not equally imply misery as well. For instance, the modern world is proving every day that the materialistic outlook on life, which is being overemphasized by the scientist is a complete failure in making man happy. If you list the wireless, electric light, etc., among your material achievements, you must not forget the machine gun, the depth bomb and other instruments of destruction. ...true happiness can be attained only by real spiritual growth based on higher forms of ethical principles. Neither the utilitarian nor the humanitarian ethics (of

Comte) are sufficient actuating powers to secure happiness. Morality cannot stand without its spiritual background."

Such views as the erudite Swami presented might well have been considered unorthodox and even radical to the divergent ethnic and church-going population of Providence. They might also have promoted controversy and interest. Success followed. As Swami Shivananda, the President of the Ramakrishna Order, had written in a letter of March 12, 1929: "I was exceedingly pleased to learn that your work is progressing steadily and that you are able to attract people's sympathy (attention). If you have purity, love and detachment and above all complete dependence on Him, you will gain co-operation from all. Be convinced that both our personal lives and our monastery are based on these qualities."

The 6th October, 1929 Evening Bulletin announced a lecture, "Philosophy of Reincarnation," at the Biltmore Hotel, Mezzanine floor for the next evening. Other articles appeared in the Evening Bulletin in which Swami Akhilananda contested the views of Sir Arthur Keith, commented on the opinions of the atheists, and refuted Dr. Mordecai Kaplan's position "that each faith is a separate psychological entity that need not be compared with any other faith..."

For his services Swami Akhilananda gave talks on the Gita on Tuesday evenings, practical lessons in meditation on Friday evenings. For his Sunday sermons he had a variety of topics: Incarnations, science of breathing, today's religion, yoga, self-discipline, harmony of East and West, power of thought, etc. In his lectures he had a universal approach to religion, stressing the spirituality in each of them. He was no provincial Hindu. This brought him into sympathy with everyone -- Christians, Jews, unbelievers, etc.

As the Providence Journal on October 6, 1929 reported him as saying: "My mission in Providence is not to convert Christians or others to Hinduism, but, if possible, with the teachings of the Gita, to inspire persons to take up their religious life, to refresh their minds and to revive their interest in spiritual things. The Vedanta movement is that of a universal religion."

He had a wonderful capacity for making friends. Wherever he went, people were immediately impressed. This was true from his early days at Providence. One of his students, Robert Louis of Santa Barbara, some years later described an incident that was characteristic of the Swami at any time in his life. "We were at the Illinois Central Railway station in Chicago," he writes, "where we were to meet and pick up Swami, who had given a lecture that day at the University of Illinois at Urbana.

"It was about midnight when the train pulled in, and at first we thought Swami had missed it; at the end of a line of passengers, there was Swami arm in arm with two men, talking and laughing like a group of old friends.

"It turned out they were all strangers having met on the train just a few hours ago. But here they were, walking with Swami as if they were life-long friends."[7]

"Be merry with men,"[8] Ramakrishna had said. So he was.

With his ministry moving along so favorably and the assurance of continued support, in late 1930 a house was purchased at 224 Angell Street, which became the Chapel and the living quarters for the Swami.[9] Swami Shivananda had cabled earlier in the year: "Delighted. Blessings. Everybody wishes work prosperity."[10] Gatherings of ministers and other religious leaders were held at the Center. Helen Rubel wrote to her aunts in Switzerland in October, 1931: "And I wish you could visit our Swami's house and feel how peaceful the atmosphere there is. He is friends with many ministers of many religions and also a rabbi. Even the ministers and the rabbi as they came in remarked on the wonderful atmosphere."

Now established in a permanent place of worship, the Vedanta Society had its first meeting for being incorporated on February 2, 1931.[11] How did Swami Akhilananda structure his Sunday service? Every Vedanta Center in the United States has its own pattern for the Sunday morning program. In Providence it would start with his chanting a short Vedic hymn in Sanskrit. This would be followed by the congregation reciting the following prayer:

We offer our salutations to the All-Loving Being who endows all beings with consciousness. We meditate on the Lord, Who is the origin of the Universe. Lord, Thou abidest in all; Thou art all; Thou assumest all forms; Thou art the origin and goal of all; Thou art the Self of all; Thou art Existence, Knowledge, Bliss. Salutations unto Thee. May the world be peaceful. May the wicked become gentle. May all creatures think of mutual welfare. May their minds be occupied with what is spiritual and abiding. May our hearts be immersed in selfless love for the Lord. Peace, Peace, Peace be unto all.

The Swami might then read a few scriptural passages that were in harmony with his sermon. He would launch immediately into the sermon that would last almost an hour. Then would follow the offering and the benediction:

May He who is Father-in-heaven of the Christians,
Holy One of the Jews, Allah of the Muslims,
Buddha of the Buddhists, Tao of the Chinese,
Ahura Mazda of the Zoroastrians, and Brahman of the Hindus,
Lead us from the unreal to the Real,
From darkness to Light, from death to Immortality.
May the all-loving Being manifest Himself unto us, and
Grant us abiding understanding and all-consuming divine love.
Peace, peace, peace be unto all.

There was no singing at any time during the services. On the altar an inscription read: Truth is one, men call it by various names. Above it was a picture of Ramakrishna. Near the altar, on the walls, were pictures of Holy Mother, Swami Vivekananda, and Swami Brahmananda.

Elsewhere on the walls of the chapel were plaques with scriptural passages from the different religions. For Christianity: "The kingdom of God is within you." "Be ye perfect even as your Father which is in heaven is perfect." "Ye love one another as I have loved you." Christ. For Islam: "Your God is one God, the merciful, the compassionate. He is the light of the heaven and earth. Remember the Lord within thyself humbly." Mohammed. For Judaism: "God created man in His image." "The eternal God is thy refuge." "He is mighty who makes his enemy love him." For Buddha: "Let a man overcome anger by love. Let him overcome evil by good. Happy is he who has found the Truth. There is no saviour in the world except the Truth." From the Vedas: "Truth is One, men call it by various names. There is one Supreme Being, the soul of all beings, who makes His one form manifold. The wise who perceive Him as existing in their own self, to them belongs eternal Bliss."

A plaque for Ramakrishna read: "There is but one God, but endless are His names and aspects in which He may be regarded. Call Him by any names and worship Him in any aspect that pleases you. You are sure to realize Him."

The first time Mrs. Elizabeth Bertini went to hear Swami Akhilananda, she looked at all the plaques on the walls and read the sayings of the founders of all the great religions. Hearing the Swami speak, she thought, "I've come home! So many questions can be answered truthfully here."[12]

Charlotte Morrison, who assisted Swami Akhilananda with secretarial work, has written that two Providence ministers were attracted to him and his message shortly after he started his ministry. One was a Methodist, Dr. Allen Claxton, who became a life-long friend. The other was Rev. Frederick A. Wilmot, the religious editor of the <u>Providence Journal</u>. Both were instrumental in introducing him to various church organizations and religious groups, Christian and Jewish.[13] As he became acquainted with the clergy and educators of the community, he was invited to speak before church groups. He was requested to speak to the students and faculty in the area, especially R. I. College, Providence College, Brown University, where he became intimately acquainted with the professors and administrators, including the President, Dr. Clarence Barber and the Vice-President, Dr. Albert Mead, and at the University of Rhode Island. He received invitations to join the following organizations: R. I. Ministers' Union, The Universal Club of Ministers, R. I. Philosophical Society, R. I. State Council of Churches, World Affairs Council.

Throughout his ministry the Swami attracted educators, doctors, philosophers, psychologists, theologians, scientists, and religious seekers, some of whom were troubled and sought his peaceful presence. Prof. Robert Ulich of Harvard University remembers: "Without any pose he moved among us simply, modestly, and naturally. ...When I met him for the first time, I intuitively felt the presence of an unusual personality. He was a lover of life and man.[14]

Both Helen Rubel and Mrs. Anna Worcester assisted the Swami at the time of the services and with other work at the Center. Now and then when the Swami was away Helen Rubel took an evening class, speaking on spiritual personalities. She had written to her family in Switzerland in October, 1931: "These years I have been living in Providence with Mrs. Worcester and her daughter. ...We have a very nice little six room apartment and do our own work."[15]

For the summer they tried to get away from Providence. In 1930 Swami Akhilananda, Mrs. Worcester and daughter, and Helen Rubel and some other close devotees spent one month on the coast near Providence. Helen Rubel has written that they "went down to stay as long as everyone could at a nice hotel. There was swimming and boat-ing and we had classes every day..."[16]

However, while enjoying their vacation it appears that Swami Akhilananda was not always feeling well. In early June Swami Shivananda, the president of the Order, had written to Mrs. Worcester, or Annapurna as she was called: "Akhilananda wrote me in one of his various letters that he is suffering from stomach trouble." Perhaps, the Swami writes, this was due to eating too many Indian dishes.[17] In the fall of the year, 1930, Swami Akhilananda was hospitalized for an op-eration. By November 19th Swami Shivananda was writing that he hoped Akhilananda had recovered completely by that time. Again in a letter of December 4th, he wrote to Mrs. Worcester: "Your letter of the 9th November last gave us much relief. For it gave us news that Akhi-lananda is out of the hospital and is on the fair way to recovery." And then he remarked; "Akhilananda is one of the purest souls. Coming in contact with him many souls will get peace."[18]

Vacationing continued. In the summer of 1931 Bhakti again wrote to her Zurich family: "It was Mrs. Worcester, her daughter, our swami and a young man also interested who went on the Western trip this summer. We went from one of the Centres to the next, and sometimes the other swamis joined us on part of our travels. Everywhere they were more hospitable and kind than can be imagined. It was a wonderful experience..."[19] In California Swami Akhilananda and Swami Prabhavananda were happy to see each other and to greet Swami Ashokananda. He had recently arrived on July 4th. He would be assisting Swami Vividishananda who would be the head of the San Francisco center. Swami Dayananda, who had been in San Francisco for five years, was returning to India. It was in August that Swami Prabhavananda paid a visit and so did Swami Akhilananda, a close friend of Swami Ashokananda from their Madras days. All three swamis had known each other there. All the five swamis, Akhilananda, Ashokan-anda, Dayananda, Prabhavananda, and Vividishananda enjoyed an outing at the Golden Gate Park. They gave a farewell reception to Swami Dayananda on Sunday, August 14th.

Swami Ashokananda was not quite at ease in America. He needed proper coats and suits. So Swami Akhilananda suggested that he would buy Vividishananda and Ashokananda each a new overcoat and suit. No ready-made black suits were available so they went to a tailor, who made their suits, each with two vests, one with a clerical collar and the other for shirt and tie.[20]

Swami Akhilananda, Mrs. Worcester, Helen Rubel and their guest also met Swami Gnaneswarananda in Chicago where he had opened a center in January, 1930.[21] For the summer of 1932 they vacationed at Chesterton, New York, near Lake George.[22] In June, 1933 Helen Rubel wrote: "We expect to go to the Adirondacks to about the same place as last year. It is a little bit mountainous there and much cooler. Only this summer there will be two or three more swamis visiting with our swamis."[23]

In late 1932 Swami Nikhilananda who had been assisting Swami Akhilananda for a while left Providence for New York City. Swami Vividishananda then came to Providence. As Swami Shivananda wrote: "'so that... the work may not suffer."[24]

Although it had been thought that the following incident did not happen until late 1933 or early 1934, it has been determined that the surprise which Swami Akhilananda experienced when Helen Rubel dropped by the Center with a suitcase full of investments probably would have occurred in the late spring of 1932.

The suitcase, which she had brought to Swami Akhilananda, contained a fortune for him to do exactly what he wanted with it. Both the Swami and Mrs. Worcester were astonished. He, devoted to his teacher, Swami Brahmananda, knew that Brahmananda wanted a temple to Ramakrishna to be built at Belur Math. It had been designed by Swami Vivekananda. Swami Akhilananda contacted the President of the Order, Swami Shivananda, about the gift. Could it be used for the construction of the temple? Swami Shivananda cabled to Swami Akhilananda that that was why Sri Sri Thakur had sent him to America.[25]

This received a confirmation when in 1936, Swami Akhilananda wrote to Belur Math: "I said about the proposal of Sri Maharaj (Swami Brahmananda) to Rev. Mahapurush Maharaj (Swami Shivananda) at the end of June, 1932. ... Rev. Mahapurush Maharaj sent his blessings by cable."[26]

Helen Rubel

Mrs. Anna Worcester

Providence Vedanta Center, 1930s

From the left, Swami Vividishkananda, Mrs. Worcester, unknown lady,
Swamis Ashokananda, Akhilananda, Prabhavananda, Devatmananda

Dr. Allen Claxtron

7

PROVIDENCE, PART TWO

That Swami Akhilananda might have become the leader of the Vedanta Society of New York we learn from the letters of Swami Bodhananda, who had taken care of him when he was ill in 1927 and who loved him as a younger brother. It has been rumored that if he had one weakness it was Swami Akhilananda. Marguerite Fleischman in a letter of March 18, 1994 wrote about Swami Bodhananda: "He also once said: 'My preferred Swami is Swami Akhilananda. I still have this weakness.'"[1]

It was as early as July, 1932 that he wrote to Swami Akhilananda: "... I like you to be my successor so that during winter I can return to India after 26 years and spend final years with my people. Hope with the grace of Thakur this wish will be fulfilled and the work of Swamiji and Thakur will continue in this big city."[2] It would seem that Swami Akhilananda was willing to come to New York. Swami Bodhananda again wrote to him on July 19, 1932: "I am happy to know that you agree to take care of twenty thousand dollar mortgage as well as the full responsibility of the Vedanta Society." Throughout the summer he continued to write in this vein. Letter of August 5th: "My earnest wish is if you can take the responsibility of work in here and get to know all aspects of it." And again on August 15th: "I am very glad and extremely restful to know that you are willing to take up the responsibility of the Vedanta Society of New York as per the itemized written statement made by me." He had written that for 20 years he worked in New York "for doing Thakur's and Swamiji's work with his heart's blood."[3]

But it was not to be. Swami Bodhananda would continue as head of the Vedanta Society until his death in 1950.

Perhaps the main concern of Swami Akhilananda until the late 1930s would be the building of the Temple at Belur. Swami Shivananda had enthusiastically accepted the proposition of building the Sri Ramakrishna Temple, which had been planned by Swami Vivekananda.[4] At the Marshfield Ashrama one summer Swami Akhilananda in talking with his friends recalled that Swami Brahmananda, about three weeks before he died, had commented: "Well, the temple for Vivekananda is now finished. We should make the temple for Sri Ramakrishna."[5] Now the time seemed auspicious.

For this purpose Swami Akhilananda decided to go to India. The Providence Journal for June 23, 1934 announced that he would be sailing from New York aboard S. S. Ile de France, July 7 for Plymouth, England and would stop a few days in London and in Paris. He planned to visit Munich, Germany and the Passion Play at Oberammagau. He expected to join friends in Zurich and Geneva, Switzerland and visit the shrines of St. Francis and St. Anthony at Assisi and Padua with side trips to Venice, Florence and Rome, where he hoped to see the Vatican.

Sailing from Brindisi, Italy on August 12th he was expected to arrive in Bombay August 23rd. From there he was to travel by train across India to Calcutta, arriving August 27th. He would be leaving Bombay for New York on November 8th, arriving November 28th. Mrs. Anna Worcester, her daughter, Frances, and Helen Rubel (Bhakti) accompanied him.

Arriving in Bombay Swami Vishwananda welcomed Swami Akhilananda and his party. A gathering in his honor was held the following week on Sunday morning at the Ramakrishna Center in Khar, just outside Bombay.[6] There towards the end of August he gave a talk to a large gathering at the Blavatsky Lodge on "What India can teach America". An unnamed Indian newspaper article, reporting from Bombay, which appeared on August 27, 1934 quotes him as saying: "Another war means the complete destruction of modern civilization. Only one country can prevent this catastrophe. And that country is India." Describing some aspects of American life, the limitations of Communism and other "isms", the Swami concluded with: "Karma yoga with its emphasis on the spirit of service was the gift of India to the world and a proper understanding of this message would be the salvation of humanity."[7]

Another talk was given in New Delhi in early September. The Hindustan Times. September 12, 1934, reported: "America's Response to India's Message" was the subject of an inspiring lecture delivered by Swami Akhilananda under the auspices of the Talkatona Club tonight when the Club Hall was crowded to the full. The Swami had recently returned to India after a prolonged stay in America. ... Swami Akhilananda pointed out that while America led the world in economic prosperity, they lacked in poise and a balanced frame of mind. Hence there was a great desire among the Americans to learn the technique of Indian spirituality and a meditative frame of mind."

Meanwhile Swami Akhilananda had been extremely eager to see both Swami Akhandananda, the President of the Order, following the death of Swami Shivananda and Swami Vijnanananda, the Vice-President, so that plans for the Temple could be carried out. When Swam Akhilananda and his friends reached Calcutta, Swami Akhandananda was at the Sargacchi Center. Swami Vijnanananda was in Allahabad, who then came to Belur Math to work on the plans for the Temple. Swami Vivekananda had designed this temple before his death. The fledgling monastic organization was not at that time in a position to build it. But the monks were not forgetful. The Temple hovered in the background. In 1898 when Swami Vijnanananda was at the Belur Math drawing up plans for the monastery and Temple, Swami Akhandananda was visiting at the same time. They were staying in the same room and the two would often discuss these plans together.[8] Now, almost 40 years later, coincidentally, they both would be involved in the construction of the Temple. Even before Swami Akhilananda's departure for India, plans for it had been sent to him. He looked them over, returning them to Swami Vijnanananda, now the vice-president of the Order.[9]

With Swami Akhandananda not coming to Belur Math, and with the plans of the Temple needing to be discussed, Swami Akhilananda decided to visit the Sargacchi Center. This was an orphanage founded by Swami Akhandananda in 1897.[10] At that time while he was walking on pilgrimage, he came across starving people in Mahula, a place ravished by famine. Deeply moved, weeping at the misery, he helped them as much as possible. He saw how destitute some of the children were. Wanting an orphanage for them, he wrote to Swami Vivekananda who replied, giving him "a thousand embraces and blessings".[11] The overjoyed Swami chose a rural locality outside of Mahula with the expectation that those living there might be benefited.[12]

"During our visit," writes the Swami, "he (Swami Akhandananda) and Swami Vijnanananda both emphasized that the Temple must be built and completed as soon as possible. They were most anxious to have the Temple finished. In fact, each one told me separately that I must see it completed by all means. This encouragement was a thrilling experience on my part. In fact, both these great Swamis made my part in the construction of the Temple clear to me as Swami Shivanandaji had done earlier in his cable to me before his passing away. Certain ideas about me were also expressed by Swami Akhandanandaji to others in my absence. But I came to know about it from the persons to whom he made the statements. One day I was amazed to find that he was even listening to a lecture I was giving at the Math, as Swami Vijnananandaji had done at a public meeting in Calcutta. I could not believe he would do anything like this."[13]

With glowing words he describes his visit: "It was indeed a unique occasion in my life. What love he expressed! He told me many glorious incidents from the lives of Sri Ramakrishna, Swamiji and Maharaj (Swamis Vivekananda and Brahmananda), as well as his own experiences with them. He also spoke about the early period of the Order, about Swamiji's cooking, singing, and so on; and about his relationship with Maharaj.

"Swami Akhandanandaji gave me a kind of formal dinner with silk clothes, new dishes, and so on. It was both embarrassing and extremely thrilling, to say the least, that this great spiritual giant should do these things for me, a servant of the Order. What love, consideration, and sympathy he showed to me! It was really an unbelievable occasion. This incident can never be forgotten."[14]

It was not long before Mrs. Anna Worcester, Helen Rubel, and Mrs. Worcester's daughter arrived at Sargacchi where they spent the day. Swami Akhilananda recalls: "He treated them with deep love and sympathy almost beyond description. He also showed concern about their welfare, not only in that small place, but also during their entire stay in India."[15]

When they were about to leave Sargacchi "He came to see us off at the railroad station. Those things that he did are almost unbelievable from a Hindu point of view - for a great spiritual personality like him to do these things for devotees and younger Swamis!"[16]

Swami Akhilananda and his party had returned to Calcutta. He writes: "After a few days, this great personality accepted our request and graciously came to Belur Math, the headquarters in Calcutta. I was indeed amazed at the way he treated the American devotees... He even went to their hotel and ate food there. He used to go with them for drives. His kindness to them was unbelievable!"[17] This visit of the great Swami was a surprise to the American ladies as well. Helen Rubel writes: "One morning when we arrived at the Math we were greeted with the happy surprise that Swami Akhandananda had arrived during the early morning. For a few days we enjoyed visiting with him and hearing about Sri Ramakrishna and Swami Vivekananda."[18]

While Mrs. Worcester, her daughter, and Helen Rubel were staying at the Great Eastern Hotel in Calcutta and Swami Akhilananda was at the monastery at Belur Math, Helen Rubel took the opportunity to visit a maternity and child welfare Centre, the Sisumangal Pratishthan of the Ramakrishna Mission located in Calcutta. She had considerable interest in this type of service for, in a letter from Providence, dated Nov. 23, 1930, she had written to her aunts Helene and Cecile in Zurich; "I have lately been carefully considering an idea. Their Order in India is starting a Child Welfare Center such as we have all over the U.S. ...The Centers are places where mothers expecting babies can come to be taught methods of care, and where they can bring their babies to get medical instruction... You know how hard India is struggling and how badly they need Child Welfare Centers. I want to use some of my share of the Foundation (she is referring to the Rubel Foundation) income for those Child Welfare Centers. I feel that in that way the money will do the greatest good to sufferers much greater than we have here in the U.S. If you want to know what I have really at heart to do with the income, that is my feeling."

When Swami Dayananda came to the U.S. in 1926, he began to study the child welfare activities in the United States. Returning to India, in 1931, he submitted a comprehensive scheme for this kind of service. Its work started in July, 1932 with the mothers beginning to register in September. Qualified nurses offered to go to India to help with the work.[19] The chief donor, Helen Rubel, wrote to her aunts in Switzerland in a letter, October 13th, 1934: "The other day we visited the work and I am very very much pleased at the way it is being carried on, and the big need it is filling. It is the first-work of its kind here and very much needed."

While living in Calcutta the three American women would go almost every day to Dakshineswar to visit the temples there and to see the shrine of Ramakrishna. They also became better acquainted with Indian life. The <u>Providence Sunday Journal</u> for June l6, 1935 reports that "Few visitors see the interior of Hindu homes. The Providence trio were honored guests in cultured families during their entire stay and wherever they went in the peninsula. They absorbed Hindu life in a way that the usual visitor to India never does." The three women early on decided to wear the Indian sari as their usual dress.

Helen Rubel was enchanted with India. The months they spent there were too short for her. She was very impressed with the Indian people, how they lived, and their outlook on life. Returning to Providence in early 1935 she wrote a letter to Swami Gnaneswarananda of Chicago about her Indian experience.

Jan. 20, 1935

Dear Swami Gnaneswar,

...Indeed, I should very much like to tell you about our stay in India. I like the country as I have never liked any other, and the time spent there has meant very much to me. A lady, hearing that we cared for India so much, said, 'Oh yes, naturally you had sympathy for the Hindus and wanted to help them! 'No,' I answered in astonishment, 'but I was continually impressed by how much they had to give us', - much more than I could conceive of. I wondered that her thought had never occurred to me while in India.

There seems to be a meaning back of life that people in India are aware of. Every day they do actions showing the reality of this to them. We saw them up early while it was yet dark, sitting to meditate on the roofs, in the streets or anywhere. In the evening the conches were blown and the temple bells rung for the evening worship, and the Mohammedans, who had been waiting around collected in threes, turned to the West and prayed aloud.

We were also very much impressed by the gentleness and contentment in the faces of the people. Even our own, I think, lost a little of the hurried worry. Their poverty is beyond conception, yet, we saw them living quietly: sleeping in rows on the edge of the sidewalk, in stations, or in any sheltered place, storing mat and cover in some shop for the day.

Greetings are very warm in India, and we were escorted off the boat at Bombay amidst flowers, gayety and joy such as we were not accustomed to. Then at Khar came our first glimpse of a Ashram with the little temple spreading its influence out over the land.

In Bombay I was very much struck at the ease with which different races live together keeping their individual customs. We enjoyed picking out one from another by the dress. The bells of a Hindu temple would ring near us, and not far off we would see Mohammedans going into one of their mosques. Every day we saw bodies carried along the bay road to the Hindu cremation ground. Not far beyond is the Parsee Tower of Silence. Another few miles and we saw a coffin going to the Guanese Christian church.

When we returned to Bombay at the end of our trip, it hardly seemed Indian at all. Mussori was of little interest because then were no Swamis there. At Hrisikesh we first went down and touched the Ganges.

We especially liked Calcutta. Of course it is the kindness and attraction of the Swamis that made us enjoy and get so much out of the trip. When we arrived, the station was like a sea of Swamis. Even you were hard to recognize in the bewilderment.

The first day at the Math when we went from one temple to another it seemed like going through a whole life-time -- consecration, emotion, turmoil and finally peace in the temple of Swami Vivekananda. I like to think of the quiet way, you know, that we often sat on the porch of the Math with some of the Swamis during the long glow of the Eastern sunset, and watched the shad fishers laboriously paddling up the Ganges and swiftly drifting down mid-stream with their nets out. Then the incense was brought around and the evening song of Swami Vivekananda began.

Our visit to the house of Balaram Bose will always remain in my mind as the visit to a shrine. There was the room where Sri Ramakrishna met many of his disciples, and next to that the room which means so much to the chosen ones of Swami Brahmananda. The ladies also were most kind in entertaining us in their quarters and allowed us to pay our respects at their shrine.

It gives a thrill to see some of the ideals of Swami Vivekananda coming to life in the different institutions connected with the Mission such as the many medical clinics and student homes attached to the different Ashramas, the hospitals at Benares and Kankhal and the various educational institutions. The Sister Nivedita School had such a wonderful atmosphere that I liked to be there among them. The Child Welfare Centre is a good beginning, and will be unusually valuable in training nurses and mid-wives to carry the work in the villages.

Swami Vijnanananda first took us to Dakshineswar. The tower rise so majestically on the bank of the Ganges as one crosses Bali bridge. As he told of his first meeting in Sri Ramakrishna's room and showed us where Sri Ramakrishna sat and told what was said, he seemed to live it all over again. You know that, after many trips we were finally allowed to salute at the Kali temple. All through the Durga Puja we went there every day in Indian dress. The attraction of the atmosphere and of the experience is something that I do not think can be explained, but is just what I miss most on leaving India.

One morning when we arrived at the Math we were greeted with the happy surprise that Swami Akhandananda had arrived during the early morning. For a few days we enjoyed visiting with him and hearing about Sri Ramakrishna and Swami Vivekananda. To our great joy he decided to go to Bombay where we later met him and had two weeks to hear stories and go out riding with him at sunset time when there was the peaceful hush of an unseen living presence over all. At the end, when we boarded the boat, he and other Swamis came on to visit, and we should dearly have loved to take him with us at least a little way. The parting was too affecting to remember.

In Benares we only spent a day and a half, but I agree that it feels like a place outside the world. A peace seems to reign over the whole town. I do not believe that I could do my own will there. We walked by the bazaars where they sell little altars and beads. Just before sunset we took a funny almost round boat on the Ganges and sat on the roof with some 25 Swamis. Very slowly we were paddled along the bank and saw the many people sitting on the temple steps to meditate. They were not so engrossed, however but what they were able to stare at us. Further along, the smoke curled up from the pyres on the cremation ground as it grew darker and darker and the Ganges flowed ever on. It would be nice to end there like that. Anyway, Benares has left a very strong attraction to go back and find out what it all means.

At Allahabad, before we were able to enter the town, we had to spend an hour in the dark fighting with the 'Octrol' (town customs office) about passing our baggage which we had just had mounted precariously on the curved top of a gary, the only available vehicle. But next morning made up for all this when, in the company of Swami Vijanananda, we drove without a road up over the bank of the Jamuna and down into the dry river-bed toward the confluence with the Ganges.

Agra was of little comparative interest. Just after dawn one very cold morning we jogged off in a tonga and reached the Taj Mahal by sunrise. It was an impressive way of seeing that wonderful piece of art. Of course it is not a temple, but still, I was surprised at the lack of feeling inside, and preferred to stand on the portico in the sunlight and look far out over the river.

Delhi was very picturesque with its big Mosque and the camels in the streets. We tried to imagine the early empire. But best we liked the view from the Ridge road even to the Jamuna.

We needed not to roll in the Brindaban dust; it came up in clouds for us to eat. It is the most beautiful fine sand that I have ever seen - not gravel although it rises so lightly. Again in Indian dress, we spent one last long evening going from one temple to another at Arati time. Brindaban is a dream place where it is very easy to dream that dream that transforms life into sport. But the parting is very sad; and little by little the train slipped relentlessly past the small villages where the cows go back and forth with the cowherds every morning and evening, and the women still wear Radha's costume.

When we had taken the train leaving Calcutta I had thought, 'If only the train would keep going on and on until it goes all around the world and stops again at Calcutta! I still feel that way

Special things I noticed were; warmth of feeling in the people, social customs some of which are based on devotion which is not considered silly; worship sometimes of the divinity back of people, not always of the persons themselves; the conception of a wife and mother of a family as a separate ideal from that of lovers. But always I am most impressed that people there are conscious of a meaning back of life.

I hope I have changed a little too, and that some day I can go back. I am so glad to be able to tell all this to you who can understand.

With greetings and best wishes to you and to the friends.

Signed in her handwriting (Bhakti)

India was such a wonderful experience for her. But now, to return to the remainder of their trip.

In early October, 1934 a public reception was held by the citizens of Calcutta, who presented an address of welcome to Swami Akhilananda before a large crowd at the Albert Hall, as was reported by Forward on October 4th. "The function was attended by a large number of Swamijis of the Ramakrishna Mission and the Belur Math. Sj. Bejoy Krishna Bose on behalf of the Reception Committee presented the address of welcome and in doing so he related the activities of the Swamiji in the West as also in India." In his reply Swami Akhilananda remarked on the enthusiasm Americans had for Vivekenanda and his message. He also mentioned how co-operative the Americans were.

Before they left Calcutta Mrs. Worcester, her daughter, and Miss Helen Rubel fed the monks at Belur Math one day with many special delicacies.[20]

When they were ready to leave and travel to Bombay on their way to America, Swami Akhandananda, who had been visiting in Calcutta wanted to go with Swami Akhilananda and his party to Bombay to see them off. He could be with them a few days more. Swami Akhilananda was concerned about his health, but the doctor said if Akhandanandaji wanted to go, he could.[21] In seeing the Swamis off from Howrah station Akhilananda's cousin writes: "We all went to see them off. Swami Omkarananda and Satyan Maharaj (Swami Atmabodhananda) were also present at the station to bid them farewell."[22] While staying in Bombay, Swami Akhilananda wrote that Swami Akhandananda would go out every day in a car with the American devotees and us for a drive. Those few days were very memorable for all of us. He told us so many inspiring incidents from the lives of Sri Ramakrishna, Holy Mother, Swamiji, Maharaj and other great Swamis. Swami Akhilananda continued: "On the day of our departure from India, he came to the pier to see us off. It was indeed a very moving and touching experience in my life and in the lives of the American devotees."[23]

The India they were leaving was still British India. When Swami Akhilananda would return to the U.S., he would speak of his experiences in India and the role Gandhi was playing. It would appear that on this first visit to India, he visited with his family. His brother writes: "On one such occasion he visited Netrakona, his father's place, accompanying Swamis Atmabodhananda, Omkarananda (Ananga Maharaj) and others and he and Swami Omkarananda delivered lectures at a largely attended public meeting."[24]

8

PROVIDENCE, PART THREE

As far as it can be determined, Swami Akhilananda and his followers returned to Providence in January, 1935 after a six month absence, having sailed on the S. S. Europa from the Continent. While in Europe, Swami Akhilananda had visited Zurich, possibly Germany. Also Italy and Paris. While in Italy he traveled to Assisi and the chapel where St. Francis had his spiritual experiences. "Not the big cathedral," he remarked, "but the little one around the corner:", was the church where he had felt that spirituality was still present.[1] Remembering later, he recalled: "In Assisi we visited some monasteries and you cannot imagine the disciplines that they practice."[2] He also went to Padua, for he was not only an admirer of St. Francis, but he was also very fond of St. Anthony, "to whom he was compared by an intimate friend because he combined intellect and devotion as did the saint of Padua."[3]

In Paris, he would visit his brother monk, Swami Siddheswarananda, a disciple of Brahmananda, who had lectured at the Sorbonne on St. John of the Cross. When Swami Akhilananda visited Germany, which he did a few times while enroute to India or the U.S., this was another pleasant experience and he was well treated.[4]

After his return, the Providence newspaper reported: "The Hindu leader will speak at the Vedanta Centre tomorrow evening at 8 o'clock on 'My Experiences in India', and next Friday evening at 8, the Society will hold a reception for friends to meet the Swami. Special music will be furnished on the latter occasion by Henri J. and Marie B. Faucher, pianist and violinist.

"The Swami said that Christian missionaries in general had changed their approach to the Indian people a great deal since he was last in India,, ... The Swami spoke before many gatherings of Indian youth while in the Far East and said that the average Indian young man and woman of university age was modernistic like our own youth, but would accept a religion that was rational and at the same time touched life - 'a practical dynamic religion, not merely an emotional outburst.'"[5]

Resuming his classes on Tuesday and Friday evenings, his Sunday service and his interviews and local lectures, Swami Akhilananda also continued on occasion his ministry in Washington, D.C. Charlotte Pellini has stated that he began this effort in 1929, traveling to Washington, D.C. monthly.[6] Carl Jackson in his book, *VEDANTA FOR THE WEST*, writes: "Buoyed by the warm reception of his lectures, Swami Akhilananda mounted still a third effort in 1930. He remained long enough to rent quarters for a Center, then summoned Swami Vividishananda from San Francisco, to take charge."

Vividishananda worked there until May 1936 when he left for Denver to start another center. "Swami Akhilananda then resumed his duties at Washington, being partially relieved from his work at Providence by the arrival of Swami Satprakashananda at the end of 1936."[7]

Swami Akhilananda also made an effort in Philadelphia where he lectured in conjunction with his trips to Washington, sometimes as frequently as weekly.[8] There a group was formed, the stability of which, enabled Swami Yatiswarananda to establish a Center there in the early 1940s, in December, 1942.[9]

In Providence Swami Akhilananda's Sunday sermons, which attracted many people, were stimulating, for their contents were provocative, yet reasonable; a challenge to the listener. They clarified religion. Such topics as Psychology and religion, Was Christ a yogi?, Power of mind, Self-Surrender, Meditation, and so on.

One of the most important topics that he would touch upon was the subject of a lecture as reported in a newspaper article in 1935 when he addressed the Universal Club at Faunce House, Brown University on the Gandhi movement. "'If men say that Gandhi's movement will fail, they are implying that Christ's teachings have failed already,' declared Swami Akhilananda ... in an address on Satyagraha -- Taking Hold of Truth..." He went on to say that editorial writers in American newspapers either "misunderstood or misrepresent Gandhi's movement. ... They say that it is a negative and passive thing and do not emphasize its dynamic aspect at all.

"Satyagraha means 'taking hold of truth.' Here 'truth' means that which abides without change in the past, present and future. Truth is the soul -- God -- whereas that which is transitory -- the relative world --- is not true." He went on to describe the three aspects: non-cooperation, non-violence, and soul-force. "Some 3000 to 5000 years

74

before Christ," said the Swami, "the Vedas taught the conquest of evil by love. Some 2600 years ago Buddha taught -- Hatred cannot be conquered by evil but by good. Gandhi has not introduced any new movement in India as far as Hindus are concerned. The new feature of this movement is that it is the first time in history that a great mass effort has been made to put into practice an individualistic spiritual principle."[10]

Years later there was a student at Boston University with whom the Swami discussed and advocated satyagraha. That student was Martin Luther King.[11]

At the end of June, 1935, a gathering of swamis from different canters in the United States was held at the Vedanta Center. Swami Gnaneswarananda of Chicago, Swami Paramananda of Boston, and Swami Vividishananda of Washington, D.C. were guests of Swami Akhilananda.

All were speakers at a dinner at the Center. Swami Gnaneswarananda maintained that "What the world needs is a new type of human being; one who shall combine enough of the energy and speed of the best to tackle the practical problems of life and of the spiritual contemplation of the East to have a purpose in his activity." Swami Paramananda said: ..."for the first time as a nation we are beginning to be spiritually conscious of the deeper values of life." Swami Vividishananda, the final speaker, gave encouragement to science urging us not to take a hostile view towards science.[12]

Later in the year, the Swami, we learn from a letter of Swami Virajananda, 5 December, 1935: "by invitation delivered lectures at St. Louis, Philadelphia and Cleveland, which increased their level of enthusiasm to the point that they want to establish permanent centers in those places." These lectures in October were to be followed by a second series of four lectures, Nov. 18 to 20.[13]

Along with his outreach to different cities, his work in Providence had brought invitations by radio stations W.J.A.R. and W.F.C.I. to speak at different times and conduct morning devotions at intervals with other local clergymen.[14]

The year 1936 was special, marking the centennial of the birth of Sri Ramakrishna. There were several newspaper stories. Probably it was the <u>Providence Journal</u> that reported; "A good-will symposium on the mystical experiences of great personalities of Roman Catholic,

Protestant, Jewish and Hindu faiths, centering around the centenary celebration of the birth of Sri Ramakrishna, greatest of modern saints of India, will be held in Plantations Club Auditorium. Abbott Park Place, Sunday evening, Feb. 23 at 8 o'clock. The public is invited.

"The speakers are: Rev. Arthur H. Chandler, O.P., LL.D., dean of Providence College, "Catholic Mysticism of St. Thomas Aquinas"; Dr, Ralph 0. Harpole, "Practical Mysticism of Horace Bushnell"; Rabbi William G. Braude, "Mysticism of the Master of Goodname"; Swami Akhilananda, "Mystical Experiences of Sri Ramakrishna, Prof. Joachim Wach, Ph.D., Th.D., Brown University, "Unity in Easter and Western Mysticism,"' and Rev. Frederick A. Wilmot. "Mysticism and Social Justice". There was a brief violin recital by Prof. Henri J. Faucher, accompanied by Mme. Marie Faucher, pianist. This was the first of the several centennial observances in Providence. As one of the opening programs, it was a fitting observance also of Brotherhood Day - Christians, Jews, and Hindus coming together.[15]

Charlotte Pellini wrote of this affair at the Plantation Club that it was "celebrated publicly with eclat... As far as we know, this was the first time that a Roman Catholic priest had participated publicly in a mixed religious forum in R.I."[16]

For the public meeting at the Plantation Club, Swami Akhilananda spoke on "Sri Ramakrishna and modern psychology". He began with a short sketch of Ramakrishna's life and how he approached religion, wanting to verify the teachings of the scriptures,[17]... "He (Ramakrishna) systematically followed the methods of different religions and actually left scientific records of the experiences for us to go through in order to realize God," and the Swami continued: "He was in fact a product of this modern age. He would not accept even God-consciousness until he had himself verified it, until he had realized the fact."[18]

"He stands actually for the Hindu ideal of life," the Swami said. "Again, he also stands for the Western scientific and rationalistic mentality. We find in him the development of intuitive realization, which we call superconscious experience, as well as the scientific approach to the problems of life."[19]

Although Swami Akhilananda had never seen Ramakrishna, he lived with Swami Brahmananda in the monastery and with other disciples of Ramakrishna. He and his brother disciples saw the high states of spiritual illumination that Swami Brahmananda had. Not only his, but other brother disciples. Swami Akhilananda was too modest and humble to speak of his own experiences. So he said in his lecture: "From the life of Ramakrishna, we find that mystic experiences are not mysterious entities or hallucinations. It has been a common mistake all over the world for so many centuries to think when you meet a man of God... that he is peculiar or has hallucinations."[20]

He continues and remarks on the spiritual experiences of Saint Theresa of Avila, quoting her:... "whereas a genuine heavenly vision yields to her a harvest of ineffable spiritual riches and an admirable renewal of bodily strength."[21] He notes that she became a transformed personality. And, "From the life of Sri Ramakrishna, we fully realize that mystic experiences do not make us insane but make us better men and women. They illumine and make us pure, unselfish, loving and humble and efface our egotism."[22]

He brought out the narrow views and concepts of some of the then present day psychologists such as the behavorists and dogmatic psychoanalysts.[23] He felt strongly that a new kind of psychology was needed. He said: "If we want to develop a complete psychology, we have to discipline ourselves first. ... Until you can discipline your mind, and train yourself wholly and completely, you have no access to the mystic experiences of the superconscious realm. Until you take up the methods that will lead you to mystic realization, you have not the slightest idea of the existence of the superconscious realization nor of its effects."[24]

Directly or indirectly, this would be a vigorous challenge particularly to the psychologists. In time there would be many psychologists like Dr. Gordon Allport of Harvard who would feel Swami Akhilananda's influence. In his lectures Swami Akhilananda would bring to his congregation the need for the renewing of one's mind. All through his ministry he would lay stress on spiritual practices and experiential religion. For him, as for Swami Vivekananda, "Doctrines, or dogmas, or rituals, or books, or temples, or forms are but secondary details."[25]

A description by someone unknown of the entire program of the centenary celebration is included in the Appendix.

After the festivities in Providence, Swami Akhilananda was in New York City at the Vedanta Society in mid-March where on the 15th the Society held a banquet at the Ceylon-India Inn for the centennial observance of Ramakrishna's birth. On that occasion Swami Akhilananda met the French writer, Jules Bois, who had befriended Swami Viveka-nanda when he was in Europe. A photograph was taken of Jules Bois seated between Swami Akhilananda and Swami Bodhananda. Swami Akhilananda heard Bois give a talk that evening on Vivekananda. It is said that he spoke feelingly about the great Swami.

With all the success that Swami Akhilananda was having in Providence, there were those who thought Vedanta, and particularly a Swami, were almost beyond the pale. Swami himself used to regale his audiences by telling the following story, which, of course, was told to him. One of his friends was out walking one day when she met by chance another friend. They stood chatting, and finally Swami's friend said she had to be on her way. Where was she going, the other friend inquired. To see Swami at the Vedanta Center was the reply. "Oh, do you go to that funny place?"[26]

Then there was the Southern woman in Washington, D. C. who thought the Swami was a wonderful man, but it was too bad that he hadn't been baptized.

In the summer of 1936 he traveled to the West Coast, first visiting Hollywood and Swami Prabhavananda and then on to San Francisco. He wrote to one of his followers in Providence, Charlotte Morrison, who later became Mrs. Pellini, in a letter dated July 9, 1936: "Mrs. Worcester, Miss Rubel and Frances sailed on June 29th from Los Angeles. They were on their way to India. I stayed on in Hollywood till 3rd of July. .... I enjoyed very much in Hollywood. The Swami and his friends were very loving to me.

"The Swamis and the devotees in San Francisco are also very kind and loving to me." ...At Ashokananda's suggestion, he and Swami Akhilananda visited Yosemite Valley, taking with them Ediben Soule and Al Clifton. Ediben Soule pointed out to Swami Akhilananda, who sat beside her in the front seat of the car she was driving, the spectacular sights of Yosemite. They stayed overnight at one of the luxurious hotels and next day they visited Lake Tahoe.[27] Swami continued his letter with: "I delivered a lecture last night and then they had a reception. I have many dinner engagements. Well, I shall try to have a little rest when I go back to Providence. ... I shall go to Portland by the end of next week. ... Hope you are doing well through Lord's grace."

Swami was seeing his old friends. He continued on his way to the dedication of the Sri Ramakrishna Ashrama in Oregon on July 26th. It was about 20 miles from Portland. Swami Devatmananda, another disciple of Swami Brahmananda, was the spiritual leader. While he was en route to Denver, Swami Akhilananda wrote to Charlotte Morrison on July 31st: "I had so many engagements in San Francisco and in Portland..." Then he went on in a more personal way giving encouragement: "I am indeed very very happy to know how you feel the influence of my humble activities. Our Lord is doing everything. I am only an instrument in His Hands. So you all are blessed that He is making you feel in this way. He is certainly attracting your mind to Him. May he ever protect you and bless you is my earnest prayer." He continues describing his trip. "I went to Yosemite and Lake Tahoe with Swami Ashokananda and four of his friends. ... The scenic beauty of Northern California is really wonderful... I had a very nice time with Swami Devatmananda in Portland. I shall meet Swami Vividishananda tomorrow and spend five or six days with him. I am expected in Chicago on August 7th. Then I go to Wisconsin for a week... Back to Chicago and then to Bodhananda in New York." In his letter of August 4th, he wrote while in Denver: "They are giving me reception tonight."

Construction had begun on the Temple at Belur Math. Charlotte Pellini recalls: "After the construction was commenced, a cable was sent to Swami from Headquarters in 1936, requesting his presence at Belur to expedite the work which was lagging due to human complications."[28] Before Swami left New York, Mrs. Anna Worcester, her daughter Frances, and Helen Rubel arrived in Madras from Colombo by the Indo-Ceylon Boat Mail on August 8th. They were received at the Egmore Railway station by Swami Saswathananda, President of the local Ramakrishna Math, and his party.[29]

Swami Akhilananda would soon leave the U.S. They would meet in Calcutta.

Temple to Ramakrishna at Belur

Swami Akhilananda in the late 1930s

Swami Akhilananda and his brother, Swami Ramananda in India, 1930s

Swamis Akhilananda and Ashokananda, 1936 in California

Swami Akhilananda at Lake Tahoe

9

THE TEMPLE

B efore they would meet in Calcutta, there would be his ocean voyage and visits along the way in India for Swami Akhilananda. He
wrote, recalling his last visit to India in 1934-35: "A year and a
half later, I received a cable in September that I must go to India for the
inspection of the construction of the Temple. My humble services were
needed very badly. In a couple of days I sailed."[1] Aboard the "Bremen"
enroute to Europe, he wrote to Charlotte Morrison on September 27,
describing an unusual incident: "You will be glad to know the Hinden-
burg was flying over us this morning at about 11:30 am. It was indeed
very exciting. We all went up to the sun deck. Some were even with
their night dresses. You can easily imagine how excited they were. The
people from the airship were waving to us and we returned our greetings to them. What a sight!"

He also told her: "May Lord be your all in all is my prayer. He is
with you and will guide you even though I am away." The conscientious guru giving encouragement and solace to his student.

When he arrived in India, he stopped at Allahabad on the way to the
Math and visited Swami Vijnananandaji. Annapurna, Bhakti and Fran-
ces had arrived six months prior to that time. After he met Swami
Vijnananandaji, he went to the Math, and then to Sargacchi to meet
Swami Akhandanandaji.[2]

On his arrival in Calcutta, he received the following letter from
Swami Sankarananda, written October 28, 1936: "Letters of Khirod
(Swami Akhilananda's brother) and Bhakti inform me about your safe
arrival and that you are very tired and busy. ...Inform me about your
program and how long you plan to stay at this time. I know that you
have come to clear a few points regarding the construction of the 'Sri
Temple'. I am sure everything will be all right with His blessings.

"I am worried regarding the health of the ladies. I am very much
concerned and feel sad knowing that they are suffering from occasional
fever. ...I am happy to know you are keeping well."

When Swami Akhilananda came to India in 1934, his first visit regarding the Temple, the plan for it was completed and the contract was given out.[3] Later, after his return to the U.S., it seems as though there were some minor problems for the financing of the Temple.[4] In addition, as he told his devotees at Sarada Ashrama, Marshfield, August 5, 1958: "Some of the younger Swamis opposed, feeling that the money should he used for philanthropic work."[5] These were perhaps some of the "human complications" that Charlotte Pellini referred to.

As soon as possible Swami Akhilananda went to Sargacchi to visit Swami Akhandananda, staying only a few days. "One day he asked me to take him to America," he recalled. "He said he would like to stay with me. I knew about his heart condition... So I only looked at him and did not say anything. ...

"Then I came back to the Belur Math headquarters to carry out the instructions of these great personalities (Akhandananda and Vijnanananda). I remained only to supervise the work of construction on the Temple for about five months. I had felt for the last few years that Swamiji and Maharaj (Swamis Vivekananda and Brahmananda) wanted us to see that the Temple was completed. Then these two other Swamis lovingly ordered me to carry out the construction. Fortunately I found the architect and contractor extremely co-operative during this period. As the construction was again under way as it should be, I decided to return to America for a few months."[6] During this period Swami had had an office in a corner of the partly completed structure. After returning, Charlotte Pellini recalls, he would grin, doft his hat and say in a most amusing way, "I have become businessman."[7]

The thoughts of having such a temple occurred to Swami Vivekananda in 1890, when having returned to Calcutta from Ghazipur and Baranagore, he wrote on May 26 a letter to Pramadas Mitra, a scholar with whom he had been corresponding. In that letter we get the first hint of a temple. Vivekananda wrote: "What greater regret can there be than this, that no memorial could yet be raised in this land of Bengal in the very neighborhood of the place where he lived his life of <u>sadhana</u>... It is impossible with a sum of Rs. 1000 to secure land and raise a temple near Calcutta." A dream of Vivekananda's that would not be fulfilled for over 40 years.

It was in 1897 that Swami Vijnanananda drew up the original plan for the Temple as envisioned by Vivekananda, who had studied the architecture of northwest India, wanting to incorporate its best features in the temple to Sri Ramakrishna. It would then be an epitome of Indian culture. The foundation stone was laid on Ramakrishna's birthday, March 13, 1929 by Swami Shivananda, although no funds for construction were available. The foundation stone was re-positioned in July, 1935 by Swami Vijnanananda.[8]

The Temple at Belur Math, the monastic headquarters a few miles north of Calcutta, was not far from the River Ganges. Close enough so that a sea wall was being erected to contain the high tides.[9] We get a glimpse of the early construction through a letter of Josephine MacLeod, a staunch friend of Swami Vivekananda, who wrote, November 24, 1935: ..."this place has become a workshop creating the finest temple in modern India.

"It is good seeing these hundreds of workmen about and the growing of this great Ramakrishna Temple - 320 ft. long, 120 broad and 112 ft. high - the hundreds of bamboo scaffoldings reminding me of Milan Cathedral... The new Temple will not be finished till 1937... The money to erect this temple is given by two shy modest America women from Providence..."[10] But it was only one shy, modest American woman who gave the money. Josephine MacLeod wrote several years later to a friend: "I... enclose a letter to Swami Akhilananda who has given the 200,000 dollars for this great new Ramakrishna Temple. ...When I was at Almora, I met Miss Rubel - 'Bhakti' who gave the money to Swami Akhilananda to do exactly what he wished to do with it, so she said to me, 'I have nothing to do with the Temple. It was Swami Akhilananda's gift.'"[11]

Before he left India in 1937, Swami Akhilananda visited with Swami Akhandananda once more. He writes: "Just as I arrived I saluted him and reported to him the progress of the construction with feeling and encouragement. He at once said to me that he would not see the completion and dedication. I was very much shocked. ...I was in a way frightened by this, but still hoped and prayed that he would be with us at least for the dedication of the Temple. Then I left for America."[12]

In doing so he had to spend Vivekananda's birthday on board ship. He arrived in New York City on February 10, 1937. On that same day Swami Sankarananda wrote to him: "Happy to receive your letter written from Paris on February 2. ... was relieved to receive at noon today your cable sent from New York bearing the news of your safe arrival.

"This time you had to undergo lots of troubles. 'Many obstacles result in good endings.' Because the Master is having such a great undertaking done through you, He has endowed you with adequate capacity, patience and forbearance in order to get the work accomplished. Keep your mind free of worries after surrendering everything to Him. ... It is according to His wishes that you had to spend Swamiji's birthday anniversary aboard the ship."

From an undated Providence newspaper clipping there are a few more details about this return trip. That he sailed on the S. S. Europa from Cherbourg, France. "He left Bombay January 18th, arrived in Venice, January 29th and spent a few days with friends in Zurich, Switzerland and in Paris." On March 13, in 1937 the Providence Journal announced that Swami Satprakashananda had come to assist him.

Swami Akhandananda's prediction about his death came true. Mrs. Worcester, Miss Helen Rubel visited him about two weeks after Swami Akhilananda. They also were informed that he "was leaving" in two weeks. They were shocked and overcome with emotion. Swami Akhilananda writes: "Afterwards he treated them in a very endearing way and went to the station to see them off. As they were leaving, he said to them: 'We are brought together by the Spirit and we shall remain together always in the Spirit.'" ...as they arrived in Ceylon they received a telegram from Headquarters that the great Swami had entered into Mahasamadhi.[13] "He had passed away."

As on his previous return from India, the Providence newspaper reported on Swami's observations while abroad. "Everywhere in Europe there is intense military preparations but no one seems to want war," said the Swami. "In Switzerland lights are put out at night in practice preparations against air raids. Food is being conserved and rationed in preparation for eventualities in many countries."[14] He again resumed his schedule, lecturing Tuesday and Friday evenings and his Sunday services.

In a few months he would again leave for India. Swami Shankarananda kept him informed of the progress in the construction of the temple through his letters. Many details in that regard were given. In his letter of August 5, 1937 he wrote: "I came to know that you are leaving for Europe on 27 August,, ... Necessary arrangements for welcoming and taking care of Rev. Wilmot will be made. I shall inform Math quite early that they will be present at Math during the installation ceremony. It seems you all will come together." The party would also include the three women, Mrs. Anne Worcester (Annapurna), her daughter Frances, and Helen Rubel (Bhakti). Rev. Frederick Wilmot was religious editor of the Providence Journal. His wife accompanied him.

Enroute they would stop at Geneva, Italy and stay at the Hotel Colombia. There Swami Akhilananda wrote to Charlotte Morrison: "We met one of our Swamis in Paris and spent 4 or 5 days very happily. Exposition was also very enjoyable, ...Then we went to Berlin. I can not help appreciating the reception we got in Germany. They were very kind to us. You can feel friendly atmosphere... We did not like Vienna so much. But we had a lovely time in Zurich. We met some friends and a Swami there. I had a lovely time with Prof. Wach in Dresden. We are to sail tomorrow at 3 pm. I shall send a cable from Bombay."[15] Years later in 1948, he would remember this visit to Dresden: "We were in Prof. Wach's home in Germany. It was palatial and what beautiful things there! There were people visiting all the time. What a wonderful atmosphere was there!"[16]

He continued with this letter to Charlotte Morrison: "Yes, I shall be more than happy when the Temple will be dedicated. I shall tell you quite a few things about it and its history after the dedication. I am blessed that Sri Ramakrishna allows this servant to serve Him. What can I say? It is too deep to express."

While being in India during the cool season of 1937-38, it was probably then that he met Sir Arthur Eddington, scientist/ philosopher, the author of *SPACE, TIME, and GRAVITATION; PHIHLOSOPHY of the PHYSICAL SCIENCES;* and *SCIENCE and the UNSEEN WORLD.* It was at the monastery, Belur Math, that Swami Akhilananda gave him tea and they conversed. He wrote: "A great scientist of this country related to us a conversation he had with Einstein, who told him: 'I do not have a glimpse of the Absolute but Eddington has it.' We had met Eddington in India during 1937 when he accompanied a Calcutta scientist to our monastery. From his facial expression then we had the distinct impression that he was on the borderline of spiritual realization."[17] The great scientist that Swami refers to was most likely Prof. Harlow Shapley of Harvard University, a Nobel prize winner and a noted astronomer.

He wrote another letter to Charlotte Morrison on November 8th, 1937: "You will be sorry to know that the Temple is not ready for the dedication. We hope it will take place by the end of Dec. or so. The contractors are working hard nowadays. I shall let you know the date later on. Mr. and Mrs. Wilmot will sail from Bombay on November 10th. They left Calcutta on Nov. 3rd." Evidently they could not wait for the dedication, which at that time was uncertain.

While in India, the Swami was busy lecturing. In his letter of December 22, 1937 to Charlotte Morrison, he wrote: "I have been traveling here and there and everywhere for the last four weeks and lecturing once or twice a day. Hindu University in Benares and Dacca University invited me to give lectures. I have been enjoying to meet the people but life has become very strenuous. I am now on my way to Calcutta. I hope to stay there until the dedication of the Temple on January 14th. Of course, I was in the Math once or twice in the meantime. My thoughts are in the Temple. I have no relief until the dedication is over. May Lord make everything all right is my prayer."

"At long last, on January 14, 1938," wrote Swami Gambhirananda, "the Temple was dedicated with elaborate religious rites, and the ashes of the Master laid in it by Swami Vijnanananda. On the new altar was placed an image of the Master in samadhi pose executed in white Italian marble by a reputed Calcutta sculptor Mr. G. Paul. The completion of the front portion took some months more."[18] Vivekananda at one time in a conversation with Swami Akhandananda had envisioned that the altar of Ramakrishna would have a glorious OM beset with precious jewels.[19] OM being a symbol of God.

The *HISTORY OF THE RAMAKRISHNA MATH AND MISSION* describes the Temple as facing South, constructed of pinkish white Chunar stone 112 1/2 feet in height. "The prayer hall is 152 feet long, 72 feet wide and 48 feet high... The total length of the whole structure is 233 feet from north to south."[20]

The Temple had elements of Buddhist, Islamic, Hindu and Christian features in its layout and in its different details. "The windows and balconies of this hall (the prayer hall) and the arches around the sanctum recall the Rajput and Mogul styles of architecture; the pavilions suggest the usual Hindu temple in Bengal; and the central dome the renaissance type of European architecture. The ground plan of the prayer hall, with its vestibule and shrine placed one behind the other, gives the impression of a Christian cross. ...The sanctum is roomy, airy and well-lighted..., the temple has about it a modern air of spaciousness that stands in striking contrast with the usual stuffiness of its traditional prototype."[21]

For the dedication, "Devotees came from remote parts of India and were staying at the Math for some days to be present on the historic occasion. Nearly 50 thousand persons joined in the celebration, and the vast crowd included the 'elite and, the most distinguished persons in the city'." Swami Akhilananda's family also was present at the dedication. About the occasion, his cousin Shirish Sanyal writes: ..."we all came to Calcutta. Akhilananda's father also came to participate in this ceremony with his family."[22]

In late 1938 Josephine MacLeod wrote to a friend about the Temple: "Thousands now come to see it daily."[23]

Earlier during Swami Akhilananda's first visit to India in 1934 when the plans for the temple construction were completed, Swami Akhandananda had remarked: "Swamiji (Vivekananda) himself completed this work through Akhilananda."[24]

The two women in Swami Akhilananda's party had been staying at the Grand Hotel in Calcutta. His cousin recalls that after the dedication "they invited the members of Akhilananda's family for tea at the hotel. I also happened to be present there. Ms. Bhakti herself served the sweets and tea to all. Everyone was quite impressed with her modesty. Ms. Annapurna and her daughter were also at the party."[25]

After the temple dedication celebrations, they went to Holy Mother's house. His cousin Shirish writes: "all of us in our family went to the House with Akhilananda. Satyan Maharaj was then in charge there. That day special prasad arrangements were made. After partaking the consecrated food there, we all went to take rest at Satyan Maharaj's room." His cousin was much impressed that Swami Akhilananda could lay down on the floor and fall into a deep sleep immediately. Then awaken by himself and get up after 15 minutes. "We were all amazed to see this."[26]

What more could be said about the temples to Ramakrishna than what G. Venkataramana Reddy, retired architect and town planner from Hyderabad, who had designed Ramakrishna Temples, writes: "The greatest thing about the temples of Sri Ramakrishna is that to enter into these temples, there is no bar to any religious sect of any country, to the rich or the poor, to the literate or illiterate, to the atheist or theist, to a Brahman or 'Sudra' of the lowest order, to men or women. Everyone has right to pay his homage to Sri Ramakrishna in his own way. These temples are the seats of prayer to all religions. They are the tangible embodiments of the truth, 'As many faiths, so many paths.'"[27]

That could be the last word about temples to Ramakrishna.

Before leaving India Swami Akhilananda would visit his birthplace. His youngest brother remembers: "On another visit to India he went to Netrakona again and then to his native village Noapara in a small country boat and the writer, his youngest brother accompanied his beloved brother during that tour. He delivered speech in a largely attended public meeting held at the local high school. Whoever came there were deeply impressed and attracted by his loving, magnetic and glowing personality."[28] This visit took place before the Temple at Belur was dedicated. He and Swami Atmabodhananda were given an address of welcome, which reads in part:

"To Revered Swamijis Akhilananda and Atmabodhananda
the most reputed Sannyasins of the
Sri Ramakrishna Mission
Reverend Swamijis

It is with feelings of the deepest devotion and love that we, the staff and the students of the Noapara High English School, avail ourselves of the high privilege of approaching with this humble address to Sannyasins, like you who have dedicated their consecrated selves for carrying out -the high mission of Sri Ramakrishna, the God-incarnate of the age.

We recall with pleasure the day ever memorable to us when three years one of you - Reverend Swami Akhilanandaji kindly consented and joined us on this very spot with an address expressive of your deepest feelings of religion.

It is thus appropriate in the highest degree that on the present auspicious occasion we should be anxious to extend to you such enthusiastic welcome as lies in our power.

The staff and the students of Noapara H.E. School
Noapara 20 Dec. 1937

Earlier in December on the fifth, he was given an address of welcome from the citizens of Narayanganj, which read in part:

To His Holiness
Sreemat Swami Akhilanandaji Maharaj
Revered Swamiji
We, the citizens of Narayanganj, beg to accord you our heartest welcome in our midst on your return from America. It is through the grace of God that we have been able to avail ourselves of the rare opportunity to express our sense of reverence and gratitude for what you have done in the East and the West towards the fulfillment of the great mission of Sri Ramakrishna and the illustrious Vivekananda.

On the twelfth of the same month he was given an address of welcome from the citizens of Mymensingh, which read in part:
To His Holiness
Sreemat Swami Akhilanandaji Maharaj
Revered Swamiji
We, the citizens of Mymensingh accord you our heartiest and most respectful welcome on this occasion of your memorable visit to this town.

We take particular pride in the fact that we can boast of you as one of the worthiest sons of this District of ours and our welcome to you is not a matter of convention, but is prompted by genuine affection and esteem for your noble self.

The Commissioners of the municipality of Netrakona gave him an address of welcome on the 14th December, 1937 which read in part:
Dear Swamiji
Being animated with a mixed feeling of triumphant pride and just satisfaction over the splendid humanitarian services you have been privileged to render to advance the cause of Universal Religion, both inland and outside, we, the humble representatives of your native town. most eagerlv avail ourselves of this opportunity of offering you an address of welcome on the occasion of your auspicious visit to the town of your birth after your momentous sojourn in America.

The members of the Ramakrishna Medical Education Society for Women on the fourth of February presented an address of welcome to Mrs. Anna Worcester and Miss Helen Rubel for their generous contribution towards the cost of the Temple. The same society gave an address of welcome to Swami Akhilananda.

Addresses of welcome were presented to Swami Akhilananda and to Mrs. Worcester and Helen Rubel on the 31st of January, 1938 by the citizens of Calcutta. A news report in PRABUDHHA BHARATA for May, 1938 has some of the details:

The citizens of Calcutta presented an address to Swami Akhilananda, founder and head of the Vedanta Society, America, and to Mrs. Anna Worcester and Miss Helen Rubel, two munificent donors of the new Ramakrishna Temple at Belur, at a crowded public meeting held at the Albert Hall, Calcutta, on Monday, the 31st of January, under the auspices of the Vivekananda Society. Mr. Sanat Kumar Roy Choudhury, Mayor of Calcutta presided. "... The Mayor then presented the addresses in costly caskets to Swami Akhilananda, Mrs. A. Worcester and Miss H. Rubel amid prolonged cheers. The Swami and the two American sisters thanked the organizers in suitable speeches for the addresses presented to them. ... The women of Calcutta were also not behind in showing their appreciation of the princely donation of these two American disciples of Swami Akhilananda. As many as nine Women's associations of the city... gathered at the Grand Hotel at Chowringhee on Friday, the 4th of February and presented garlands and addresses to them..."

10

THE RETURN TO BOSTON

Before they were to leave India there took place another event that was of great interest to Swami. That was Swami Akhilananda's meeting with the Swiss psychiatrist, Carl Jung. Swami Akhilananda accompanied by Swami Pavitrananda and Mrs. Worcester went to Jung's hotel in Calcutta. There in the dining hall the Swamis and Jung conversed very pleasantly.[1] We don't know all the wise and humorous words they spoke that day.

But we do know a little. This was a time when the field of psychology was being explored in new ways. J. B. Rhine's *NEW FRONTIERS OF THE MIND* had been published. Extrasensory perception was a topic of immense interest to many. The conversation between them turned towards dreams and their interpretation. As Swami Akhilananda had discovered in his life, he had his own reason to believe dreams could be significant. Evidently Jung felt the same way. In a lecture some years later in 1949, Swami told the following: "Prof. Jung was telling, when we saw him, about a dream. A friend of his, an engineer, knew he was interested in dreams and one day when he met him on the street said to him: 'Well, what do you think of this dream that I had?' And he told how he dreamt he was flying over the mountain tops. Prof. Jung asked him not to go mountain climbing for some time. But the fellow did not make much of dreams and told Prof. Jung that and they parted laughing. Later on when the engineer was climbing a mountain and got to the top he had the urge to jump across to the other peak and he did. And you can imagine what happened. He fell below and was torn to pieces."[2]

There was a time in his life when Jung thought that spiritual illumination, a superconscious experience, was a deep unconscious state. In 1946 Swami Akhilananda pointed out in his book *HINDU PSYCHOLOGY* how wrong this interpretation was.[3] It's doubtful that they touched on this subject. Instead their conversation naturally drifted to meditation. The Swami recalls: "We had the pleasure of discussing this very point with the psychiatrist, Prof. Carl Jung and we talked about the utility and effect of meditation in personal and collective life. He seemed to understand its utility and after our discussion he said, 'Well, I understand, Swami, that you mean this. If I do not keep my garden clean and orderly I cannot go out and tell my neighbor to keep his garden clean and orderly.'"[4]

But the meeting was not without its humor. At one point Jung referred to a well-known philosopher saying, "I hear our friend (B.R.) is making matrimonial experiments," this being recalled in his lectures laughing with great good humor by Swami Akhilananda.

What other incidents they might have exchanged is regrettably lost. There is a rumor that after Swami Akhilananda and Mrs. Worcester left the table Jung turned to Swami Pavitrananda and remarked that Akhilananda really did not understand Western psychology.[5] Anyone with a superficial acquaintance with Swami Akhilananda might think that way, but those who knew him well knew otherwise. Gordon Allport, professor of psychology at Harvard University and author of *PERSONALITY. A PSYCHOLOGICAL INTERPRETATION,* wrote *an introduction to Swami Akhilananda's HINDU PSYCHOLOGY, ITS MEANING FOR THE WEST*, which would be published in 1946, where he says: "Understanding and appreciating the significance of much of Western psychology, he is able to point shrewdly to certain improvements that Eastern psychology can offer..."[6] G. Hobart Mowrer, research professor of psychology, University of Illinois, wrote in his introduction to Swami's *MENTAL HEALTH AND HINDU PSYCHOLOGY,...* "the author is an accomplished scholar, not only in the field of classical religion, but also in respect to the theories and theoretical dilemmas of contemporary psychiatry, psychology and sociology."[7]

In India at their departure time, Helen Rubel saw Swami Akhilananda and Mrs. Worcester and her daughter off from Bombay on February 15th. They would be stopping in Zurich on their way to the United States. Helen Rubel had decided to stay in India. She wrote to her uncle Eduard in Switzerland..." I was very anxious to make this separation, thinking it better for all, besides wishing above all things to see and learn in India... You know that I am doing the thing that means most to me in life."[8] Although she would not be in Providence, she was not indifferent to Swami's welfare, his needs, or the work of the Center.

She wrote to him frequently, trying to help him financially. On December 6, 1938: "If in April a few hundred would help you, let me know."

Swami was to know another separation. In 1938 Swami Satprakashananda, who had been assisting him, left Providence and established a permanent Vedanta Society in St. Louis, Missouri.[9] Swami Akhilananda would not have an assistant until 1954 when Swami Sarvagatananda came in October.

In the summer of 1938, Swami Akhilananda visited San Francisco again. Swami Ashokananda was having a cabin built at Carnelian Bay, Lake Tahoe with a grand view of its lake. The new cabin was scheduled to be dedicated in the early part of August, on the 8th. The ceremonies were performed in the cabin's living room, before the fireplace with Swami Akhilananda as the worshipper for the homa fire ceremony, which included chanting and meditation. Other Swamis were there, of course, Swami Ashokananda, Devatmananda, Prabhavananda, Satprakashananda, and Vividishananda.

Two years later in 1940 Swami Paramananda, the leader of Boston's Vedanta Society, who had purchased 20 acres in Cohasset in 1929 as an ashrama for Boston, collapsed with a fatal heart attack while walking in its woods on June 21, 1940.[10] The question arose as to whether another Swami would succeed him. The biography of Swami Paramananda, *A BRIDGE OF DREAMS*, states; "The other Ramakrishna Mission swamis were eager to replace him with another Swami. Swami Paramananda's community, distrusting the attitude of some swamis toward women, refused to accept any new Swami. They applied to Belur Math authorities to be allowed to continue as a Sisterhood, with Sister Daya and Gayatri Devi conducting the public services as they had done in Parmananda's lifetime... When after much soul-searching, Paramananda's two centers chose not to accept a new swami as their leader, they were severed from their parent Order."[11]

The President of the Ramakrishna Order, Swami Virajananda, sent a cable from Belur Math in early 1941 for "Akhilananda to start Boston work."[12] The city which had seen Swami Vivekananda could not be without a representative. In the meantime Swami was busy lecturing in Boston. In a letter of November 4, 1940 from, Belur Math where the Ramakrishna Order was located, Swami Sankarananda wrote: "I am happy to know that you have been invited to give lectures at the Metaphysical Club before large audiences. ... I heard that you are delivering lectures in a rented hall."

A printed program lists the December lectures;
Sunday, Dec. 11
8 pm Self conquest
Sunday, Dec. 18
3:30 pm Meditation and realization
8 pm Place of emotion in life
Sunday, Dec. 25
3:30 pm Divine incarnation
8 pm Was Christ a yogi?
Sunday, Jan 1
3:30 pm Scientific basis of religion
8 pm Soul and over soul
Tuesday, Dec. 13.20, 27 8 pm
Class on Gita
Thursday, Dec. 15, 22, 29 8 pm
Meditation and practical lessons
Swami Bodhananda will lecture in Boston Jan. 15th. He was the President and leader of the Vedanta Society in New York City.

The following year in April 1941 Swami Akhilananda received a cable from Swami Virajananda, the President of the Order, on the inauguration of Vedanta work: "May it radiate perennial peace, benediction, love among all truthseekers."[13] An undated newspaper article reports that

"The opening services of the Ramakrishna Vedanta Society will take place tomorrow at 11 am and 3 pm in rooms taken by the society at 687 Boylston St., the Kensington building, ... Another swami, Vishwananda of Chicago, will participate in the formal opening tomorrow morning and will speak with Swami Akhilananda. The subject will be "Principle of Vedanta". In the service tomorrow afternoon the subject will be "Yoga Practices", Tuesday a weekly class will be inaugurated at 8 pm on "Spiritual Problems of Modern Man", conducted by Swamis Bodhananda and Vishwananda, and Thursday at 8 pm there will be a lecture on "Masters of India".

A permanent location for the Center was necessary. Swami Akhilahanda with the help of Mrs. Worcester began the search. They became interested in a property on Deerfield Street, number 58. She had a dream about how much should be offered in order to buy the property.

Swami wrote about this dream in his book, *HINDU PSYCHOLOGY, ITS MEANING FOR THE WEST,* p. 66-67:

"A friend of ours had a most amazing dream just before the Vedanta Society of Boston acquired its present building. We had been negotiating through a real estate company to buy this property, and one morning we requested our friend, who was interested in the negotiations, to make an offer for the house. She said, 'Swami, if I am to make an offer I shall give the amount of which I dreamt.' It was almost less than half of the sale price. We felt that the Society would lose this opportunity to have the place if such an offer were made. However, our friend insisted on it, and when we went to Boston the offer was given to the real estate agent. He was vexed and almost decided to drop the matter without relaying the offer to the owner. We finally persuaded him to take a check with the offer to the owner, who would have the chance of refusing it. The next morning the real estate agent telephoned and told our friend that her dream was true, as the owner had accepted the offer. The house was acquired as indicated previously in the dream."[14]

Of course dreams are of interest to everyone. Swami Akhilananda knew how different and various dreams could be and how skeptical people were about them. Were there dreams that had any meaning? He writes: "Dreams need not necessarily be created by inhibitions, repressed conscious or subconscious urges... Dreams are not always retrospective... Some dreams are progressive and creative; others, again, give evidence of spiritual unfoldment. Still others leave tremendous impressions upon the mind amounting to spiritual joy and realization. Jung is of the opinion that some dreams are progressive. He relates many instances in which they gave knowledge of future events."[15]

The unexpected strokes of luck in acquiring 58 Deerfield St. were followed by another. World War II was intensifying. A Mrs. Rasalia Abreu was in France and while visiting there she approached Swami Siddheswarananda offering to help him. He suggested that she help Swami Akhilananda.[16] Returning to America, that is what she did, supplying the necessary funds for the purchase and remodeling of this neo-Georgian house and its rooms to create a chapel.[17] All of it was a delight to the Swami situated as it was overlooking the Charles River in the Back Bay.

In 1942 on April 1st this new home for Vedanta was dedicated. The evening program, described by an unknown person who was there, tells the story of that occasion, and its impact. Swami Akhilananda had invited Prof. Edgar Brightman of Boston University to be present, but he was not able to be there. He wrote to Akhilananda: "Your spiritual aims are so pure and noble, and your purpose so close to my own that I should very gladly have shared in the dedication...."[18]

Congratulations came from the President of the Order, Swami Virajananda; from Swami Prabhavananda, Ashokananda, Devatmananda, Nikhilananda,[19] from Rabbi William Braude[20] of Temple Beth El in Providence, from Dr. Allen Claxton[21] of the Broadway Temple in New York City, and others.

This account of the dedication had lain undetected in an unknown student's notebook for almost sixty years. It is included in the Appendix.

As is shown by his lecturing at the Metaphysical Club, Swami Akhilananda was not a stranger in Boston. While he was in Providence, Dr. Allen Claxton, the Methodist minister at Grace Church, had introduced him to Prof. Edgar Brightman of Boston University and he also met Dr. Earle Marlatt, the Dean of the School of Theology. Slowly, year after year, his circle of friends particularly in the academic community increased. AS Prof. Lavely of Boston University describes Swami:

"Because of this kind of devotional ecumenicism, he was able to appeal to a surprisingly wide spectrum of intellectuals in the Boston area. I think the thing that impressed me most about the Swami was the number of great minds he knew, in a personal way. For many of these he performed a pastoral function which no local clergyman could have. Of course, he was able to hold his own in sophisticated philosophical discussions (he was, for example, an active member of Philosophics Anonymous, an informal group of Boston area philosophers and theologians), but perhaps more important was his gift of providing practical guidance in spiritual matters. His was indeed a great ministry over the years in Boston."[22] This was just about to begin.

Boston Ramakrishna Vedanta Center, 1940s

Dean Walter G. Muelder of B.U. School of Theology

Dr. Paul Johnson of B.U. School of Theology

Dr. Edgar Brightman of B.U. School of Theology

11

BOSTON BRAIN OF AMERICA

With Swami Akhilananda returning to Boston in the early 1940s, New England had been no stranger to Vedanta. Boston, the hub of the universe, and what Swami Vivekananda called "the Brain of America.". It was here that Swami Vivekananda came before he spoke at the Parliament of Religions in Chicago in 1893. He had been invited by Kate Sanborn, a well-known author of her time, when she met him on a train traveling from Vancouver to Chicago. He visited her in August, 1893 at her home, Breezy Meadows, in Metcalf. MA. At that time he would also visit Annisquam, MA invited by Professor John Henry Wright of Harvard. Leaving there, he would go to Salem, MA where he would speak. He would return to Annisquam in August, 1894 for another visit of about three weeks. That was the time when he said he gave his first public address in America the previous year in the Annisquam church.

Another disciple of Sri Ramakrishna, Swami Saradananda, came to the Boston area in 1896-97 and stayed on several occasions at Mrs. Ole Bull's house in Cambridge where she had a studio house for her guests. While there he gave a series of lectures at the Procopeia, 5 Park Street, Boston in December, 1896. He also spoke on <u>Ethical Ideals</u> on November 29th at the Cambridge Conferences. Swami Abhedananda, another disciple of Ramakrishna, came to Boston in June, 1896, staying with Mrs. Bull in her studio house. He, too, spoke before the Cambridge Conferences in the summer of 1898 on <u>Unity in Variety.</u> He was to speak again the following year on <u>Religious Ideas in Ancient India.</u> And, of course. Swami Paramananda disciple of Vivekananda, had been lecturing in Boston from 1910-1940.

Swami Akhilananda's ministry in Boston had an auspicious beginning with the early friendship of Dean Earle Marlatt, B. U. School of Theology, and its professors, Dr. Edgar Brightman, Prof. of philosophy, and Dr. Paul Johnson, Prof. of Psychology of religion. As the years went by, Swami Akhilananda would be friends with other professors at Boston University. He would also be of service to MIT, where he would become acquainted with President James Killian, Dean Francis Bowditch, and other Deans. At Harvard it would be a similar story, being close friends with Prof. Pitirim Sorokin, the world famous sociologist; Harlow Shapley, well-known astronomer and Nobel prize winner, and Gordon Allport, Professor of psychology. Gradually he would become known to other educational institutions in the Bay State and beyond. In the years to come he would be spreading his energies far and wide.

It was a time of expansion. The Vedanta movement of Ramakrishna's and Vivekananda's teachings had accelerated in the 1930s. Vedanta societies were established in St. Louis, Chicago, Hollywood, Portland Oregon, and a second Center in New York City. In the years following, there would be several more Centers in the United States, in Europe and in South America.

You might say that Swami Akhilananda was blessed with good luck for he survived the economic stress of the Great Depression in the l930s. Not only did he survive it, but he gave financial assistance where it might be needed to other fledgling Vedanta societies such as Chicago. As long as he was alive, he underwrote the finances of that Center to relieve Swami Vishwananda of any worry.[1]

Whatever it was that made for Swami Akhilananda's success in Providence, it followed him to Boston. He met the needs of the people. He served them. He loved them. He not only gave the message of Ramakrishna "so many faiths, so many paths" to God, which would tend to lessen the antagonism and bickering between religious groups, but he saw early on as he remarked in his first visit to India, that the Americans "lacked in poise and a balanced frame of mind." They wanted to learn "the technique of Indian spirituality and a meditative frame of mind."[2] Meeting these needs and inspiring individuals to strive for a life of spiritual realization were the twin prongs of his ministry. People were enthusiastic for the latter and grateful for the former. He would delve into the heart of any spiritual problem and meet the needs of the people. Two sisters who attended his services told a friend: "I now understand what Christianity is all about."[3] People found peace in the chapels, in Boston and in Providence. As Swami Shivananda had written in a letter of December 4, 1930 to Mrs. Anna Worcester: "Akhilananda is one of the purest souls. Coming in contact with him many souls will get peace."

Swami would become very busy at Boston. Unfortunately we do not have a complete record of his life and events. He didn't have the newspaper publicity in Boston as he did in the early days of Providence. His annual engagement diaries for the 1930s up to 1944 were probably lost. They have not been found either in Providence or in Boston. There were devoted followers in Boston as there were in Providence. As for those helping him at the Center, Mrs. Worcester, who could be somewhat formidable at times, managed the Center in Providence and continued to serve him in Boston. Her daughter and granddaughter lived with her in the Boston Center during a portion of the 1940s. This continued into the late 1950s, when the daughter remarried. There were others who served him in Providence such as Italo Pellini and Mrs. Charlotte Morrison, who, in 1959 became Mrs. Italo Pellini. In Boston, in addition to Mrs. Worcester there was Granville Sheldon, who dubbed himself as being "on call", a true English gentleman.

We do know from letters to a student, John Duane, that in December '42, Swami visited Philadelphia[4] and in March '43[5] he was "expected in Philadelphia on Friday next at the Ethical Society". In a letter to the same individual he wrote on February 11, 1943: "you will be happy to know Boston University (School of Theology) has been very nice to me. I have many lectures and discussions there. They have a few very fine men in the Department of Philosophy and Religion."[6]

That summer of '43 Swami had a serious illness. The nature of it is not known. He wrote to John Duane in a letter of August 7 '43: "I am much better now through Lord's grace, Mrs. Worcester will let you know everything. It is now past. Evidently our Lord wanted me to stay here and to be of His service. May His will be done, I am gradually gaining strength although I am still quite weak. I am allowed to read my mail and to write one or two letters. Mrs. Worcester worked very hard even without sleep and food. She is still doing so many things for me. Mr. Pellini also did his best for me." And in September he wrote: "I am improving in health quite a little, The doctor was very happy to see the report of X ray, etc. last time. I have to take medicine regularly for some time more. But I gained strength through Lord's grace."[7]

His spirits improved. Within a month he wrote to John Duane: "Swami Bodhananda of New York, Swami Yatiswarananda and Swami

Satprakashananda of St. Louis came to visit with us last week. They spent a few days in Boston and in Providence. We had a lovely time together. We talked so much of our Master and other great Swamis - the disciples of our Lord. Ah, what joy one gets to talk of these things."[8]

Every now and then, or every few years, Swami Akhilananda would have an illness which would incapacitate him for a while. He worked untiringly. His sleep amounted to four hours a night. He said in a lecture of January 11, 1949: "Swami Brahmananda used to say that to sleep more than 4-hours is laziness. And we never used to sleep more than 4-5 hours utmost. But this does not apply to you people. The American people need at least eight hours sleep a night. A friend of ours would like us to have more sleep, but you cannot force yourself out of a habit of 40-50 years."[9]

If the faculty at Boston University, School of Theology, was keeping him busy with lectures and discussions, he had numerous other engagements in addition to the services at Providence and Boston. There would be speaking engagements where he would talk on comparative religion, or the religions of India. Interspersed between all his commitments would be luncheons and dinners mostly at the Boston Center, where he cooked for his friends from the colleges and universities. Swami Akhilananda's personality was such that it was really impossible for anyone to resist his friendliness. His many dinners and luncheons were one way he expressed his love. He kept in touch and his friends did likewise. He could have been writing about himself when he said: "We know of a young man who, from his boyhood, was optimistic, sweet, and friendly to everyone. His genial temperament attracted men and women to him in great numbers. He expanded his life immensely, and his circle of friends increased so much that it is difficult for him to find time to satisfy the emotional cravings of his friends who are constantly seeking his loving expressions."[10]

Before 1944, there is no clear picture of his engagements. Or of his luncheons or dinners. At that time the first luncheon he had was with his old friend Prof. Joachim Wach of Brown University on January 4th in Providence. On the 14th Dr. Paul Johnson of B.U. and family came to dinner in Boston. In addition there were requests for him to speak and attend meetings. To enumerate for the month of January, 1944; On Jan. 2 at 6:00 at the Matheson street church in Providence he spoke on spiritual life, on the 3rd he had lunch with the committee of the church, on the 7th he had lunch with Dr. Edgar Brightman of B. U. on the 8th he had a special meditation class at 11 am at the Boston Center and a dinner party for Pedro Abreu.

He was at the Pawtucket Methodist church Jan. 9 for a talk. He gave an early morning radio talk in Providence, station WFCI, on the 10th. On the 16th he had lunch with Mr. and Mrs. G. A. Guyer. The 17th was Swami Vivekananda's birthday with special worship. Dr. Raymond Willoughby of Brown University came for lunch Jan. 18 at 12:30. On the 18th in the afternoon Rabbi and Mrs. Braude came to visit. On Jan. 20 Swami Akhilananda had lunch with Dean Clarence Skinner of Tufts and at 2 pm Swami gave a talk at Tufts School of Theology. His special group class for meditation took place on Jan. 22 at 11 am. On the 24th at 3:30 he spoke on comparative religion at E. Providence high school. He was at Brown University Jan. 25th at 2:45. On the 27th he had a special worship for Swami Brahmananda's birthday. On the 28th he had lunch with Dr. Edgar Brightman at the University Club in Boston. On the 29th his special meditation class. He attended on Jan. 31 at 10 the Minister's Council of R.I.: at 12 he had lunch and a meeting with the executive committee of the Minister's Union and at 3:30 a lecture at the Universal church in Providence.[11] There were half-a-dozen lunches with various devotees. In addition he gave 35 interviews during the month by appointment. No doubt there were also those who spoke to him after the services.

Again in early February on the 2nd he attended the B. U. Philosopher's Club, and on the 3rd at 12:30 had Prof. Harold DeWolf to lunch. On the 4th at B. U. he gave a talk at the Chapel service on mystical experience. He was a guest for lunch at Dean Earle Marlatt's house on February 5th and he gave a radio talk on Station WFCI in Providence on Feb. 7th. Rev. Van Dyke came for lunch Feb. 8th and Swami gave a lecture at YWCA the next day. So his daily schedule went with further meetings and other engagements.

Rev. Allen Claxton, the Methodist minister in Providence had introduced Swami Akhilananda to Prof. .Edgar Brightman. The Professor and the Swami used to meet frequently for lunch at the University Club in Boston. As the Swami has said: "This friend of mine and I meet every week or 10 days and we always discuss this point - Personalism and Absolutism."[12] At another time he remarked: "Some of the personalistic philosophers such as Prof. Brightman are very good friends of ours." In this country,[13] Brightman, according to Swami Akhilananda, was the greatest exponent of Personalism, a philosophical movement putting ultimate value and reality in persons, divine or human. In one lecture the Swami remarked: "We often argue with Prof. Brightman 'When I want joy I want unlimited joy and how can a finite being give me that?' Then we say also for the sake of argument 'Let us not quarrel, Let us start from any point of view and build up our spiritual nature, then we will know.'"[14] In 1944 alone he had close to 20 luncheons with Prof. Brightman. They became an established custom. In addition there were dinners at 58 Deerfield St, Boston for Prof. Brightman and his family with Swami Akhilananda serving them his delicious Indian dishes, such as curried lamb, rice, dal, etc.

Prof. John Lavely of Boston University writes of their friendship: "I can still see them as clearly as though it were yesterday: engaged in animated conversation, deeply serious yet strangely light-hearted, pressing a point and yielding a point, never in perfect agreement but always learning from each other. One could only envy a friendship which produced such conversation, what a model for the relation of East and West, this friendship between the American philosopher and the seer from India."[15]

"Dr. Brightman had an especially deep and personal appreciation and affection for the gifted leader of the Ramakrishna Society in Boston," writes Prof. Harold DeWolf of B. U. ..."Brightman generously acknowledged that the Swami was a helpful spiritual guide, a guru to him. ...But his belief that God reveals Himself also in nature and especially in human nature in all times and places made him welcome the evidence of God's grace in Swami Akhilananda's kindly testimony and personality."[16]

Swami treasured the friendships he made. As Swami Prabhavananda has said about him: "having wonderful love for everyone",[17] he would have many lunches and dinners throughout his ministry. They were incidentally a way of disseminating the meaning of Vedanta in the present world.

Another friend, Peter Bertocci, who was a Borden Parker Bowne Professor of philosophy at B.U. writes:

"Swami Akhilananda on several occasions was a dinner guest in our home, Mrs. Bertocci, our three sons, and I bowed our heads in prayer as Swami at our request said grace. There was a brief silence, and the Swami intoned; '0m! - and immediately took our nerves and minds with him to another dimension of Being. 'Oh God, who art our Father, Oh, God, who art our Mother!' once more he broke through our stereotypes, and yet he used symbols of a special tie we had with each other and with the Universal One."[18] Besides cementing friendships, his luncheon and dinner engagements served another purpose. People felt they could open their hearts to Swami. He spoke of one such event in one of his lectures.

"The other day we had a young man to our place in Boston for dinner. Just the two of us were there and we ate together. This young man has been institutionalized and they have tried to find out why he drinks. The best psychiatrists have tried to discover yet they cannot find out the reason for his drinking. There does not appear to be any reason for it. He comes from a very fine, highly educated family. He was telling us 'You know, Swami, when the psychiatrists start to ask me questions, I close up. I know that whatever I say they will interpret.' Somehow or other that young man has confidence in us and trusts us through and through. ... The reason for his drinking is a very deep-seated one. ... He has to be told that he is not as bad as some people may think he is. He has to have confidence in himself. ...He told that when he drinks he goes to the worst place to drink - the lowest type of place, the most disreputable. He goes because in such a place the people will not criticize him. They will not condemn. ...Now he seems to be on the road to recovery. We invited him to our place to eat with us and we talked. That is our humble way."[19]

Although Swami Akhilananda dined with well-known personalities, he was not what you would call a name-dropper. We have learned from the lecture notes of an anonymous devotee, May 29, 1949, about one of those times. The Swami was in Europe. This is what he said:

"When we were in Europe years ago, we had dinner at the home of a great scientist in Switzerland. He is a botanist." Well, of course, we all wondered who that might be. The scientist went on to tell about a meeting in Italy with scientists from different parts of the world. What a wonderful time they all had. The scientist continued: "'and yet a group of religious people cannot get together. There is quarreling and prejudice...How do you explain that?'"...

And from the same source a year later (March 5, 1950): "We had lunch recently with two brilliant scientists. One of them is now teaching at Harvard. He was Einstein's successor. In his home in Germany, he had wonderful library...He feels very bad about losing his library...but his wife says that it was too much bother to take care of them anyway. (laughs)...We cannot be certain of anything here..."In his lectures there would be tantalizing moments! Who were these men?

Swami loved to reach out.Visiting New York city and Phildelphia, including Rochester, NY in 1944 gave him an opportunity to see those who were devoted to him and to give the truth of Vedanta to others. On all these trips he spoke. He did so when in New York City at the Vedanta Society and had dinner with a number of friends including Mrs. Rasalia Abreu and Rev. and Mrs. Allen Claxton. In 1944 he had, as far as it can be determined, his first contact with MIT when he was to see an unnamed professor at 2pm on July 17th.

It was in 1945 that he met Dean Walter Muelder of the B. U. School of Theology, who would be another close friend. Dean Muelder writes:

"My relationship with Swami was many-sided. Quite regularly we had lunch together either at the Center or in some pleasant restaurant like the Window Shop in Cambridge. We discussed the major ideas he was wrestling with in the American cultural scene, the secular challenges to religion, psychologies that seemed insensitive to the realities of spiritual experience, particularly troublesome issues in counseling, the needs of theological students, and the writing we were doing at the time."[20]

Dean Muelder relates how Swami Akhilananda told of clients who had disappointing experiences with psychiatrists. The Swami was critical of some professional people who did not really love their patients nor did they see the need for couples to love at the spiritual level. Swami had great faith in mature religious experience. All of his pastoral ministry was, to him, in the framework of the All-Loving Being.[21]

Dean Muelder tells of Swami's visits to their home.

"He always expressed keen interest in the children and their problems and development. He was sensitive toward the anxieties of mothers who carried heavy responsibilities of child-rearing as the wives of professionally ambitious and success-oriented men. He was pastoral counselor for youths and young adults from a number of such homes and for those from broken homes.[22]

"Professional men also came to see him. Professors of religion and ministers of the gospel were among those who cherished his friendship, his wisdom, and his guidance in spiritual practices. He took the initiative also in calling on them when ill and he remembered their family festivals. We often discussed the kinds of spiritual disciplines which he felt were appropriate for busy people in the American culture. In such matters his caring included respect for their religious traditions. He was well read in the writings of Christian mysticism. With his guidance I read, as time permitted, in the literature of Vedanta and we discussed its methods in relation to Christian devotional living."[23] Dean Muelder concludes with "Swami Akhilananda was a truly spiritual person and the power that was released within him radiated blessing among those with whom he practiced his mission."[24]

In July 1945 on the 19th, Mr. Nalini Sarkar, the former mayor of Calcutta visited Swami, who feted him at the University Club and introduced him to his friends. While in Boston, Mr. Sarkar was a news-event, having his picture-taken with the would-be Senator Leverett Saltonstall and other dignitaries, which was published in the Boston Globe.[25] He stayed a week and then went to New York City where he met Swami Akhilananda again. They were old friends.

Swami Akhilananda's cousin, Shirish Chandra Sanyal, has written of one such occasion:

"Once before, Mr. Sarkar came to America and visited him, Akhilananda took him to Harvard, Boston and other universities, showed him around and introduced him to many recognized scholars and professors there. Mr. Sarkar was amazed and charmed to see how these distinguished people treated Akhilananda with so much respect and reverence. Upon returning to India, Mr. Sarkar told all these experiences to Akhilananda's elder brother, Lalit Chandra, in great details."[26]

On June 24 the Swami traveled to Syracuse, New York where he spoke to members of the Lisle Fellowship, Inc., an organization founded in 1936 to promote and provide intercultural understanding. A volunteer organization with programs in different countries, it has a program in India every year. Staying for three days, Swami spoke on "Hinduism and meditation" on Monday, on Tuesday "Post-war reconstruction", and ended on Wednesday with "What we plan to do." From there he went to New York City where he stayed until June 30th, meeting Swami Bodhananda and having interviews and dining with his various friends.

In the spring of 1946 Prof. Sarvepali Radhakrishnan visited Swami on April 4th and had lunch with him. Swami gave him a dinner party and later Prof. Radhakrishnan gave a lecture at the Boston Center for the evening class. Earlier in the afternoon he had delivered a lecture at Brown University on the British Empire and India. Swami was to see him again the following day for a brief visit. At 8 in the evening Swami Akhilananda gave a talk on Ramakrishna and Christ at the Trinity church in Pawtucket. Soon Swami Akhilananda was to turn another corner of his life in New York City on East 33rd street at Harper & Bros.

12

HINDU PSYCHOLOGY, IT'S MEANING FOR THE WEST

W hen Swami Akhilananda's *HINDU PSYCHOLOGY, ITS MEANING FOR THE WEST* was published in 1946, the year after World War II ended with its post-war turmoil, Christopher Isherwood wrote a letter to him in December saying: "It is certainly one of the most important things published this year."[27] Now 60 years later it is out-of-print. But what Swami Akhilananda had to say about Hindu psychology might very well make this book a small classic. Its publication began with a number of his friends, both in academia and his followers in Boston, Providence and elsewhere, who felt that his work should reach a larger audience. The thoughts of Sri Ramakrishna and his disciple Swami Vivekananda and some of his other great disciples brought a challenge to every religious seeker. Swami Akhilananda's broad presentation drawing on incidents in every religion was a welcome approach. It would seem to be inevitable and it was. The value of Swami's Sunday sermons would not be lost. In 1946 when Harper and Brothers published his book Swami wrote in his Preface:

"Some friends were anxious to have a record of these lectures and employed stenographers to take notes on them... as the lectures were received enthusiastically by the audiences, our friends were anxious to have a permanent record. Our late friend, Dr. Raymond Willoughby, formerly of Brown University, attended some of the lectures and read the notes. He told us: 'You... have something to give us for the-training of the mind.' So the lectures were edited and elaborated for publication..."[28]

His good friend, Gordon Allport, Prof. of psychology at Harvard, wrote the introduction; "In some respects, I am convinced, American psychology would improve in richness and wisdom if it accommodated in some way the wise things that the author says about meditation and the necessity for an adequate philosophy of life."[29] Prof. Edgar Brightman of Boston University's School of Theology wrote the Foreword in which he said: "The principles which the Swami Akhilananda sets forth in this book are universal, not sectarian. They are based on the results of centuries of experience and spiritual experiment as truly as science is based on the work of centuries of physical experiment."[30] The chapters would focus on cognition, emotion, the subconscious mind, will and personality, meditation, the effect of meditation, ESP, the superconscious, religion and psychotherapy, and philosophy of life.

Swami Akhilananda in his early chapters reflects on the history of psychological thought in the West. Swami takes note that Western psychoanalysts began their research in abnormal states of mind and he mentions Charcot, Janet, Freud, Adler and Jung.

"It should be remembered," he remarked, "that it is extremely unsafe, to say the least, to generalize the findings from the study of abnormal mind and apply them to fairly normal minds. Freud and others made superficial remarks about the religious tendencies of man in terms of sex, and they try to find the 'death' or 'destructive' tendencies even in normal and supernormal minds. Actually, the supernormal minds function in a manner quite different from normal and abnormal cases. This is the reason that the unfortunate generalizations of many of the psychotherapists regarding spiritual experiences are extremely inaccurate and unscientific. They are far from the truth."[31]

He wrote: "Most of the American psychologists seem to give extreme emphasis to the motor aspect of the mind...their chief interest is to know the activity...in order to find out how the mind acts and reacts...Hindu psychologists try to understand and strengthen the whole mind."[32]

The development of Hindu psychology is so interesting as presented by Swami Akhilananda that to be fair to him one should quote the entire chapter. As he said:

"The science of psychology was developed mainly by the Hindus as they studied the methods by which they reached the highest religious experience - the superconscious state or samadhi. It is the only method of understanding and controlling the mind in order that a higher consciousness may be reached. According to the *YOGA APHORISMS OF PATAJALI*, the mind becomes thoroughly illumined and can transcend even the limitation of the nervous system when it is controlled and unified in the course of concentration and deep meditation. The mind can

114

immediately and directly reach another plane, the superconscious state, in which it experiences reality."[33]

In his chapter on emotions Swami delineated how they affect our physical and mental health. There will be conflicts and the mind will be restless. The nervous system will also be affected.By the power of concentration a man may dissolve his conflicting urges and emotions. This may take a litle time as the mind has been scattered and needs to be disciplined. A change will occur. Swami Brahmananda, the teacher and guru of Swami Akhilananda has said: "'But if you persist, as in the taking of a medicine, you will find it a perennial source of joy, pure and unalloyed.'"[34] Needless to say this is meditation. Meditation was a topic that Swami Akhilananda was never tired of talking about. This is how he defined it in his book:

"When concentration is very deep and the mind does not waver but remains focused on the object of thought, that is meditation.... According to Hindu psychologists meditation is not merely a nice thought, a poetic flight, or loose fancies of even pleasant experiences; it is the depth of concentration in which the mind flows continuously to an object without any cessation as 'oil poured from one vessel to another.' It is not a succession of many thoughts of the same object. The mind must not waver whatsoever. So a man is really meditating when his mind is freed from all other thoughts and is wholly focused on the object of his concentration."[35]

In one of his lectures in 1950 on February the 12th he said:

"Meditation is the activity of the total mind. Most of the time we use only a portion of the mind. When the mind becomes concentrated on one point the total mind becomes active. Meditation is not just sitting back lazy. It is a very active state. The mind has to struggle to be concentrated because we are in the habit of scattering our mind on different things. We are not in the habit of thinking of one thing consistently. We may think of one thing but we think of different things relating to that thing. We think successive thoughts and so it is not easy to focus the mind on one point."[36]

"Meditate, meditate, meditate," he would say in his sermons. He wrote; "Without the practice of concentration and meditation, no man can ever expect to reach the highest state of spiritual evolution. When we study the lives of the great Christian, Jewish, Hindu, Buddhist and Mohammedan mystics, we fully realize that they reached the highest spiritual consciousness through the development of the power of concentration."[37]

Swami told of his own initial interest in meditation. "In India, when we were small boys, we learned the practice of meditation from the older members of our family, namely, the parents or grandparents who used to practice it. We became interested in the practice of meditation through them. When we were small children, six or seven years old, we used to see them meditating, looking quiet and serene, absorbed in their ideal, and we used to imitate them. This was the beginning of our spiritual life."[38]

We will have a beginning to our spiritual life. As Swami was inspired, so we all can catch inspiration from a great personality. Our growth will be enhanced. Meditation helps to keep the mind steady. Swami is guiding us when he says:

"When a person grows up, he seeks the highest values of spiritual culture in love, unselfishness, and other such elevated ideals. His nature goes through a transformation. When a man constantly thinks and acts on the higher planes of existence and manifests higher values in his activities, and when he is in a state of divine realization, his whole system is thoroughly changed and transformed...Human beings possess a peculiar relationship with God and until they have a definite realization of that connection there is no peace."[39]

As he wrote in *HINDU PSYCHOLOGY*, "… in India, psychology is the basic science of spiritual evolution."[40] The mind and the emotions are everything in spiritual life. They, plus the will, are the dynamo that pierces into the realm of Reality, the realm of Truth. And then there is the Grace of God. "Blessed are the pure in heart, for they shall see God."

Nowadays writings on meditation are more sophisticated, more secularized. Swami Akhilananda always felt that meditation with a spiritual orientation was best. The mind of someone who has had hard knocks and had been troubled, longs for the calm of a Buddha, the love of Jesus, or the bliss of Ramakrishna. Swami Akhilananda's teachings on meditation for mental health gave strength, new vigor and an optimism to those who followed his instructions. It brought out to a degree their own latent spirituality.Pitirim Sorokin wrote a letter, December 10, 1946: "My cordial congratulations with your book: it is simple and clear and really sound and wise, not to mention its competence." Alfred

116

Werner in the <u>Christian Century,</u> wrote: "...gives a welcome glimpse into the mental world of a great Asiatic nation."[41] There were review comments by F. S. G. Northrop, author of *THE MEETING OF EAST AND WEST* and by Professor Edgar Brightman, who said: "Few indeed will be those who study it and try even a few of its suggestions without experiencing some new calm, peace, and strength in the inner life."[42] Aldous Huxley wrote: "A clear, sensible well-informed account of the rival working models of the mind - the Western... and the Hindu..."[43] Professor Paul Johnson, writing in <u>The Journal of Bible and Religion</u> for January, 1947:

"The holistic and interpersonal trend of recent psychology is evident in the psychology of India. A third emphasis in Hindu psychology is the therapeutic interest in mental health. ... Our restless minds, distracted and frustrated in the stresses and anxieties of urban living, may gain much from the calm sanity and helpful instruction of Swami Akhilananda."[44]

HINDU PSYCHOLOGY was to be published abroad. It would be published in Swedish with a lengthy review in <u>Svenska Dagbladete.</u> In a letter from Stockholm, dated January 21, 1958, Bengt Paul, who had translated HINDU PSYCHOLOGY into German writes; "an extensive and very positive review of your book, as it well deserves it." The publishers, Routledge and Kegan Paul, Ltd. wrote on January 8, 1948 that they had decided to publish it. On March 16, 1948 from Amsterdam, the Netherlands, came a letter from a publisher, Uitgerevij Theosofische: "We have decided to publish your book, HINDU PSYCHOLOGY in the Dutch language. We find it exceedingly worthwhile that your work shall be printed also in Dutch."

Walter Houston Clark, Professor Emeritus of the Psychology of Religion, Andover Newton Theological School, wrote in 1973:

"...his *HINDU PSYCHOLOGY*, which appeared in 1946, was far ahead of its time, and I cannot but speculate that, had it made its first appearance today, it would have achieved a much wider circulation. That there are far more psychologists and general readers now open to its message is partly due to the patient spade work done a generation ago by the Swami and his collaborators."[45]

Swami Pavitrananda used to tease Swami Akhilananda about his interest in psychology.. It was another source of amusement.[46] They were good friends. A bridge-builder between East and West, perhaps it can be said that Swami Akhilananda tried something that had not been tried before in writing *HINDU PSYCHOLOGY*. It can bring to mind the American poet, Robert Frost, who wrote a poem in which he said that the road he took made all the difference. So it did for Swami Akhilananda.

Dr. Gordon Allport of Harvard University

13

THE ASHRAMA

I t was in the year 1946 that Swami Akhilananda purchased 61 acres of forested land in Marshfield Hills, MA as an ashrama, or retreat, for the members of the Boston and Providence Centers. It was about 30 miles southeast of Boston, and 2 miles or a little more or less from the ocean. As part of Marshfield Hills, its land would be a little elevated and at that time one could see Humarock beach from the front of what would be the Swami's cottage. With the wind in an easterly direction what doubt could there be as to the nearness of the beach and its sea water.There were two houses on the property out of sight of each other in those scattered woods, one called the "old homestead" and the other the "Stanton" home. Both had only a few rooms, a porch, and they were used only for summer residents.

In 1947 two houses for summer use were built on the property. One would house the Swami and the other was for women who would attend the ashrama. The two houses already on the grounds would be for visiting Swamis and male devotees. In the summer of 1947, a "homa" or fire worship service with chanting and meditation was held at Marshfield with Swamis Vishwananda, Devatmananda and Swami Akhilananda participating. The ashrama was dedicated to Sri Sarada Devi, the Holy Mother. A few devotees were present.

Those visiting would comment on the quiet of this oasis in the midst of suburban life. The woods muffled the noise of outlying roads - their traffic. Only the songs of the birds went thru the trees. Someone once heard the watchful deer stamping their feet at night. An ideal spot for an ashrama. Here one could struggle with one's mind and try to meditate. No excuses.The newly built woman's cottage with four bedroons was out-of-sight of the other cottages. Evergreen trees, mostly pine, some medium height, some tall were on all sides. Towards the East fifty yards away in the midst of scattered foliage was the old Rishi tree. So the women named the very tall, impressive pine tree with only a few branches of green at its top. It almost asked for reverence.The first occupants of the women's cottage were Jesse Baxter, Editha White,

Ilona Dorothy Lesnyak, Mrs. Hershey;[1] and Mr. Prescott for the men's cottage. The month of July was reserved for the Providence members and August for Boston.

It was a very serious attempt by Swami Akhilananda to build up the spiritual life of sincere seekers. As someone once said - he gave his life-blood for Marshfield. Time spent there was not in any way a vacation. A schedule was put into effect where time was allotted for meditation in the morning, followed by breakfast, and then various duties. There was a period of free time for the devotees in the afternoon. A morning class was held at the cottage, the Swami staying about an hour. Classes were informal as a rule.

As a student recalls it: When Swami Akhilanannda came to visit the devotees and talk with them, he would arrive about 9 o'clock in the morning. He would drive up in his car and we would all go out to greet him. He would be his usual happy person, full of warmth and friendliness, asking about us all. After we had meditated, on one occasion one devotee inquired about Sri Ramakrishna giving initiation. Swami talked about Ramakrishna, Vivekananda, and Brahmananda initiating people. They could give initiation by touch. Swami said: "Maharaj was walking and a devotee, who was a lawyer, Kedar Babu, was coming towards him. Maharaj said: 'Hello, Kedar Babu, hello', and it was finished for him, Swami said, snapping his fingers. Swami knew of other instances when Maharaj gave illumination. ...Mrs. Chadwick inquired whether electro-magnetic currents of the body were changed by this illumination. Swami smiled and replied that there was a change in the structure of body and mind, a basic change."[2] There were always questions about the direct disciples of Ramakrishna.

A morning came with all of us being very attentive when Swami Akhilananda went into the difference in emotional structure between men and women. When women love, they love one-pointedly and when they hate, the same way. That one-pointed love is necessary to establish society and to have stability. For it is the women who build up society. At another time Swami Akhilananda told of the passing away of Swami Vivekananda; how Swami Brahmananda knew that Swamiji was planning to go, and how he deliberately stayed around to prevent that. Swamiji knew that Maharaj was planning to prevent his going, so he sent Maharaj on an errand to Calcutta. Maharaj realized what was in back of that, so he told Saradananda to keep watch. Swamiji also sent

Saradananda away. Than he went and sat for meditation, told the boy to stay outside, and it was over. When Maharaj returned by boat from Calcutta, the monks met him at the landing place, and he was so moved he could not get out of the boat. They had actually to lift and help him out. The disciples of Swamiji and other Swamis were crying when they met Maharaj, but he in spite of his sorrow and condition, rubbed the chest of each, saying "He is there", and all their sorrow vanished. Swami said that Swami Bodhananda had told him this story, who was there at the time.[3]

Following this Swami Akhilananda spoke about the passing away of Swami Premananda and how Maharaj had wiped away the sorrow in Swami's heart. Swami said that these Swamis were very unusual. We were all so touched, we could not talk when he finished.[4] He said he would come tomorrow about 9:30 or so. Then we all went out with him towards the car.

Other Swamis would come to visit in Marshfield and give talks and hold classes. In the summer of 1954 Swami Satprakashananda, the leader of the Vedanta Society of St. Louis and a brother disciple of Swami Akhilananda stayed at the ashrama for the summer. One morning following the meditation period the author asked if there was any condition in God's grace. The Swami replied that some people said there was and some others that there wasn't. As far as he was concerned, God's grace had its own way, just as love has its own way, or wheat growing in a field has its own way. That there was a difference between grace and justice. Grace was a different thing, another realm in which the cause and effect of justice was not operative. Grace was dependent on resignation, on the abandonment of the ego, the "I", the "I" of our feeling that we are the doer, the master of the place. When the windows of the room are closed, the wind cannot come in, he said. And sometimes the windows are hermetically sealed, and he laughed and laughed. The same was true of ourselves. When we implore the Lord for His mercy, He gives. He is always ready to give his grace, but our egoism, pride, etc. do not allow His grace to operate. Grace has its own way. Justice was always within the law. But God's grace takes us into another realm above the law. Law operates thru karma, or cause and effect.[5]

All meals were within one's own cottage. There was no socialization with the villagers. There was only limited contact, if any, with those in other ashrama cottages. Why should this be so? So that new students and others would not be distracted from their spiritual practices. It helped to foster a spiritual elan vital.In rare cases, when there were only a few students, visitors from another cottage would be made part of a class, or a meal.

Once there were just the two of us at the ashrama, Mrs. Editha White and myself.So we decided to try and have Swami Akhilananda come to lunch if he would. He was happy to agree. At the Center he would cook food on special occasions. "Eat well," he would say as he was serving us. And glance to see if we wanted more. Now we had a chance. So we set the table. One prepared a delicious meal and the other sea-moss pudding for dessert. We three chatted: what others were doing, the health of Swamis. Nothing profound.

Swami Akhilananda always stressed meditation and prayer. There were four periods during the day for meditation: morning, class time, late afternoon, and bedtime. After the evening meal, devotees would gather together to read some scripture: the GOSPEL, or Mother's conversations, Brahmananda's teachings, etc.

It was far from usual, but there would be at times little troubles between residents of a cottage. They may have been friendly before they came, or they may have been strangers. At such times, Swami Akhilananda was the personification of tact, love, and patience. As he wrote in *SPIRITUAL PRACTICES*: "A spiritual teacher must be extremely patient. We do know human weaknesses, and we know how human minds behave. Suppose a spiritual teacher gives instructions to a student, do you think he can at once change his mind? He may be inspired; he may get temporary enthusiasm. But so far as the mind is concerned, it takes time to be changed... to be frank, a teacher is like a mother. As you know, a real mother has tremendous patience with her children."[6]

It was amazing to Swami how Sarada Devi, the Holy Mother, would behave towards persons, with difficult problems. When a young Swami complained about another's behavior, and asked her "What do you say, Mother?" her only reply was "What can I say? I am the mother."[7]

Nor had Swami Brahmananda been indifferent to interpersonal conflict. "We know many episodes of a very serious nature when he removed conflict and stopped hateful activities by being patient and by asking those persons to intensify their spiritual practices. On one occasion, he told us: 'If I tell certain things to such-and-such a person, he will go away.'" It was not lost on Swami Akhilananda how Brahmananda handled situations with deep love, sympathy, and patience.[8]

The quiet retreats at Marshfield were always booked. Its schedule of mixed activities and the self-discipline necessary in small quarters kept no one away. Swami Akhilananda was enthusiastic and hopeful that Marshfield would be well-attended, its students and devotees anxious to return for another year, as most of them, if not all, were. His final word in regard to rules for the ashrama were:

"The devotees should always remember that the Ashrama is for spiritual development. So all activities and behavior should be governed by this ideal. Let society be benefited by our living examples. We must always be careful that we do not have any wrong attitude or action. We should work in harmony and co-operation."[9]

Swami's love made everything seem easy. Some of us worked for hours at a time cutting back on the bull-briars, which were full of thorns and seemed to cover every inch of the forest floor. There were those who would do the shopping, paint the houses, and clean out closets, reline drawers. In the evening some devotees would talk about their own lives or speak of those moments of spiritual awakening not to be forgotten. Various devotional books were read and enjoyed.

It was always painful to leave Marshfield. The ashrama, full of peace and serenity, its woods, the companionship of friends and Swami's visits and all of its unacknowledged pluses would have to wait for another year. At the close of one season a couple of us one Labor Day washed and simonized Swami's big Oldsmobile car. The weather was perfect for this. Within a day he would be driving his big Olds to Providence and then to Boston. He would drive to some of his appointments. People's needs kept him very busy. One day he said: "I'm rushing around like a crazy man." He was in such demand. There was always something. It was just a lot of fun. One hot August night a devotee and I decided to sleep on the porch of the cottage. Cots were moved. But sleep? Impossible. A chorus of hundreds of "katy-did, katy-did katy-did" all night long put sleep to sleep.

Swami Akhilananda picnic

The Old Rishi Tree

14

TIME GOES BY

S wami Akhilananda loved to cook. Every year there would be a
dinner honoring Sri Ramakrishna in Providence, possibly at the
Plantation Club, and also in Boston, where early on it was held at
the Center, but after 1951 at the University Club or at the Hotel Shel-
ton, for about 100 people, many his academic friends. From
Providence, Elihu Wing, Jr., the son of Dr. Wing, Swami's physician,
writes of these occasions:"How can one think of the Swami without
remembering the delightful birthday anniversary dinners of Ramakrishna. How lovingly he prepared the food and served it, personally
tending to each one's needs. These dinners were always highlighted by
inspiring talks given by brother Swamis and friends from the clergy
and universities. Throughout all of these activities he maintained a deep
spiritual commitment in a totally God-centered life."[1]

To be God-centered was not to be grim. Swami Akhilananda enjoyed life. His friendliness spilled over giving a sense of joy and
acceptance to everyone. And he reached out. On January 3, 1947 he
went to New York City where he met with his good friend Dr. Allen
Claxton and his family, and Mrs. Rasalia Abreu. He also had lunch
with Dr. Ordway Tead, vice-president of Harper and Brothers, whom
he saw again when he was in New York City on the 31st of January for
the Lisle Fellowship dinner. He was to be in NYC several times during
the year, meeting with Christopher Isherwood on May 16th, having
traveled from Chicago where he met with Prof. Joachim Wach.

He gave a number of talks and lectures at different places in 1947.
He gave talks in Providence at several churches and at a Jewish syna-
gogue. He lectured at different colleges, Brown university, Harvard,
Boston University, Hillier College and he returned to Harvard to give a
lecture on the Indian contribution to American civilization at the
School of Business Administration.

Earlier in the year he went to the Boston Dispensary on February
6th and had lunch with Dr. Joseph Pratt and the other colleagues in the

psychological clinic. He was invited to the South End House, a settlement house, on December 1st.

The year 1948 - again the same number of lunch and dinner engagements and the trips to New York City. One might say it was business as usual: the sermons, the classes, the trips and speaking engagements. If he got exhausted, he would never complain. Perhaps most draining for Swami Akhilananda were the interviews where the individual had serious problems. Swami had a number of such persons. Maybe the interviewee thought Swami could bring about a miracle. At times a miracle might occur. But Swami Akhilananda would say: "It was His grace."

Once in his talks he told of Holy Mother, how she could attach herself and also detach herself. When Swami Premananda or some other disciple of Ramakrishna passed away, she wept as if her heart would break. But, should something unexpectedly come up, she could, at an instant's notice, compose herself and give all attention to the new situation. Swami Akhilananda had this capacity to empathize and to love and care for the interviewee. But he could also be detached. What Dr. Dana Farnsworth of Harvard University saw was Swami's patience and tolerance with the weaknesses and foibles of the people he was trying to help.

"He could see through pretense and insincerity without becoming moralistic and judgmental because he respected every person even though he could not approve all his behavior."[2]

The hectic schedule was beginning to take its toll. Such rare men are a treasure. So his physician, Dr. Elihu Wing, in the early summer of 1948 wrote to the President of the Ramakrishna Mission in Calcutta about Swami's health: "Over the past few years I have been conscious of the fact that Swami Akhilananda has been carrying too heavy a load. He has long looked over-tired and very seldom takes any vacation. He travels frequently and has been doing a great deal of valuable work in connection with several of the local universities. Even during the summer he carries on extensive work for his friends, not to mention the many conferences, committee meetings, and other responsibilities.

"As his medical adviser, I write to you, asking if there isn't some way in which the Swami could be given some assistance in carrying this burden. In making this request, I assure you that it is prompted by my initiative and not the request of Swami himself, I am sure that many of his friends would join me in this request. It is our desire to see the Swami keep his health and extend his good work, which is felt not only here in New England, but in many sections of the United States."[3]

The reply he received from Swami Virajananda said in part: "Can you not kindly persuade the Swami to curtail his activities a little till we can send him someone."[4]

Dr. Wing then advised the Swami "to arrange for a vacation and to limit his working hours so that he might obtain more rest." It had been the Swami's habit to work almost twenty hours a day.

In September of 1948 Dr. Wing was gratified to receive a letter from Atlantic City in which the Swami wrote:

"I know that you will be glad to see my new address. I came here on Friday, September 10th, after the conference on science, philosophy, and religion in New York. I am resting very well and doing nothing. You are right. I needed this change and rest, although I did not like to admit it as so many things had to be done. You know I cannot refuse to do some things when the people have so much suffering. However, I am doing what you and others wanted me to. ...By the way, you will be amused to know I meet people even here who really need interviews."[5]

The twenty hour day, however, did not completely stop. It would go on like this for the next ten years. Swami had two services on Sunday, one in Boston and later in the day in Providence. Claude Stark, one of his students, writes of at least-one occasion: "... during the automobile ride from Providence to Boston after an evening lecture Sunday night, he would suddenly awaken abruptly from a nap in the back seat and say. 'We must get liver for the cats!' No stores were open Sunday night for liver, so upon arrival at Back Bay, the hour nearly midnight, and the Swami exhausted from the day's platform work, he would proceed carefully to pick the chicken off some cooked chicken bones so that the two cats could enjoy a chicken dinner instead of canned cat-food."[6] Humility was one of Swami's dominant characteristics. Nothing was unimportant to him.

Earlier in the year in March 1948, on the 2nd, 9th, 23rd and 30th he attended Prof. Pitirim Sorokin's Seminar at Harvard. He was one of the world's leading sociologists, author of *SOCIETY, CULTURE AND PERSONALITY, THE WAYS OF POWER AND LOVE, THE CRISIS OF OUR AGE*, etc. In 1947 he was doing explorations in the unex-

129

plored field of the phenomena of altruistic, creative love.[7] The result of this was his book *RECONSTRUCTION OF HUMANITY*. He became a close friend of Swami Akhilananda.

Going to Hartford, Connecticut, Swami Akhilananda on March 22 gave a lecture at the School of Theology on Hindu culture. On May 7th he journeyed to Rochester, NY to meet with friends and to speak at Rochester University. On Monday May 10th he had a lecture at Rochester's Baptist Temple. The following day at the University in the morning at 9am he lectured on Plato and Hindu philosophy with student interviews at 10 o'clock. In the evening he took a late train to Chicago, where, on the 13th he met with Prof. Joachim Wach and had lunch with the faculty at Chicago University. A lecture on ethical values followed at 2 and then a seminar lecture at 3. In the evening he had dinner with Swami Vishwananda of Chicago. Swami Akhilananda's friend and devotees from California, Mr. and Mrs. Robert Louis were also there with whom he had lunch on the 14th.

Swami Akhilananda had another early contact with MIT when he met with Dean Chalmer on June 11, 1948. He had lunch with him on November 4th. On the 16th of November he had lunch at 12:30 with Dean Baker of MIT. These meetings might be considered a foreshadowing of his close association with MIT in the mid 1950s.

The year 1949 brought with it the usual, the unanticipated, and what might have been an exciting course of events.But it would be in January that we found out what the word "swami" was sometimes thought by many people to connote: a fortune-teller, a reader of tea leaves. In reading the lecture notes of an anonymous devotee for January 11th Swami Akhilananda shared with us this story: "The other day a lady called us up. Evidently her son had been having psychiatric treatment and was not getting any better. At first we thought she wanted something like psychiatric help. She said that Rev. so-and-so had told her that the swami could do something. (He probably told her to call me because he knows I'm deeply interested in psychology). He goes out of the body and then can find out what the trouble is. When she told me that I said to her, 'I am sorry, madame, you have the wrong person (laughing). I do not go out of the body. I stay in the body."Yes,there were the customary lunch and dinner engagements with the academics around Boston and Cambridge. Unanticipated, perhaps, was that on March 30 Mayor and Mrs. James Michael Curley of

Boston came to dinner. As Swami Akhilananda says: "Well, we had Mayor Curley to our place in Boston one day. We gave him curried rice and chicken and the poor man poured out his heart to us." It was then that he disclosed that he went to prison because of political maneuvering. "We are not saying that he is honest." said Swami, "far from it - but he was not imprisoned for his dishonesty. Well, that is the way with politicians."[8] At present no indication of how they became acquainted.

Swami Akhilananda had dinner with the board of directors of Mt. Holyoke College on April 19 and on May 8th participated in the Temple Emanuel brotherhood Sunday. An extended trip followed with his leaving for Chicago May 30th. When he arrived he saw Prof. Joachim Wach, had dinner at 6:30 at the Faculty Club at Chicago University and gave a talk "Hindu View of Christ." He left for Kansas City where he would participate in the Institute of Human Relations. He had dinner with officials there and gave a lecture at 8pm at the Institute. On June 3 he traveled to Los Angeles where he met Swami Prabhavananda. On the 6th he went to Trabucco Monastery and on the 7th to the convent at Santa Barbara. He met Swami Ashokananda at San Francisco on June 8th where at 8 o'clock he gave a lecture.

After visiting Olema on June 9th and 10th, he was at Lake Tahoe where he stayed until June 18th for all day sessions of the Pacific Institute of Philosophy. There he gave a lecture on the 13th. He returned to Boston via Chicago. The rest of the summer of '49 was a quiet one with two radio talks in August from Providence a visit to Andover-Newton Theological School on August 4th, and to Harvard and MIT on August 6th for business unknown.

There were several visiting Swamis in 1949. Yatiswarananda, Vishwananda, Aseshananda, and Rudrananda, the latter two having been influenced by Swami Akhilananda to join the Order. A third friend whom Akhilananda influenced was Swami Jnanatmananda, who has told how this came about: "...a friend of mine, Nirode Sanyal,...came to me one day and said, 'A few of us, friends, are going together to a beautiful place. Why not come along with us?'" He soon found that they were at Belur Math and there he would meet Swami Premananda. There was much talk and discussion, at the end of which, Swami Premananda: "(Sri Baburam Maharaj), simply sat there sedate, his face radiating divine bliss. It was this event, I think, that first planted the seed of religion in my heart, quite unknown to myself."[9] He was not to be at Belur for two or three years. He writes: "But my friends, especially Nirode, would not leave me alone. Ultimately one day he brought me to the presence of Swami Turiyananda. I was charmed by his sublime appearance and sympathetic words. Quite unknown to me, my sleeping religious inclination started waking up..." [10]Later, on October 21st Jawaharlal Nehru, the Prime Minister of India was at MIT in the afternoon, and at 5 o'clock a grand reception for him was held at the Boston Center. Many came. One friend said later that Nehru must have appreciated the quiet moments in the shrine where the Swami had brought him.

In acquiring the Boston Center in 1941/42 and with the publication of various books, the Vedanta movement had inched a little further into the American psyche. In 1944 the Swami Prabhavananda and Christopher Isherwood translation of the *BHAGAVAD GITA* had been published by Harper & Bros. It would later come out as a Mentor paperback selling in the hundreds of thousands. Isherwood edited *VEDANTA FOR THE WESTERN WORLD* in 1945 published by Viking. Swami Akhilananda's *HINDU PSYCHOLOGY*... came out in 1946. It was in 1948 that the abridged *GOSPEL OF SRI RAMAKRISHNA* came out as *PROPHET OF NEW INDIA,* published by Harpers.

In 1949 Swami Akhilananda saw the publication of his *HINDU VIEW OF CHRIST*. The question may arise: how could he write about Christ? Why not Akhilananda, though a follower of Ramakrishna, who spoke of Jesus the Christ as Love Incarnate?[11]

15

HINDU VIEW OF CHRIST

"I remember", Swami Akhilananda said, recalling his days as a late teenager, "the first time we had Christmas celebration at the monastery. Maharaj was there. It made a tremendous impression on us - the effect was tremendous."[1] It was a memorable Christmas eve with Swami Brahmananda going into samadhi, "creating an intense spiritual atmosphere."[2] The Swami was to write in his *HINDU VIEW OF CHRIST*: "This and successive celebrations of Christmas were so elevating that even now the effect remains with us."[3]

The whole Ramakrishna Order has a reverence for Christ. At one time Ramakrishna was deeply attracted to Jesus the Christ and meditated on him. Ramakrishna became completely devoted to him. He did not even enter the Kali temple at this time. His one-pointed devotion culminated in the Panchavati, a grove of sacred trees, where "the Son of Man embraced the Son of the Divine Mother and merged in him."[4] Ramakrishna fervently believed, knew, that Christ was an Incarnation of God. Christianity was a way to bring man to God.

The celebration of the birth of Christ became a tradition in the Ramakrishna Order. With the new monastic Order forming after the death of Ramakrishna in August 1886, it was Swami Vivekananda, who, on an auspicious day, related to his brother disciples the life story of Jesus and bonded them into a brotherhood. They later found it was the eve of the birth of Christ.[5] In choosing his disciples, Ramakrishna cast his net wide. One of them, Swami Ramakrishnananda told an American devotee: "My Master used to tell me that in a previous life Saradananda and I were Christ's disciples."[6]

Once a Christmas celebration was held in Madras. Swami Brahmananda was visiting, the time possibly 1908 or 1909. Sister Devamata, an American devotee was there and she was requested to have a Christmas day party. With everything ready, she relates what happened: "Swami Brahmananda asked me to read the story of Christ's birth and I chose the account of St. Luke. When I had finished reading, the intense stillness in the air led me to look towards Swami Brahmananda. His eyes were open and fixed on the altar, there was a smile on his lips, but it was evident that his consciousness had gone to a higher plane..."[7] Swami Brahmananda later said: "I have had a great blessing here this afternoon. As you were reading the Bible, Christ suddenly stood before the altar dressed in a long blue cloak. He talked to me for some time. It was a very blessed moment."[8]

Other Swamis of the Order, Vivekananda, Saradananda, Abhedananda expressed their appreciation of Christ. With Swami Akhilananda it was in listening to his lectures on Christ that at times one felt he was trying to say something without really saying it, as if he knew something, as if he had something precious to give, to say, as when he spoke many times of the early Christians thrown to the lions in the Roman arena, who would rather have died than lose the level of consciousness they had attained. Or when he spoke of the catacombs in Rome. "The power of Christianity," he wrote, "lies in the catacombs where the martyrs sacrificed every ounce of their blood for the truth, for God. There lies the strength of Christianity."[9] In a lecture he remarked: "One of the Swamis who was in this country and on the way back to India stopped in Rome on the way and visited the catacombs, etc. He wrote how much he was thrilled to see those things and how familiar things looked to him. We wrote back maybe some of us were there in the past - I knew something else, too, which I am not going to disclose now."[10]

Again in his sermon 'Christ and the Cross' on April 21, 1946, Swami Akhilananda noted that those who had followed Christ and who were martyred: those buried in the catacombs - that there was the center of Christianity. Their deaths helped to establish Christianity in Rome and eventually in the West. He would refer on many occasions not only to the catacombs, but also to the hymn "In the Garden", which evidently had meaning for him. He would mention it lovingly off and on in his sermons on Christ. Whatever he had to say about Jesus was said with reverence. The question would often arise - did he have a connection in a past life with the early Christians? This speculation cannot be answered, but what can be acknowledged is his sympathetic understanding of them and the times in which they lived. One might say it was in his spiritual genes. As when he was questioned about Jesus, what He said or what He had done, Swami's answer revealed insight and understanding. One day a young American woman came for an interview and told of her mother's spiritual experiences. When it came to her mother receiving the Cross, which she did in a dream, the Swami explained: "Suffering and endurance."[11] Or when a Christian minister asked him why Jesus condemned the fig tree, Swami's reply was that it was in reality a blessing.

In 1949 his book *HINDU VIEW OF CHRIST* was published. Swami Akhilananda was intensely serious in writing about all aspects of Christ, his teaching and the meaning of his life. For these troubled times when things are falling apart, the Swami's well-taken observations are timely even 50 years later. With an overlay of deep-rooted secularism and anti-religious sentiments plus cultural conflicts, preserving modern civilization will need a periscope to find its spiritual roots. People are skeptical and disillusioned with religious organizations. That doesn't mean there isn't a basic faith in the people, but they are not happy with the way things are. Swami Akhilananda did not stress the organization, but the teachings. It was the individual, the seeker, that interested him. Much as times change, people remain much the same.

He writes: "It is needless to say that we cannot remove tensions and other disturbances without basic understanding of the different cultures and religious groups. If we really want to preserve modern civilization, we must go to its foundations. The main purpose of this presentation is to establish harmony and understanding among religious groups and show the common background of the various religious ideals imparted by the founders of the different religions. It is a humble attempt to establish harmony of religious ideals."[12] As Dean Walter Muelder of B. U. School of Theology says in his introduction: "Swami Akhilananda unites East and West in a moving appreciation of Jesus Christ and his significance for the whole world."[13] It was a landmark publication.

Audacious as it was, according to Swami Akhilananda, to try and discuss the life of a personality like Jesus the Christ, he attempted to do so. An Incarnation is aware of his purpose on earth, to fill the need of the age, where and when righteousness has declined. Jesus came to re-establish the spirit of religion. His teachings were powerful and inspiring. Incarnations are embodiments of love, sympathy and forgiveness. Swami Akhilananda writes: "The love we find in them cannot be duplicated anywhere else in the world... a tidal wave of love flows from them."[14]

The Swami goes on to say that Jesus was the ideal of typical Oriental life. The Swami had a warning: "Jesus first emphasized the love of

God... pure social gospel or philanthropic activities are noble indeed, but they must be used for the main purpose of religion...it has been found that if the primary objective of religion is not kept brightly in view, our minds gradually become entangled in the meshes of egoism and our sense of superiority."[15]

Was Christ a yogi? According to Swami Akhilananda, a yogi is someone who can say, "I am the Self... I and my Father are one."[16] One who practices yoga must follow "the science of restraining the mind from breaking into modifications."[17] Jesus was a master of all kinds of yoga. When he said, "I and my Father are one", and "I am in my Father, and ye in me, and I in you",[18] he shows the oneness he felt and experienced. Not only was he a bhakti yogi, a karma yogi, he was also a jnana yogi, in which there is superconscious union, a state of unity, which is above plurality, a oneness of consciousness and being.

Spiritual practices! Swami Akhilananda was absolutely in accord with the words of Jesus: "But, thou, when thou prayest, enter into thy closet, and when thou hast, shut thy door, pray to thy Father which is in secret..."[19] Swami Akhilananda stressed love of God and noted: "Jesus Himself practiced the path of love and repeatedly told His disciples to do the same... Consider His parable of the ten virgins and their lamps."[20] For the story of Martha and Mary where Jesus said that Mary had chosen the good part, Swami wrote: "These incidents clearly indicate that spiritual practices and cultivation of love for God are prerequisites of the second commandment of Jesus."[21] Swami Akhilananda warned us that it would be a mistake to think that spiritual practices can be undertaken without cultivating the love of God. They are meant for the refinement of our urges and emotions.[22]

Jesus gave the Lord's prayer to His disciples. He told them to watch and pray, that the spirit is willing, but the flesh is weak. One must be alert. As Swami Akhilananda wrote: "Slipshod or mechanical methods will not change the human personality. That is the reason Christian mystics who followed in the footsteps of Jesus were so emphatic about spiritual practices."[23]

Nor did Swami Akhilananda feel that religion should be divorced from the problems of everyday living. One should be aware of God in our lives. He felt that a cultural crisis was taking place in our civilization, affecting us intellectually, politically, and spiritually. He deplored, very politely, the neo-orthodoxy of Reinhold Niebuhr. "If the religious leaders," the Swami wrote, "lose their spiritual ideal, there will not be anyone left to inspire and elevate the followers."[24]

When it came to the crucifixion of Christ, Swami Akhilananda maintained: "Jesus completely forgot the iniquities and harmful tendencies of the people who crucified Him."[25] This was due to His awareness of the presence of God. He died on the Cross freely. "He refused to resist evil or use His miraculous powers to prevent it."[26] He employed the spiritual method, not the method of force, in overcoming a problem. "As an incarnation of God," the Swami felt, "Jesus set an example to the Jews and Gentiles that physical force will not solve the problem of violence."[27] Jesus' followers, like St. Peter, who was crucified, and St. Paul who was killed, adhered to the example of Jesus.

Most people cannot, or do not understand, this high ideal of life. As the Swami said: "Go and talk spiritual truths to most people, and they will look at you and think you are an insane person. A spiritual person is regarded as an abnormal person in modern society."[28] Swami Akhilananda felt that Pilate and the Jews should not be blamed for crucifying Jesus. If Jesus should come today and teach as He did, He would be crucified. "So it is a mistake to condemn a group of people of the first Century A.D. because they committed a mistake. The same mistake is being made by people today, why? Because they think that evil should be conquered by evil."[29]

Spiritual life is a struggle. "We have to struggle," wrote the Swami, "intensely with tenacity." We have to conquer ourselves. "Death can be defied only when we have that realization of the abiding presence of God in us. So we learn from Jesus at Easter that we can defy death only by realizing the truth."[30] As the Swami said in one of his Easter sermons: "Becoming aware of our eternal nature is the spirit of Easter."[31]

As Swami wrote in his book, there are people who want to know about the real power that is behind religion. Particularly the social scientists who would like to improve society. Religion would be helpful if we could understand it thoroughly and apply it to our individual life. "...religion must affect the lives of individuals. It is true that religious practices are considerably individualistic, yet the individuals who are transformed by them contribute greatly to society."[32] Emphasis should be given to individual growth. Community life is also important.

"We fully recognize," wrote the Swami, "the utility of community life, understanding at the same time that people's spiritual growth is individual. As they develop individually, they become powerful agents of community development."[33] In teaching and preaching, Jesus sent His disciples, to whom He had given power, to go and share what they had learned. Such teachers can take the responsibility for the students' spiritual welfare. Others can share their knowledge and understanding. And some are too enthusiastic to save the souls of people. Finally, one can do some good by silent spiritual living and by sharing experiences with others. Swami Akhilananda's conclusion was: "...if we want to stabilize the family or society, we must express religious dynamics ourselves."[34] We have to live the life.

In his last chapter, the Swami discusses the missionary work of Christians, Buddhists and others. He wrote: "...the mutual exchange of ideas and ideals through integrated spiritual personalities is absolutely necessary."[35]

The Swami received letters from his friends. One of the extant ones is from the Dean Emeritus, Boston University School of Theology, Albert C. Knudson, who wrote on October 10, 1949: "A great many thanks for the copy of your *HINDU VIEW OF CHRIST*, which you were so good as to send me and which I have read with special interest. I found it very informing and stimulating. You have rendered an important service toward a larger degree of mutual understanding between the spiritual forces in India and America. As I read the book I was reminded of a remark once made by President Lowell of Harvard to the effect that all spiritual movements meet at the top. They may not be in complete accord with each other, but that are headed in the same direction and this gives ground for the hope of eventual agreement on the essentials of religious faith."[36]

Some of the reviews were noteworthy.

A review in "Philosophy East and West" for July, 1952. p. 172, states in part: ..." Swami Akhilananda is a liberal in his view of both Hinduism and Christianity. It is true that he accepts the principle of divine incarnation - a principle which is especially cherished by Western conservatives; he is a liberal who prizes the past. But his test of truth is always experience, rationally interpreted and applied." This review being by Dr. Edgar Brightman covers all aspects of the book. At the close he writes: "The swami fails to oblige those Christian theologians who regard the Cross as an offense. He finds in the voluntary submission of Jesus to death on the Cross evidence that Jesus is an incarnation - 'a person who is thoroughly established in the All-Loving Being. The Cross, then, is a manifestation of 'soul force'. Likewise, the Swami finds in the Easter experience the attainment of Christ of 'eternal bliss'. Which is, of course, eternal love."

Charles Braden of Northwestern University writing in the "Journal of Bible and Religion," April, 1950. p. 135: "This is not the first time a Hindu has written of Him. It is, however, the first time that a Hindu has written so comprehensive a book about Him." He concludes his review after evaluating in a positive manner the Swami's contentions: "In this book the Christian has an opportunity to acquaint himself with what Hinduism at its best thinks about Christ, the center of his own faith. To the reviewer, it is a challenging book."

A review in "Prabuddha Bharata," August 1950: "Swami Akhilananda has won a place for himself in the hearts of all cultured persons through his original presentation of *HINDU PSYCHOLOGY*, and now, with the same catholic outlook and rare insight, the Swami's interpreting the personality of Christ as seen through the eyes of a Hindu who has realized the highest truth. The inner approach of the Swami unlike that of writers on comparative religion in the West is born of intense personal religious experience. So convincing and so refreshing."

Reading the following comment by Dr. Frederick May Eliot, President, American Unitarian Association and Chairman, board of trustees, Mt. Holyoke College, might shed some light on why his book was considered a landmark publication:

"In the field of religion it is extremely difficult to provide for competent but disinterested criticism and evaluation. Either the critic is an 'outsider' whose disinterestedness militates against his thoroughgoing competence, or else he is an 'insider' whose competence militates against his disinterestedness. This is a familiar paradox, but its familiarity does not make it less serious for those who would come to the kind of understanding of religion that is only possible in the light of expert, objective study.

"This book by Swami Akhilananda comes as near as any piece of writing I have seen to fulfilling both requirements. Here we have an examination of the person who is central in the Christian tradition by one who is both an outsider and an insider - an outsider technically, but by virtue of his extraordinary spiritual sympathies one who has created for himself a quality of perception and insight which entitle him to be in reality considered an insider.

"No Christian should read this volume unless he is prepared to face the results of honest, thoroughgoing, sympathetic, yet unsparing critical study. If he is willing to face that experience the result will be, I think, that his own appreciation of the essential worth of the Christian tradition will be enhanced and he will feel that he is under permanent obligation to this Hindu scholar and man of spiritual insight.[37]

It is obvious that it is almost impossible to say anything about the inner life of a person. Swami Akhilananda had that spiritual insight into Jesus, perhaps, for many reasons. Carole Moreau, the grand-daughter of Mrs. Anna Worcester, and who lived at the Center in Boston for the first twelve years of her life recalls in her reminisce about Swami Akhilananda that "He delivered no sense of superiority - even as he had seen Christ!"[38] He said this to her himself. Being a modest man he would not say this publicly. But in talking about Christ, he often gave the impression of wanting to say more. He embodied within himself, with all his merriment, something which brought to mind Christlike qualities. Dr. Richard Evans, pastor of the Presbyterian church in New York City, attended a large banquet in Boston in honor of Sri Ramakrishna in 1956. He was one of the guest speakers. He talked about Swami Akhilananda at some length calling him "The most Christ-like man he had ever met."[39] Swami knew that the meaning of the Cross was "suffering and endurance."

Prof. James Houston Shrader of Eastern Nazarene College, who worked with Swami on various committees writes: "His spirituality was deep-seated. He never spoke about 'believing' this or that. He knew. I once asked him whether he had ever enjoyed the experience of breaking through and contacting Reality known as mysticism. He said that he had. This gave him an assurance that was stimulating to behold."[40]

Had Swami Akhilananda crossed over the great divide that separates religions? Writing in 1928 in "Prabuddha Bharata," Swami Ashokananda said: "the doctrine of religious harmony has an aspect in which it teaches a new spiritual ideal. The ordinary idea is that every man should realize a single aspect of God. This teaching wants that every man should realize as many aspects of God as possible. That parable of Sri Ramakrishna, in which a dyer produces various colors from the same tub of dye is very significant. Each of us has to be like this dyer, capable of realizing God in all his aspects. This is the type of man the new age wants, a man capable of universal sympathy, not merely sympathizing but identifying himself with all religions just as Sri Ramakrishna did."[41]

Over 50 years later the same sentiment: "... no man's knowledge of God is complete unless he gains some experience of Him through other paths besides his own. The more his experiences of God, the fuller becomes his spiritual life and the greater his contribution to the enrichment of collective life."[42]

In 1977 a book was published in West Germany with the approval of the Catholic Church written by a Catholic priest, Heinrich Barlage S.V.D., on Swami Akhilananda and his *HINDU VIEW OF CHRIST*. The book was entitled *CHRIST, SAVIOUR OF MANKIND*.

In his preface, the author begins with "'Christ, Saviour of Mankind!' Swami Akhilananda as well as many other Hindus and Christians can agree with this formulation. The real problem arises when we try to add an article: Swami Akhilananda says 'a' Saviour of Mankind and Christians 'the' Saviour of Mankind... Our theological reflections are all centered on this problem." [43]

What the author says about his own scholarly book is correct. He felt that Akhilananda's book should be taken seriously. However, Swami Akhilananda's approach to Christ and to religion is primarily psychological. "Blessed are the pure in heart," said Jesus, "for they shall see God." The Catholic Father's: primarily theological. With all his scholarship and theologizing and analyzing of Akhilananda's liberal approach, the last page of his book reflects his outlook: "It will be Christ himself who must integrate the 'true and holy' of Hinduism by inflaming the hearts of the wayfarers with the fire of his Spirit so that they may realize the new life that he has brought into this world. Hindus and Christians alike will be able to understand what the author of the Letter to the Hebrews writes at the beginning: 'At various times in the past and in various different ways. God spoke to our ancestors through the prophets; but in our time, the last days, he has spoken to us through his Son, the Son that he has appointed to inherit everything and through whom he made everything there is.'"[44]

Now let us see what Swami Vivekananda has to say:

"The universe ... is moving in cycles of wave forms. It rises, reaches its zenith, then falls and remains in the hollow, as it were for

141

sometime, once more to rise, and so on, in wave after wave... What is true of the universe is true of every part of it... In every nation's spiritual life there is a fall as well as a rise... a huge wave comes, sometimes a tidal wave - and always on the topmost crest of the wave is a shining soul, the Messenger... He puts forth his tremendous power upon society...These are the Prophets of the world, the Messengers of life, the Incarnations of God.

"Man has an idea that there can be only one religion, that there can be only one Prophet, and that there can be only one Incarnation; but that idea is not true."[45]

16

CONFERENCE ON SCIENCE, PHILOSOPHY AND RELIGION

When Swami Akhilanana went to the meetings of the Conference on Science, Philosophy and Religion it was with his usual calm and serenity. Every step would be with anticipation as he walked into Columbia University in September, 1952 for the meetings on Symbols and Values. So many scholars would be there presenting their views on such topics as symbolism and science, the value of symbolism, Judaism as a system of symbols, psychoanalysis and symbols, and many other aspects of this broad subject.

Alan Watts had presented a paper, "The language of metaphysical experience" in which he might have mentioned the "ultimate reality" or the Absolute. Since that paper was not included in the bound volume, *SYMBOLS AND VALUES* there is that question and uncertainty. Swami Akhilananda, who commented on his presentation, wrote: "The Absolute as such cannot be the object of empirical knowledge, as all sensory knowledge is based on time, space and causal relationship. The Absolute is beyond all merely sensory categories... Consequently, it is unknown and unknowable from the sensory point of view. But it can be realized in what some of the psychologists call the supersensory or superconscious state, and in what the Hindus and Buddhists call samadhi. This state is not based on inference; it is direct and immediate realization beyond the sense functioning. It is not a void state. It is a negation and transcending of sense experiences; it can be regarded as culmination or expansion of consciousness, a state beyond time and space in which the knower and known are identical...the state is one of complete unity. This state is often misunderstood by many people and critics when they say it is void or negative. The only negation is that of empirical knowledge. It is a dynamic and positive state..."[1] With a minimum explanation Swami Akhilananda dispelled the notion that the Absolute was a void, or emptiness, or something negative.

This was not the first time he had participated in the Conference on Science, Philosophy and Religion. Swami Akhilananda's early contact with scholars expanded when in 1946 he attended the Conference on Science, Philosophy and Religion held in Chicago on September 9, 10, and 11. Rabbi Louis Finkelstein, the Chancellor of the Jewish Theological Seminary of America, organized a group of scholars in the early 1940s which "consisted of people of strong and often sharply divergent views on questions of the day. It was an interdisciplinary and interfaith group. It included Catholic leaders, such as Father John LaFarge, S.J., and Father John Courtney Murray; Protestants, such as F. Ernest Johnson of Teachers' College, Columbia, and Dean Listen Pope of Yale Divinity School, Jewish leaders such as Louis Finkelstein and his Vice-Chancellor, Simon Greenberg. There were scientists such as Nobel prize winner I. I. Rabi of Columbia University, Hudson Hoagland, Director of the Worcester Foundation for Experimental Biology, and Harvard's distinguished astronomer, Harlow Shapley. There were, too, scholars such as the University of Chicago philosopher Richard R. McKeon, the Columbia University sociologist R. M. MacIver, and Yale's Harold Lasswell."[2]

For his first presentation to the Conference Swami Akhilananda chose to speak on "Religions and their Values", stressing the qualities that real religion brings to society and analyzing why there is discord and antagaonism between different religions. "Religious values establish harmony in human society by lifting man from the selfish and egocentric plane of consciousness to the plane of unselfishness and love,"[3] he wrote. Society does not become stable as long as greed, love of power, and selfishness are not transcended.

The Swami felt that the real nature of religion was not understood, therefore there were conflicts. Variation in human nature brings about variation in types of worship and concepts. Each path is valid. "Through whatever path the worshipper sincerely seeks Him, he will find Him. Underlying all creeds and religions is universal truth."[4] Swami commented on papers presented by Dr. Krishnalal Shridharani of Columbia University, by Dr. John Howland Lathrop of New York, by Dr. Edgar Sheffield Brightman, Professor of philosophy, Boston University, Nels F. S. Ferre, Professor of Christian Theology, Andover Newton Theological School, and Franz Alexander, Clinical Professor of Psychiatry, University of Illinois.

Swami Akhilananda prepared carefully for the sessions of the Conferences of Science, Philosophy and Religion. How many late hours until the early morning were spent in writing out his addresses and critiques of other scholars. In the summer of 1947 he was preparing for the Conference on Science, Philosophy and Religion to be held in September at Philadelphia. On September 8th his paper "Religious Culture and Integration" along with those of several other scholars, including Swami Nikhilannda of the Ramakrishna Vivekananda Center in New York, were the substance of a religious discussion. Characteristically Swami Akhilananda wrote: "It may seem to many persons that the claim of religious culture for the removal of disturbances is contradictory to the existing conditions of religious groups."[5]

Acknowledging that there were problems in society and between groups, the Swami nevertheless firmly felt that religious culture would integrate the individual and society. Much of our tension and problems were caused by an egocentric attitude and competitive spirit. Swami Akhilananda maintained that co-operation in society could be attained when individuals worked with a spirit of service and dedication. He concluded with "individuals must be stabilized and integrated emotionally in order to carry on the work of co-operation and co-ordination."[6] Swami's presentation was in answer to the request of the program committee who had asked for contributions on the subject of "How can scholarship contribute to the relief of international tensions", the theme of the meeting.

Swami Akhilananda made comments on paper presented by Pitirim Sorokin, Professor of sociology, Harvard University, Nels F.S. Ferre of the Andover Newton Theological School, and Gustave E. von Grunebaum, Associate Professor of Arabic, University of Chicago. Swami congratulated Sorokin on his paper about international tensions and said in his comment:

"When a man is integrated and his reason and emotions are unified, with consequent stabilization of his personality, then alone can he disseminate the higher values of life. ...The more we have persons of superconscious realization in society, the greater will be the number of unified personalities. And those personalities with an altruistic attitude and appreciation can really remove tension from modern society."[7]

Nels F.S. Ferre, Abbot Professor of Christian Theology, Andover Newton Theological School, presented a paper on "A Religion for One World", in which he said: "Religion should make the fullest use of philosophy, but philosophy cannot become a substitute for religion. Philosophy is basically concerned with knowledge..."[8] Dr. Ferre's outlook on philosophy was responded to with Swami Akhilananda's comment:

"The word that is applied to philosophy in the Hindu school of thought is called arashana - experienced truth. Knowledge is divided into two types: relative knowledge, including science, literature, art, etc... and supreme knowledge, which leads one to the realization of the Ultimate Reality. It also means that philosophy should lead one to the realization of Eternal Truth... The prerequisite of the student of philosophy is thoroughgoing mental discipline. So philosophy not only gives us empirical, objective, coherent knowledge but it also leads us to the knowledge of the Ultimate Reality or God. Now Profesor Ferre will permit us to say that philosophy in the highest sense requires ethical training, mental discipline, and consequent realization of the Truth."[9]

The beauty of these gatherings was that it gave Western scholars an opportunity to learn something of Indian philosophy, religion, and ethics.

Here is Prof. Ferre's reply: "I have defined philosophy as rational empirical knowledge, in order to avoid some saying that I am using philosophy to support religion. If philosophers want to include 'the intuitions of eternity' and the discontinuities which necessitate faith, I am delighted to enlarge my definition of philosophy."[10]

It would be in 1948 at the Conference on Science, Philosophy and Religion in New York City, which Swami Akhilananda attended and which had for its theme: "Goals for American education" that Swami Akhilananda presented no paper of his own, but made comments on "Education and One World", by Howard Mumford Jones, Professor of English, Harvard University, and on Professor Robert Ulich's presentation, "On the Rise and Decline of Higher Education". In his comments on Dr. Ulich's paper, Swami remarked: "Profesor Dewey and such other thinkers can naturally mislead many persons in the name of truth when truth is limited to the sense realm and mere objective investigation. The supreme goal of that civilization will remain always the greatest amount of sense pleasure on the sense plane. The whole theme of Prof. Ulich's constructive thought is evidently in the opposite direction, namely, the search for eternal values. As he says: 'But what the students on the higher level of education could expect and should be confronted with is the philosophical endeavor of the mind that pierces the fleeting surface of reality in order to reach into the deeper sources of existence.'"[11]

Swami then went on to comment on "Higher education in a time of change," by Lyman Bryson, Professor of education, Columbia University and this was followed by Swami's comments on "The Role of Objectives in Higher Education," by Ordway Tead, chairman, Board of Education, New York City, in which Swami said: "The highest ideal of the greatest good for man and society cannot be carried out by higher education unless the institutions are in charge of thoroughly integrated personalities who are well established in moral and spiritual ideals and free from the control of interested individuals and groups. From the ancient days of Hindu and Buddhistic civilizations and the era of the Platonic ideal to Christian and other civilizations, scholars have been able to help society when they have had freedom as well as their own spiritual personality."[12]

A month later in October, 1948 Swami Akhilananda touched upon this conference in his Sunday sermon. Evidently the conference was not all sweetness and light, for Swami remarked: "Recently we attended a Conference on Science, Philosophy and Religion. Some very great scholars and thinkers were there and you should have seen the agony they expressed for the conditions today. Actual agony!...One man, a dean of one of the important universities got up and very boldly expressed his opinion that until the administration is changed the faculty cannot do anything with the students. I'm sure that if his university heard of the speech they would not like it. He risked his job to say what he thought. After he spoke we got up and said: 'wonderful, bold and frank and all that and then told that there has to be a basis for cooperation. There has to be a higher understanding. When the objective of the administration changes, things will change.'"[13]

Following his visit to Olema, California in the summer of 1949, it was on to New York City for Swami Akhilananda and for the tenth Conference on Science, Philosophy and Religion. The theme for the conference was "Perspectives on a troubled Decade... 1939-1949." He would comment on papers written by two of his friends, Dean Walter

147

Muelder of Theological School, and its Prof. Edgar Brightman. For Dean Muelder's paper "Power, Anomie and Personality", Swami Akhilananda wrote: "We fully agree with his clear presentation of the present situation in society. It is impossible for an individual to function properly for the good of others unless both the individual and society have what Dr. Muelder repeatedly mentions as 'field values'".Swami commented that where a society is competitive "there is no possibility for collective harmony, which allows individuals to function for the good of all."[14]

Prof. Edgar Brightman presented a paper on "Unity in Difference" for which Swami commented:

"We fully agree with Professor Brightman and other personalists that the source of personal consciousness is not in unconscious matter but in superconscious Being, or, according to the Hindus, Satchidananda, Existence-Knowledge-Bliss-Absolute. The personalities and diversities are based on that Reality. Basically, persons are not independent but are inseparably united in spite of the present manifold diversity. It seems to us that this very attitude is the background of cooperation in spite of diversity in comprehension of the real nature of the Being.

"It is quite conceivable that diversity in the understanding of that Reality will remain with us, as we perceive it through the categories of our individual finite minds. However intellectual this comprehension may be, even a glimpse of it helps our spirit of cooperation on the basis of unity. It is not necessary that because my understanding and interpretation of the truth is true to me that another interpretation will necessarily be wrong. A room seen from different angles of vision will appear different to various individuals. Nevertheless, all views are different understandings of the same room."[15]

For the paper by Nels F.S. Ferre on the "Motivational Power of Christianity for Democracy", Swami said in part:

"We would have been extremely happy if Dr. Ferre could have shown us how selfish love can be changed into Agape - divine love - either through mutuality of love or directly. Is it not possible that a selfish man with self-seeking, so called love can also be changed, as we find in many personalities who were redeemed and transformed? We are naturally looking forward to seeing the methods of such transformation.

"It seems to us that Dr. Ferre emphasizes the power of faith 'in Him' and completely denies the values of what they call mystical experiences. We wonder if he wishes to deny their utility. In that case, the dynamic experiences of St. Paul, which transformed him from Saul to St. Paul, from destructive critic to the constructive builder of Christianity, becomes meaningless."[16]

From the way Swami Akhilananda spoke in his Sunday lectures about the annual Conference of Science, Philosophy and Religion, we knew it was of special interest to him; mingling with those many notable pesonalities, eminent in their respective fields, was a stimulus and a challenge. In the beginning he was rather shy, limiting himself to infrequent questions and suggestions, but these were worthy of attention.[17]

"He spoke somewhat hesitantly," Dr. Faust remembers, "as if anxious to avoid any appearance of animus toward an individual or any impression of taking the first step in an assault on a position he intended to demolish."[18] Swami Akhilananda always stressed that one should be tactful. But he did win the respect of the group.In 1954 the approximately 175 scholars attending, from divergent disciples, again discussed the topic, "Symbols and Values". Swami Akhilananda presented comments on papers by Robert Ulich, Professor of education, Harvard: Symbolism and the education of man; Louis Finkelstein, Chancellor and Solomon Schechter Profesor of Theology, Jewish Theological Seminary: The Hebrew Text of the Bible, a study of its cadence symbols; and William F. Lynch, S.J., Fordham University: The Evocative Symbol.

For Prof. Ulich's paper Swami Akhilananda said in part: "I am afraid that many modern scholars do not seem to realize, as Prof. Ulich so nicely presented, that education is not mere technological and so-called scientific training. They also suggest that philosophy and religion have no place in education. They seem to think that education is based purely on making a person fit for society and to equip him for enjoyment of the objective world. There is considerable misunderstanding about the purpose of education... Education, from our point of view, ought to lead us to the 'manifestation of perfection that is already in man', as Swami Vivekananda declared. ...Naturally, we feel that proper understanding and use of symbols is of great value in education..."[19]

Swami Akhilananda had attended both the 1950 and 1951 Conferences on Science, Philosophy and Religion in New York City. He made comments on papers for both years. Prof. Nels F.S. Ferre of Vanderbilt University, attending the 1951 Conference, wrote on "Authority and Freedom", and although Swami Akhilananda praised his "vivid description of love - agape," he took issue with his statement that "'the authority of the church is the will of God'.[20] We wonder how Dr. Ferre can identify the authority of the church with the will of God knowing the historical background of religious movements. It is disturbing to find that an institution is being equated with the will of God...May we suggest that the awareness of God rather than the church is fundamental in understanding the will of God." For freedom Swami stressed the need of transcendent values in a democratic society.

1956 would be the last year that Swami would attend the Conference on Science, Philosohy and Religion. There is not any trace that he presented any paper or that he spoke.

17

MENTAL HEALTH AND HINDU PSYCHOLOGY

Just before his *MENTAL HEALTH...* was published in 1951, Swami Akhilananda had returned from a trip to India. It had been a bleak day in mid-November 1950 when he left Boston and sailed for England. He was on his way, taking with him Mrs. Anna Worcester and another elderly devotee Jesse Baxter. The Swami wrote to Charlotte Morrison on November 23rd, having reached England: "We are just now sailing for Bombay. I came to London on Saturday night. I had to worship and talked to the devotees in Paris. I had to lecture in London. You know Paris Swami and me, very dear friends" (Paris Swami being Swami Siddheswarananda).

Again, in another letter to Charlotte Morrison: "Port Said. Nov. 29, '50. We are having a pleasant trip now. But we had quite a rough ocean for about 24 hours yesterday. Most of the people were sick. Annapurna, Miss Baxter and others were not well. ... You will be happy to know that I have been sleeping often twice a day, after breakfast and lunch. I sleep once anyway. I think I am making up my sleep. You can easily imagine what is awaiting me in India after I arrive there on Dec. 8th. No more today, with love and blessings. ..."

We get a glimpse of his stay in India. To Mrs. Morrison from Nagpur on January 7, 1951: "I came to Nagpur day before yesterday. We are to go to Madras this evening. Then we go to Bhubaneswar." When he was in Nagpur, the January 9th <u>Nagpur Times</u> reported that he arrived on January 5th and delivered a lecture at the Ramakrishna Ashrama on <u>The Message of India to the West.</u> The article continues:

"Swami Akhilananda in the course of his lecture declared that the West is suffering terribly from the strain of the cold-war and needs peace of mind. The Westerners regard pleasure as the goal of life and hence they have to face mental frustration and psychological conflict. They have subordinated God to the acquisition of Health, Wealth, and

Power. In these circumstances the message of India which inculcates the superiority of Spirit over matter and advocates breadth of outlook and spirit of tolerance can alone bring peace to these Westerners.

"What they need today is the right type of Religion which according to Swami Vivekananda is nothing but the manifestation of divinity already in man. ...So far as India is concerned, what we need is character building which constitutes the essence of education."

There were other Indian unnamed newspaper reports of a short nature, unfortunately without dates of publication.

Swami Akhilananda's letter continues about Bhubaneswar. "This Center was established by Sri Maharaj. We all are very fond of this place. We are to reach Math on Jan. 13th. We leave again for ... on the 14th. After visiting Brindaban and Delhi we are to be back in Calcutta on Jan. 21st ... Annapurna and Jesse will stay in Calcutta. I have been meeting many persons in all these places." While the Swami was in India, Dean Walter Muelder of the B.U. School of Theology and other B. U. professors at that school conducted the Sunday services in Boston.

Upon their return Mrs. Worcester informed people that when Swami was in India he talked so much he lost his voice![1] He had seen a different India. He remarked.

..."The India that we knew 30-40 years ago is not the same India today in any sense of the word...A country which is dominated by foreign rule develops slavish tendencies. About 3-4 years ago when there was the famine in India, where in Bengal alone 3-4 million people died of starvation, the governor general of Bengal went to Waverly and told him to arrest 4 men, that if these 4 men were arrested it would prevent the famine. But he refused to arrest them. One of these men was the British......, another was......, an Indian, and the two others were Indian businessmen. There was starvation, privation. The people died in the streets like cats and dogs. They died in the streets of Calcutta where these 4 men lived."[2]

At the same time he said: "What we need today is man-making religion - religion that is applied to our everyday life."[3]

Returning to the United States in early March, 1951 Swami Akhilananda brought with him two Swamis - Pavitrananda for the Vedanta Society in New York, and Ajayananda to assist in Boston and Providence. Ajayananda did not feel comfortable here and soon returned to India. Swami Akhilananda was not to have an assistant until Swami Sarvagatananda arrived from India in October, 1954.

Earlier in the year before his trip to India, Swami Akhilananda had received a letter of June 5, 1950 from Dr. Max Knoll of Princeton University asking him to participate in the Princetonian "Universitas" seminar giving a lecture on Hindu psychology. Other scientists would be participating in the discussion. From the letter this occasion would have been around June 20th if all participants could be present. Since there is nothing to suggest the contrary, Swami would certainly have accepted the invitation.

On March 19-20, 1951 he was in New York City for a conference sponsored by the Josiah Macy Jr. Foundation, this being their second on Problems of Consciousness. He was there as a guest and the participants were professionals in various fields of mental health, psychology, biology, medicine, etc., such as Dr. Harold Abramson, Dr. Henry K. Beecher, Dr. Frieda Fromm-Reichmann, the cultural anthropologist Margaret Mead, M. F. Ashley Montagu, philosopher; Talcott Parson, sociologist of Harvard University; Dr. Harold Schlosberg, Professor of psychology, Brown University, and Dr. Gregory Zilboorg of New York Medical College. Swami said very little (for what would he say when the group was discussing specific schizophrenic patients) but did have an exchange with Margaret Mead on the difference between valid mystic experiences and hallucinations. As he said:

"There are some experiences which are not really religious realizations, yet they are extraordinary. They are not achieved through chemical or physical reactions but they are directly and immediately achieved, as we perceive things objectively through the sense organs. These experiences also, like spiritual realizations, are not hallucinations nor perversions of the mind and must not be classified in any category of mental disease. They are classified under extrasensory perceptions. Although these are not classified under mystic realizations of the Reality, nevertheless, both religious experiences and these extraordinary perceptions are verifiable. In fact, personally, I have verified some of these experiences."[4]

Swami was becoming well-known in the mental health field and would become more so when his *MENTAL HEALTH AND HINDU PSYCHOLOGY* was published by Harper and Brothers of New York in the fall of 1951. It was in some ways a sequel to his *HINDU PSYCHOLOGY*.Whereas that book was an introduction for Western readers of the Hindu approach to mental well-being and spiritual growth, his *MENTAL HEALTH* developed more-in-depth the therapeutic possibilities.

The <u>Psychological Book Reviews,</u> Oct. 1951, vol. 1, no. 4--2-4 has a lengthy analysis of all aspects of the book and concludes with "On the whole, the book is a presentation of the various techniques of Indian psychology. It also reveals how both scholars and students of psychology, clinical psychology, and various types of psychotherapy in the West can utilize the contributions of Hindu psychologists in the field of psychological and religious problems."

O. Hobart Mowrer, Research professor of psychology, University of Illinois, writes in the Introduction, p. xiii: "...in Hinduism psychology and religion are one and inseparable. Certainly this old and great system of thought has valuable insights and suggestions to contribute to the resolutions of our particular problems in a creative and constructive way... Swami Akhilananda... whose wisdom and kindliness have already touched the lives of innumerable persons will, in the present volume, bring new understanding and a surer perspective to many more."

Even early on it was seen that the Swami's therapeutic view of Hindu psychology would slowly spread. In 1946 when *HINDU PSYCHOLOGY* was published, he was acquainted with Dr. Joseph Pratt and his colleagues in the psychological clinic of the Boston Dispensary. "Dr. Pratt has what they call 'thought culture' classes," Swami remarked. "The patients are not patients, you know. They are students. The idea is to get them to relax. Some of the students even fall asleep during the classes..."[5] As he writes: "Even from the therapeutic point of view, the practice of relaxation and concentration is of great importance as illustrated by Dr. Joseph Pratt and his colleagues in the psychological clinic of the Boston Dispensary. They have proved that the practice of relaxation helps the patients in overcoming restlessness and eliminating functional disorders."[6]

In his book *MENTAL HEALTH* he refers to the Boston Dispensary and Dr. Joseph Pratt's practice. On the 6th of February, 1947 Swami was at the Boston Dispensary in the morning and had lunch with the group. He would often speak of Dr. Pratt and the clinic in his lectures, as he did on October 5, 1948, saying in regard to him: "He understands that the mind has to be integrated. What his classes consist of is a simplified version of Patanjali's yoga practices."[7] Swami Akhilananda was in touch with the Boston Dispensary from time to time and on June 20,

1955 he had a four hour meeting at the Pratt clinic and returned again at 6 pm.[8]

The use of concentration and meditation in a clinic as early as 1946 was not extensive and was ahead of its time. Many years later came the "relaxation response". Dr. Herbert Benson, who wrote a book on it, recalls: "In 1968 practitioners of Transcendental Meditation came to the laboratory at the Harvard Medical School where we were in the midst of studying the relation between a monkey's behavior and his blood pressure. These devotees of meditation asked whether they could be studied, for they felt they could lower their blood pressure through Transcendental Meditation. They were turned away with a polite 'Thank you'. Why investigate anything so far out as meditation."[9] Dr. Benson and his colleagues were at first not so impressed.

Swami Akhilananda's suggestions for therapy in the mental health field encompassed the depths of an individual's personality. The case histories he cited as far back as his *HINDU PSYCHOLOGY* show his approach. Let us cite one of them, illustrating the use of mental exercises.

"A woman developed a psychogenic neurosis. She was treated by different analysts but could not be cured, although at times she was helped a little." Swami Akhilananda goes on to explain the early causes of her illness. Certain unexpected developments in her adulthood brought about a serious psychophysical condition. "... the woman had difficulty in crossing the street without a companion. She was restored to a normal state by a proper understanding of the higher values of life and higher nature of man." She found a meaning in life with mental training and exercises. Autogenesis was helpful as well as a sound philosophy of life. Swami Akhilananda concludes with: "Steady practice of concentration brought out latent inner strength and created self-confidence and conviction; the mind was reconstructed and normality established."[10]

He carried the therapeutic value of Hindu psychology even further with *MENTAL HEALTH AND HINDU PSYCHOLOGY*. It will be seen that Swami Akhilananda's books were on the cutting edge of a change that would come about in Western psychology and psychotherapy.

In his very first chapter, in reviewing functional diseases, he writes:

"However, no permanent cure is possible without restoring the mental health of the patient, even though medical care is helpful. So proper psychological understanding of the causes of functional disease is of vital importance in attempts to eliminate it."[11]

He further states: "Not until functional troubles become disturbing do people seek and use psychotherapy. Religious psychology properly used at a sufficiently early stage could prevent the development of symptoms. Hence, the contributions of Hindu psychology should be properly evaluated."[12]

Swami Akhilananda shows the efficacy of mental discipline and spiritual orientation in his various chapters on overcoming anxiety, the conquest of fear, frustration, conflict and tension; the value of forgiveness, the power of the mind, the power of love, etc. He feels that the integration of personality to be most important. There are case histories: the man who stopped teaching, but resumed it following Swami's advice and instructions, the insecure boy with neurotic symptoms and functional ailments who was helped by religious psychotherapy, the lady with a toothache which vanished under the guidance of a religious teacher who gave her mental training and spiritual exercises, and a number of others.

As he writes:

"The conscious change of attitude toward life when carried out in daily activities gradually removes the cause of anxiety no matter how it may be operating in the unconscious mind. Even though the change of attitude may be on an intellectual level for the time being, by degrees it penetrates the total mind through daily living and spiritual exercises."[13]

With the publication of his two books on Hindu psychology and his first publication *"SRI RAMAKRISHNA and MODERN PSYCHOLOGY"*, privately printed in Providence in 1936, it can be seen that Swami Akhilananda was a pioneer in advocating spiritual practices for mental health. It is difficult if not impossible to trace all of his contacts with psychiatrists. We know he had a close association with Dr. Emil Gutheil of New York, Dr. Ian Stevenson of the University of Virginia, Dr. Dana Farnsworth of Harvard, Dr. David Wright of Providence, RI, Dr. Hobart Mowrer, Dr. Gregory Zilborg, and others. He was a charter member of the National Academy of Religion and Mental Health. It would not be out of place to say his work was known to many psychiatrists and psychologists.

In the late 1950s while writing *SPIRITUAL PRACTICES*, Swami Akhilananda recalled: "In a recent talk on "The Hindu Method of Training the Mind" to the American Association for the Advancement of Psychotherapy, I expounded the idea if a person is not too far advanced in his mental disturbances, the practice of concentration and meditation can completely eliminate the causes of his disturbances."[14] Swami Akhilananda was anxious to share with Western psychotherapists the value of Hindu psychology. For the psychotherapists and the general public to consider and absorb into their own systems of thought.[15]

Recognizing the limitations of Western psychology, as early as 1936, Swami Akhilananda would write: "A new study is required if we want to develop a complete psychology. We have to discipline ourselves first. We have first to have superconscious realization and experiences. Then alone shall we be in a position to give the world a complete psychology."[16] Applying the spiritual techniques, such as meditation for better mental health, was just the tip of the iceberg for someone like him.

However, a new outlook would develop with new forms of psychotherapy. In India, religion and psychology are one. Although it has come about slowly, perhaps it should not be surprising that psychology in the West would be one of the first to be influenced by Eastern thought.

Anxious that spiritual values and spiritual practices be brought into psychotherapy, Swami Akhilananda would have been happy to know of the work of Dr. Roberto Assagioli. Born in Italy in 1888, he trained as a psychiatrist taking his degree in 1910. He practiced in Italy and gradually developed his concept of the human psyche. His therapy, psychosynthesis, postulates that "the person is a soul and has a personality,"[17] a different approach from what has been customary for Western psychologies. It makes therapeutic use of Gestalt, guided imagery, meditation, and a large number of varied techniques too numerous to mention here. Jean Hardy writes: "What has remained constant is the spiritual context of the work, the assumption that the client contains his or her own wisdom and the relatively equal relationship of client and guide."[18]

Dr. Assagioli's mother became a Theosophist when he was still a boy and he became well acquainted with it. Dr. Assagioli was "widely read in the mystical traditions of the world."[19] His library had mystical and spiritual writing from all religions spanning centuries. He "received a full classical education, and the influence of classical striving for goodness, knowledge, and reality was basic to his work."[20] Plato and Dante were part of his world as well as Jewish thought and culture. So also were the Upanishads and the Gita.

In 1926 Dr. Assagioli began to make serious use of psychosynthesis in his work. It was not until 1965 that his book, *PSYCHOSYNTHESIS* was published three years after the death of Swami Akhilananda. In the 1950s psychosynthesis made an initial appearance in the United States at Valmy, Delaware as a working psychotherapy.

Swami Akhilananda's hope of introducing Hindu psychological methods to American psychotherapists may have had a bearing on a new force in psychology: transpersonal psychology which was formulated in the late 1960s, several years after his death. Did Swami and his book *MENTAL HEALTH AND HINDU PSYCHOLOGY* contribute to it? In 1994 there appeared an article of great interest in the magazine *REVISION*. Written by Roger Walsh, professor of psychiatry, philosophy, and anthropology at the University of California at Irvine, it took a new look at what-had-been. This is what he has to say:

"Born out of the laboratory and clinic, Western psychology and psychiatry had been dominated by behaviorism and psychoanalysis. These had contributed a great deal, but by focusing on simple, measurable behavior and on pathology, they had also overlooked a great deal, including psychological health and exceptional well being. Worse still, they had reduced or pathologized crucial dimensions of human experience such as spirituality and alternate states of consciousness to neurotic immaturities or random neuronal fireworks."[21]

The above might be considered almost an echo of what Swami Akhilananda had said in his lectures and books. He wrote in his *MENTAL HEALTH*: "Both orthodox Freudians and Watsonians, from their individual standpoints, attack the basis of religion without any real understanding of religion itself."[22] As long ago as 1936 he had written:

"Most modern psychologists assume that the 'idea of God' is due to childhood dependence on the father. God is nothing but 'Father transference' to overcome fear and other weaknesses. The behaviorists go a step further and want to eliminate the idea of God from human life. Some psychoanalysts dogmatically give even obnoxious and shocking theories regarding the idea of God."[23]

One of the key players in this new transpersonal psychology was Dr. Abraham Maslow, Professor of psychology at Brandeis University, who had become interested in psychological health, and who had concluded: "...it is as if Freud supplied to us the sick half of psychology and we must now fill it out with the healthy half."[24] Swami Akhilananda in his lectures many times used to refer to Freud in like terms of focusing on pathological cases. He said that Freud never had the opportunity to examine a person of superconscious experience.[25]

In contrast to Freud and some other psychotherapists Dr. Maslow appraised healthy individuals and felt that those who were healthy "tended to have peak experiences: ecstatic, unitive states of consciousness akin to those mystical experiences that have been widely reported and highly valued across centuries and cultures."[26] Prof. Walsh further states:

"It was therefore somewhat of a shock when the early transpersonal pioneers turned their attention eastward and found that Asian psychologies, philosophies, religions and contemplative disciplines contained detailed accounts, not just of peak experiences, but of whole families of peak experiences and systematic techniques to induce and sustain them."[27]

Such considerations as the above led to the formulation of the transpersonal movement in psychology in the late 1960s. Its first definition is very lengthy and involved. A partial quote: "... becoming, individual and species-wide meta needs, ultimate values, unitive consciousness, peak experiences, B-values, ecstacy, mystical experiences, awe, being,"[28] etc. By 1992, there were a number of different definitions: "Transpersonal psychology might be defined therefore as the psychology of ultimate or highest meanings and values..."[29] "Transpersonal psychology... can also be viewed as psychology of transcendence."[30] "What truly defines the transpersonal orientation is a model of the human psyche that recognizes the importance of the spiritual or cosmic dimension and the potential for consciousness evolution."[31]

What about the application of spiritual practices and meditation in transpersonal psychotherapy? Minding the mind meditation and concentrated meditation, one or both, as well as psychotherapy are utilized.[32] Stressing mental exercises and spiritual practices as an aid for mental health, it would appear that Swami Akhilananda was a forerunner of early transpersonal psychology.

So quietly did Swami Akhilananda work with so little publicity that a Roman Catholic priest, Jeremias Marseille, did not know of the Swami's work that preceded transpersonal psychology. He writes: "It was not until the late 1960s that the spiritual factor began to be reintroduced systematically in psychology and psychotherapy via transpersonal psychology."[33] However, the spiritual factor has been around since the 1930s.

Can a connection be made between transpersonal psychology and the work of Swami Akhilananda in the field of psychotherapy and psychology? From what little is known, it is possible. He knew both Dr. Abraham Maslow. Professor of psychology, Brandeis University, and Dr. Viktor Frankl, Professor of neurological psychiatry, University of Vienna, the former the leader in transpersonal psychology, and Dr. Frankl, a contributor.

Swami Akhilananda and Abraham Maslow had both worked together on the program committee for the conference "New Knowledge in Human Values", sponsored by the Research Society for Creative Altruism, founded by Pitirim Sorokin, which was held in October, 1957 at the Kresge Auditorium, MIT. They both participated in the program, Dr. Maslow giving a talk on October 5th and Swami Akhilananda being part of that afternoon session.

Dr. Viktor Frankl, who played a part in the early transpersonal movement, was also friendly with Swami Akhilananda in the mid-1950s. During World War II Viktor Frankl had been a prisoner in the Nazi concentration camps and lost his family except for a sister. Out of his dire experiences he formulated logotherapy. Mankind, he felt, wants life to have meaning. He states in his book, *THE DOCTOR AND THE SOUL*: "A psychotherapy which not only recognizes man's spirit but actually starts from it, may be termed logotherapy. In this connection, logos is intended to signify 'the spiritual' and, beyond that, 'the meaning.'"[34]

The Dr. Frankl says: "It is, of course, not the aim of logotherapy to take the place of existing psychotherapy, but only to complement it, thus forming a picture of man in his wholeness - which includes the spiritual dimension."[35] Logotherapy is for those in spiritual distress with despair over the meaning of life. In his book, *MAN'S SEARCH*

FOR MEANING, Dr. Frankl delineates it further "According to logotherapy, we can discover this meaning in life in three different ways: 1. by doing a deed, 2. by experiencing value, 3. by suffering. The first, the way of achievement or accomplishment, is quite obvious.

"The second way of finding a meaning in life is by experiencing something, such as a work of nature or culture; and also by experiencing someone, i. e. by love."[36]

Dr. Frankl had much to say about responsibility in his book *THE DOCTOR AND THE SOUL*. He writes: "We can be responsible only to an entity higher than ourselves",[37] but then he will ask the question "To whom is man responsible?"[38] The answer to which he had already given. One day while Viktor Frankl was staying in the Boston area during the mid 1950s, Swami Sarvagatananda and Swami Akhilananda visited him at his hotel. Swami Sarvagatananda recalls: "We had lunch with him. Viktor Frankl said that in addition to the Statue of Liberty there should be a Statue of Responsibility! One on the East Coast and one on the West Coast."[39] They would be the symbol of what he wrote: "Man's freedom and man's responsibility exist independently."[40] On September 20th and 21st, 1957 there was a two day program on mental health and religion which Dr. Frankl and Swami Akhilananda attended.[41] Where it was held is uncertain, possibly at Harvard.

Should we feel that Dr. Maslow, the philosophical father of transpersonal psychology, was sympathetic to Vedanta and Swami Akhilananda when he wrote as he did in his book *RELIGIONS, VALUES AND PEAK-EXPERIENCES* the following:

"... into the extent that all mystical or peak-experiences are the same in essence and have always been the same, all religions are the same in their essence and always have been the same. They should, therefore, come to agree in principle on teaching that which is common to all of them, i. e., whatever it is that peak-experiences teach in common... This something common, this something which is left over after we peel away all the localisms, all the accidents of particular languages or particular philosophies, all the ethnocentric phrasings, all those elements which are <u>not</u> common, we may call the 'core-religious experiences' or the 'transcendent experiences.'"[42]

An echo of Vedanta?

In the years since Maslow's memorable pronouncement, the transpersonal psychology movement has expanded into several disciplines such as transpersonal medicine, etc. It has found new voices such as Dr. Jorge Ferrer, assistant professor at the California Institute of Integral Studies, whose insights a Vedantist would find intriguing as when he writes in "New Horizons in Contemporary Spirituality"

"... as human beings become more whole or intuitively foresee their wider and deeper identity, a narrow understanding of the term 'transpersonal' as 'beyond the personal' may become increasingly unsatisfactory. ...In other words as we become more aware of our intrinsic vital connection with the sacred, the transpersonal gradually reveals itself to us as more and more personal."[43]

Did not Vivekananda tell the world the human soul is divine nothing but divine? Ramakrishna in speaking to his devotees would say that the Reality (the Sacred) has two aspects Personal and Impersonal.[44] Swami Akhilananda used to say that in their essence the personal aspect of Brahman and the impersonal were one.

With Swami Akhilananda's advocacy of spiritual practices as an aid to mental health and the emergence of psychosynthesis, logotherapy, and transpersonal psychology, these three having a spiritual component, it's obvious that there has been a turning, a new direction in mental health therapy.

The growing interest in spiritual workshops, retreats, the introduction of meditation periods in corporate companies, and in meditation everywhere is obvious. The Buddhists have been promoting meditation. In an interview in May, 2001 Thich Nhat Hanh said: "The Buddhists psychological approach, how the mind works, is very rich. This is very appealing to modern people."[45] Here and there, there seems to be a shift in consciousness. Will it yield a spiritual culture?

Explanations for these shifts in our culture may sound simplistic. The influence of Eastern religions, however, cannot be discounted. Wellsprings of inspiration may arise in different places. Perhaps the struggles, the prayers and meditations of many holy people are setting into motion new patterns, new paradigm that will benefit people everywhere, bringing with it greater humility and better understanding of interpersonal relations no matter where in the world. But Swami Akhilananda used to say that when an incarnation is born a new civilization comes into being. Cross-fertilization of cultures is taking place. Slightly over 120 years ago, Keshab Chandra Sen, a well-known preacher in India, asked Ramakrishna for his permission to write about

162

him for the people. In his reply Ramakrishna said: "The power and ideas which are within this body will automatically spread all over in the course of time. Hundreds of Himalayas will not be able to suppress that power."[46] Ramakrishna's words are baffling and enigmatic.

There is something mysterious about a saint. We, with our skepticism, feel inclined to discredit them, to question, even to reject. In India some orthodox Hindus used to throw stones at the young disciples of Ramakrishna. The power of an incarnation is even more mysterious. Only an illumined mind can catch a little glimpse of them. The rest of us....? As Vivekananda said on the birthday festival of Ramakrishna in 1902, speaking to one of his own disciples: "Nobody has been able to understand who came on earth as Sri Ramakrishna. Even his own nearest devotees have got no real clue to it. Only some have got a little inkling of it. All will understand in time."[47]

Ramakrishna's breadth of understanding, his foresight, he who could say sincerely, "As many faiths, so many paths", should not be dismissed. We wouldn't dismiss the words of another prophet from a different religion, would we? Not only America, but the world, now only a village, has become a place of religious pluralism. Vivekananda's stirring words at the Parliament of Religions in 1893 were prophetic. There opened up in the West the possibility of a new outlook towards religions. However a surge of interest arose when more and more Indian and other Asiatic teachers came to America. The Swamis of the Ramakrishna Order worked very quietly. Had the media displayed an interest in Swami Akhilananda's stress on meditation in the 1940s and 1950s and in his books, popular interest would have arisen much sooner than the 1960s. By that time Harvey Cox was writing *THE SECULAR CITY*, the Swamis of the Ramakrishna movement were better known and there were other Indian gurus, who might have influenced the early founders of transpersonal psychology. We can't discount the influence of Swami Akhilananda.

Not only did Swami Akhilananda address the therapists and psychiatrists about the place of spiritual practices in the field of mental health, he also spoke to those in religious education. Dr. Walter Houston Clark writes of a visit by Swami Akhilananda.

"... When I was Dean of the Hartford School of Religious Education at the Hartford Seminary Foundation, I brought the Swami to Hartford to give a lecture on the place of religion in psychotherapy. While I have now forgotten the details of that address, I can remember with much vividness and pleasure the effect of the Swami's warm personality and spiritual acumen on the students there. Some of them struck up a friendship with him that was still functioning at the time of his death. It gave me a glimpse into the sources of his influence with Christian youth, whose beliefs in the mystical values of Christianity were thereby strengthened."[48]

Swami Akhilananda's work in the area of mental health and religion was recognized when he became a charter member of the National Academy of Religion and Mental Health in the mid 1950s. Its publication, Academy Reporter, vol. 2, no. 5, May 1957 contained a guest editorial by him, "Can Religion stabilize the personality?", in which he said: "Without concentration on God which dwells within, we cannot touch the power which heals ourselves and others."

He himself had that power. In Boston alone there were several persons with serious mental health problems which he helped to stabilize. One was from a prominent nationally known business family, who from overwork, had a mental breakdown. Living in the Chicago area, he was sent by Swami Vishwananda, the leader of the Vedanta Society there, to Swami Akhilananda. He restored him to mental health. The family was so grateful they gave the Swami $10,000.00 dollars, which he then sent to Swami Vishwananda.[49] The man later married. Two others with chronic mental difficulties stayed in better health during Swami Akhilananda's lifetime.

Dr. John Parks, a psychiatrist in Kentucky, and one of Swami Akhilananda's students writes about this phase of the Swami's work:

"I first saw in Swami a personal example of sensitive unselfish love. I saw him work with many counselees - young and old - which were exceedingly difficult and trying. He was the personification of patience, love, forgiveness, faith, and a willingness to go to those in need, to unselfishly serve with no consideration of cost to himself. ...Also I saw in Swami endurance, courage, ability to stand suffering and hurtful comments of others. He had those characteristics of an indomitable spiritual will... Through Swami's service and counseling to others I saw 'love in action'."[50]

Swami Akhilananda was ahead of his time in recognizing the limitations of the Behaviorists and the Freudians, which has already been mentioned; in advancing meditation for relaxing the mind and body. "Let us meditate," he would say, "on the All-Loving Being, getting rid

of all alien and unbecoming thoughts and feelings." In constantly bringing to the forefront the wisdom of religion, of spirituality, for mental
health and a balanced outlook on life. In reminding us that we are children of God.

18

SWAMI AS GURU

Knowing the value of spiritual disciplines and the need of the times:(people were anxious to have less stress and strain in their lives,) Swami Akhilananda was always insistent on spiritual practices. His lectures and class talks were full of encouragement for the student. His "meditate, meditate, meditate" was like a mantra. So was his "struggle struggle": the work with the mind and all its scattering tendencies.

Spiritual practices are a common everyday tradition in India.The Irish disciple of Swami Vivekananda, Sister Nivedita, who went to India in the late 1890s, wrote in her book "*THE WEB OF INDIAN LIFE*", of the early morning and evening vespers, where everyone spent time in silent worship. Entire neighborhoods became quiet.

"From all around the neighborhood at sunset would come the sound of gongs and bells in the family-chapel of each house, announcing Evensong...More and more, as the spirit of Hindu culture became the music of life, did this hour and that of sunrise grow to be events of my day. One learns in India to believe in what Maeterlinck calls 'the great active silence' and in such moments, consciousness, descending like a plummet into the depths of personality, and leaving even thought behind, seems to come upon the unmeasured and immeasurable."[1]

There are those who have commented on how beautifully Sister Nivedita wrote of those hours of great active silence. Visiting Edna St. Vincent Millay and her husband Eugen, in the summer of 1945, Vincent Sheehan and the poet agreed with Sister Nivedita that India had a special atmosphere - something unusual. Recent visitors have experienced the same feeling. Spirituality can be caught. Eugen Boisevan, Millay's husband recalled that on landing in India - "She felt something in India...She felt a difference in the human consciousness."[2] And she herself said in that regard: "I did," said Edna positively, "I was aware of it the moment I stepped off the boat... there is something there that doesn't exist in our life at all... I can't explain it, but I do know that it is true."[3] What impressions the great energies of Krishna, Buddha, Sankara, and Ramakrishna have left in that land.

Spirituality can also be given.

"Sri Ramakrishna had the power to transmit spirituality to others and lift them to higher states of consciousness. This he could do either by thought, look, or touch," said Swami Shivananda, whose outstanding spirituality made him the second president of the Ramakrishna Order. The Swami continued:

"Like Swami Vivekananda, many of us used to visit the Master and we had the good fortune to be lifted to higher planes of consciousness according to our capacities. I myself was privileged to attain that high spiritual consciousness (samadhi) thrice by his touch and wish during his lifetime... It was neither hypnotism nor a mere state of deep sleep, for such realizations brought about changes of character and outlook which were more or less permanent."[4]

Or Swami Akhilananda would mention in his lectures those astonishing moments when Brahmananda or Vivekananda were inspired to say "Here is Brahman" and those in attendance would enter into ecstasy. Here is Swami Prabhavananda, Akhilananda's brother disciple, disclosing what Swami Brahmananda had to say about one of those occasions:

"...that one day Swamiji, he, and several other brother-disciples were seated on the western veranda of the Belur Math. Suddenly Swamiji said to Maharaj, 'Raja, don't you see Brahman? Brahman is everywhere!'Maharaj said that Swamiji's awareness was so intense that their minds were lifted up immediately, and they saw Brahman everywhere."[5]

Have not other great souls had similar experiences? Even though Ramakrishna had this power, he would urge his disciples to go through spiritual practices. One day he said,

"Look, the best austerity for realizing God is truthfulness. Unite the mind and speech. You must speak only what you think at heart. Otherwise, where there is deceit, God will never manifest Himself. The more the mind becomes pure through spiritual practices, the clearer it will reflect God.[6]"

Ramakrishna maintained that renunciation, loving God intensely, discriminating between the real and the unreal, yoga, uniting the mind with God by means of work, devotion and knowledge, meditation were necessities. It was not good for anyone to be one-sided.

He said: "He(God) is the sum total of all ideals and paths. I worship Him in various ways, such as knowledge, devotion, work, worship, singing, japam and meditation."[7]

God, or Brahman, was the Reality, the Truth for Ramakrishna; for his disciples as well. And for one of his disciples, Swami Turiyananda, who said: "If one realizes God, to him the world is a paradise and everything in it yields whatever he desires."[8] At another time he remarked that the joy one had in being with an Incarnation for one day compensated for the sufferings of a lifetime. "It's difficult to convince anyone," he said. "Yet I must speak out."[9] And for Swami Akhilananda, who in our age of the secular city, tried to make it a Reality to those who heard him. It is no wonder then that the caring, enthusiastic Swami would urge us with reminiscences, entreaties, enjoinders, persuasions, and descriptions of spiritual practices so that we might be inspired. Listening intently, we would try to catch every word he said. What follows is a gathering of them from different lectures.[10] The Swami immediately presents you with this:

"For this highest realization the means is meditation. Meditation corrects all the quirks of character and removes all the defects. Swami Turiyananda's own life was established in meditation. He told the students: 'Meditation is the key that opens the door to Truth. Meditate! Meditate! Meditate till the light flashes into your mind and the Atman stands self-revealed. Not by talk not by study, but by meditation alone the Truth is known.'[11]

"In deep meditation we lose our sense of time. We do not know how long we have been in meditation. We forget the body and become absorbed in the object of meditation. But still there is duality and the one who is thinking of the object. There is something more than this - when we merge ourselves in the object. This is called 'seedless samadhi'. The man who attains this state has the appearance of an ordinary person. We do not know what he is when we look at him. There are many Hindu and Christian devotees who do not want the seedless samadhi - they do not want to be merged in God. They want to remain as his devotees - to serve Him.

"There are other people who are in a peculiar position. They have the intellectual understanding of the formless, attributeless God yet

168

they are not prepared emotionally or mentally trained so as to be able to meditate on That. It is very hard for them to reconcile these two things and they have to struggle. There is no other way. We all have to meditate. We have met a few people like that in this country. They have to start with the Personal aspect of God. We say to them: 'You are teaching children in school every day on the assumption that they are all different. You see not even duality but plurality. You live every day taking name or form for granted and yet you expect to be be able to sit down and meditate on the Formless. It cannot be done so easily. The mind has to be trained gradually for this.'"

Swami Akhilananda was always after us to meditate. "How is your meditation," he would ask if he was talking with us over the phone or when we greeted him following a Sunday service.What can a spiritual teacher do for us? Can he give us a taste of God? It depends on the situation, the mood of the teacher and the temperament of the student. The disciples of Swami Brahmananda all kept quiet about their spiritual experiences. Swami Akhilananda said, "They were too sacred to talk about." However, here and there in their lectures and talks something would be mentioned that indicated a personal experiences. "One has to catch the hints," Swami Akhilananda used to say.Swami Akhilananda knew there were those who objected to meditating on a personal aspect of God even tho he recommended it. Some people would find a symbol embodying the universal aspects of God as more satisfactory. Or even meditating on the attributes of God. Then we find this: inspiring experiences and observations.

"We have to go through certain stages until we reach God-consciousness...When we get a little deeper into meditation, we come to the stage where it is Krishna and I, Buddha and I, Jesus and I, or whatever personality we take. We lose our I-ness in the ideal. Then we become aware of duality. There is Krishna and I. The next state is when we go beyond even this and are absorbed in Existence itself. That is the stage where Eckhart said: 'I renounce God for God's sake'. "He was not becoming an atheist as some of the church fathers thought. He saw the Absolute everywhere. What he meant was 'I renounce the Personal God for the God-head.' When a person reaches this state the memory of it stays with him forever. Such a person cannot do anything wrong. His life is a blessing to others. He is a changed person. His whole subconscious is changed. He becomes a center of love. His past experiences and biological urges drop off, they vanish. Outwardly he seems like the same man as in the case of Swami Brahmananda and Swami Vivekananda, but inwardly they are different. They have the apparent form of a man. A man of this state sees the different people but knows that each person has God in him. He sees God in each individual."

In the midst of reading all these selections from his talks, it's good to remember what he said while lecturing on May 29, 1949: "So God-vision is universal...But certain training is needed - just as certain training is needed for a scientist. The religious method has to be suitable to the temperament of the person...

"You all know the story. Swami Vivekananda met two of his brothers, Swami Brahmananda and Swami Turiyananda before coming to this country. He had not seen them in a long time. He was traveling incognito over India for a couple of years deeply absorbed in his spiritual life. When he met them he said to Swami Brahmananda, 'Brother, one thing I know that this (pointing to the heart) has expanded. It can embrace the whole world.' A man of God-realization embraces the whole world. He sees God everywhere...But don't be impatient. We have to develop through different stages until we reach the state of God-realization. Only then are our conflicts gone, and only then can we feel secure..."

But there could be more to concentration and meditation. The unexpected might reveal itself. As Swami says:

"A holy man by his deep concentration can easily know his past if he wants to. Sometimes the knowledge of it comes to him even without his trying to know...Sometimes it comes like flashes. (He was referring to past lives.) And not only can a holy man know his past but he can also know the past associations and lives of another...But holy men do not generally do such things. Their interest is in God. They may give advice but their main interest is in God. They may try to know the contents of a person's mind for a special purpose such as to know his actions and their motives so as to be able to advise him... A holy man can also know the thoughts of another person by making his mind a vacuum. Then it becomes like a mirror and reflects the thoughts of the other person. It is not so easy, tho, to make the mind a vacuum. It takes years of practice."

Sitting and watching Swami Akhilananda as he stood at the podium giving his sermon, one felt that he was the thing he described, whatever the spiritual condition or experience. The purity of his intentions was obvious. For all his tactfulness, Swami was simple and direct. Nothing false about him. The serious student felt blessed to have such a teacher, selfless and imbued with the knowledge and love of God. How can one describe him? He was a silent worker, modest, but he couldn't hide his certainty. Swami Akhilananda felt within himself that he had something to give, and so he did.

"By meditating on higher qualities such as friendship, mercy, love, etc. or by meditating on the person who has such qualities we gradually begin to manifest those very qualities... When a person has developed such qualities, such spiritual qualities as love, mercy, he becomes charming. People are attracted to him and not knowing why. I am speaking of spiritual charm. The charm that comes from the inside. The people who have this charm attract us in spite of ourselves.

"We have to fall in love with God...First we must cultivate the thought of God through prayer, meditation and then we realize God. When we love someone we do not have to try to think of the person. We automatically think of them. We cannot help thinking of them.. A person who falls in love with God cannot help thinking of Him all the time. He sees everyone as the manifestation of God. Then the little happenings in the world do not bother him. Thought is the expression of love."

Swami tells us a litle bit more about a person who loves:

"A man of God has his emotions thoroughly integrated. He cannot be swayed one inch from the Ideal. Ordinary men and women are considerably disintegrated personalities, if you will pardon me for saying so. They are slaves to their emotions. Their anger or jealousy can be aroused very easily. But a man of God knows only love. It does not matter whether you are a Jew or a Christian, white or dark. He loves you and you cannot take his love away from any person.

"We have to train the mind to think of God through ways that are pleasing for it. Otherwise we cannot even think of Him. The Christians think of Jesus by recapitulating the events of his life...This is good. It prepares the mind for meditation, but it is not meditation. It is not enough...We think in succeeding thoughts. What we have to do is train the mind to become unified, one-pointed."

It wouldn't be long before Swami spoke about the spiritual teacher, after a few introductory remarks:

"The mind has the deceptive nature to avoid all seriousness...It takes the easiest path. Aha, how keenly Swami Vivekananda felt for the world. The world does just the things that will cause pain. We have to do spiritual practices, keep company of the holy, etc., in order to make us desire the knowledge of Truth...The mind does not like to do. It takes the easiest path. And it is easy thing to think of the world, but not so easy to try to withdraw the mind and turn it in. First of all the student has to have the desire for knowledge. Then the teacher can do something...There has to be some contact between the teacher and student. And when there is contact the teacher pours out everything.

"And it is the duty of the student to strictly follow the methods prescribed by the teacher. The student has to cooperate...If the teacher says, 'Do this' and the student does not do or does not want to do that is where spiritual practices come in. They help to strengthen the student so that he can follow the ideal. The relationship between a spiritual teacher and student is unique. It is greater than the parent-child relationship. A spiritual teacher is not like the ordinary teacher in the colleges. That type of teacher touches only a part of the student's life, but a spiritual teacher touches his whole being. He changes his whole being. If the student has any substance at all in him he is bound to change... A spiritual teacher is the link between God and man. He leads us to God.. and the relationship is eternal and abiding.

"If we disagree with the teacher because of ignorance or egocentricity then by spiritual practices the impurities of the mind are wiped away and we see that he is right...

"We have to have a spiritual teacher to guide us. And he must be one who has the realization of God. If he does not know the way then how can he guide us? The blind cannot lead the blind...

"There is a saying that when a person is ready, when his inside is prepared and when he is craving for God then a spiritual teacher comes to him. God sends a spiritual teacher to help him. When the rosebud opens up the fragrance attracts people. And so when the flowers have the honey the bees flock there.

"Everybody wants to be a teacher... A teacher is not made. It comes from within. It is a process of evolution. He evolves.

"A spiritual teacher by his good wishes, by his unselfishness, by his love changes us. It may be slow, but we change...The teacher does not teach us for money or name or fame. He teaches us because of his love

172

and nothing else. The spiritual teacher must be free from all selfishness. 'When the teacher is great and the student is great the end is attained.'

In writing about the requirements of a spiritual teacher, Swami wrote: "...a teacher must have a clear understanding of the needs of the student. Herein lies the utility of what we call intuitive or even rational understanding of the requirements of the student. If a teacher does not understand these, he cannot give real guidance. Every student is different. If we think the world can be spiritualized in just one way, we are mistaken." To emphasize he continued: "...real spiritual awakening or real spiritual guidance should be given individually according to the requirements of each student. A real spiritual teacher who has experience of God cannot help having this insight. He has depth of understanding."[12] "We had the great privilege of sitting at the feet of some towering spiritual personalities. And they never uttered a word of discouragement. They would always encourage. One time a person asked our master, Swami Brahmananda, how long it would take to have the realization of God and Maharaj said, 'You have to do a little for a few days.' How simple he made it seem. As if it was a matter of hours or weeks or months!

"For the majority of the people the path of devotion is the best. It is the easiest. But there are a handful of persons in the world who are suited to the path of reason: Jnana yoga. To follow this path one must have a tremendous intellect and admantine will power. He must discriminate the real from the unreal. Eckhart was such a person. That is why he was able to say, 'I renounce God for God's sake. I renounce the Personal God for the God-head.'"

Usually it was pin-drop silence when Swami Akhilananda spoke from his heart about spiritual life. Would he encourage his students by speaking of his own spiritual experiences? Inspiring as that would have been, his students did not need that to feel energized in their spiritual disciplines.His instructions were stimulating. He might say to a student, "You will have everything." Or extend encouragement to another by giving special training. His optimism was contagious. The words of an illumined soul have a life of their own. As we know from the lectures of Swami Vivekananda, or the prayers of St. Francis, or the poems of Rumi. However...

"It is true that intellectual arguments, etc. are not needed for the realization of God. All is needed is faith.

...If a person has faith he has everything. And if he doesn't have faith, he has nothing. Yet to convince others the intellectualism is needed. You have to prove to them by reasoning that there is God. That there is utility to spiritual practices."

Other experiences besides that of realizing God could be had by concentration and meditation. Swami Akhilananda cautions us:

"We can get certain powers through a mantra or a name of God. There are many names of God and through repetition of a name of God we can get certain powers. But, the name of God has to be given to us by an illumined man who receives the name of God in his spiritual experiences. The name has to be suited to our particular temperament and tendencies and be short..It does not make any difference whether the name of God is in Hebrew or Arabic or Sanskrit. But the thing is it must be given by an illumined person.

"Then there are persons who mortify the flesh to get these powers or knowledge of God. There are monks who practice severe penances. In Assisi we visited some monasteries and you cannot imagine the discipline that they practice. Very rigorous disciplines. Also in Padua we saw when we visited there...There are some who take the vow of silence. They never talk...But Patanjali says that we can obtain the powers through concentration instead of whipping and starving. These things may lead to powers, but they are powers in the worldly sense and not in the spiritual sense. In fact they are obstacles to our realization of God, which is the primary purpose of every life."

But just see what power of concentration the Swami Turiyananda had and how it helped him when he faced a serious operation. Swami tells the story:

"Swami Turiyananda had diabetes and gangrene set in.

The doctors examined and had to operate but they did not like to use anesthetic as the heart was not so good. They went and told Swami Brahmananda who was then Head of the Order and then Swami Brahmananda went to Swami Turiyananda and said,'Brother, you will have to endure a little.' Swami Turiyananda said, 'Yes, Maharaj, anything you say.'

"Just before the doctors started operating, Swami Turiyananda began to talk to some young Swami about Brahman - the Absolute. The doctors operated and he went on talking as if the operation took place in another person's body so absorbed was he. Of course the doctors were amazed. This shows we can rise above the consciousnes of the body. We can withdraw our mind from the body. There is no fear of death then. If a person dies we know that only the body has gone but he is existing eternally. Death is only a change...When we expand our consciousness we realize that the real person does not die - only the body dies. Then we realize that we also exist eternally. Only a person who has the conviction that there is a soul can give that conviction to others. Only a person of peace can give peace to others."

There were always questions for the Swami to answer.

We don't know the question, but we can guess what it might have been from the answer that Swami gave:

"If we are in the habit it can happen in sleep. In sleep we can have exalting experiences. We received a letter from a friend of ours in India who had a very exalting experience in sleep. We are sure that this significant experience took place because of his steady spiritual practices... Some experiences in sleep are more valuable than in ordinary awakened state... Rhythmical breathing is practical only to make the mind quiet. At that time in the awakened or sleeping state, you have spiritual experiences. Spiritual experiences indicate rhythmical breathing."

Someone asked, "How can we ascertain a spiritual experience?"

Swami answered: "By the effect. A spiritual experience becomes self-evident. It reveals something new to you, or it may be a repeated spiritual experience. It makes you extremely happy. It affects the whole personality for a few days."

Elsewhere Swami goes on to say:

"But you can't buy God by meditation. A friend of ours, a scholar, asked us directly only this evening, 'Swami, are spiritual practices necessary for the realization of God?' We said, 'You mean are they the direct cause of the realization of God?' She said, 'Yes.' And then we explained that meditation is not the direct cause, but is absolutely necessary for the realization of God. Meditation removes the obstacles. The obstacles are inordinate tendencies, envy, jealousy, pride, etc. Our very nature is divine and flows to God, but through cosmic ignorance we do not know it. Just as when there is an embankment the water cannot flow, but if the farmer removes the embankment the water will spontaneously flow in its course. So when we remove the obstacles through meditation we spontaneously go to God."

Swami wanted to infuse us all with enthusiasm for spiritual life:

175

..."A person who has had real religious experiences is a changed person. His life changes. His emotions become unified, he becomes an integrated personality. His mind becomes alert, subtle...He becomes a stable person.

...The Freudian psychologists are greatly if not wholly responsible for the idea that association with a religion is a sign of psychoses. There have been cases where an unbalanced person associates himself with some religious idea or personality. But these persons remain unstable -- their thoughts and actions are inconsistent. A person who has real religious experiences becomes more stable, becomes integrated. He becomes purer and purer and he becomes soft as as anything.

"Science can be verified by controlled observation and so religious experiences can be verified. But we have to go through the practices systematically and verify for ourselves...It is true that we cannot know what another man is experiencing. We can have some idea by the outer expressions, but we do not understand until we go through the experience ourselves...

"A person who has deep religious experiences becomes joyous and others feel the joyous vibration around him... He has a joyous expression in his eyes. A religious person never discourages anyone. He does not say 'Don't do this.' He says instead 'do this.' It is never the negative method, always the positive. Ramakrishna never uttered a word of discouragement. You can tell in the *GOSPEL*.

"The Jewish prophet, 'Master of Good Name' had real religious experiences and his life showed it. He influenced many people around him and his influence is felt even now."

And now to return to a topic which was of great interest to him. He was never tired of talking about God.

"There are three states of realization. In the first state there is duality, God and the soul. In the second state one loses all consciousness of 'I', there is only 'He'. And there is a third state which cannot be decribed. It is beyond light and darkness, beyond finite and infinite. Ramakrishna many times tried to describe this state to his disciples, but each time he tried to describe he entered into samadhi. He said that it was the one thing not polluted by human language. Rationally speaking human language is finite. It is the product of a finite mind and the finite cannot comprehend the Infinite. To be frank I tell you as long as the mind is gross we do not even have the desire for religious experiences.

176

"We have to think of the eternal to be happy. We have to find out the god in all if we want to be happy. And once we realize our own true nature, simultaneously we see the true nature of others. The two happen simultaneously.

"As my master, Swami Brahmananda, used to say: 'It makes you feel like grabbing the feet of people and begging them to think of God'. And it is true. You feel like begging them, actually begging them to think of God. There is no happiness otherwise. "

More than once Swami Akhilananda would refer to a woman who came for an interview. She was having trouble in her marriage or some other close relationship. "What do I get out of it?" she would say. "What do you give to it?" was Swami's answer. It was an example of the self-centeredness he felt was common in America. Too common for our collective good. We needed a new outlook on life, a new philosophy.

Sri Sarada Devi, the Holy Mother

19

THE CONVENT, SARADA MATH

The searching, observing eyes of Swami Vivekananda saw a great deal of America while he was here in the 1890s. He wrote in a letter meant for his brother disciples: "Here you have a wonderful manifestation of grit and power - what strength what practicality, and what manhood![1].... Well, I am almost at my wit's end to see the women of this country."[2] Swami Vivekananda couldn't say enough good things about the women of the late 19th century. "I am really struck to see the women here. How gracious the Divine Mother is on them! Most wonderful women, these!"[3] He could also admonish: "Always remember that Sri Ramakrishna came for the good of the world - not for name or fame. Spread only what he came to teach...", warning his brother disciple not to make a sect out of Ramakrishna.[4] But Swami Vivekananda had other things on his mind.

In 1894 he wrote an impassioned letter to one of his brother disciples, Swami Shivananda: "Hence we must first build a Math (convent) for Mother. First Mother and Mother's daughters, then Father and Father's sons - can you understand this? …To me, Mother's grace is a hundred thousand times more valuable than Father's. Mother's grace, Mother's blessings are all paramount to me…"[5]

Swami Vivekananda wanted a convent, a Math, for women. Of all the disciples of Ramakrishna, Swami Vivekananda was the first to understand the unique greatness of the Holy Mother and how important she was for the regeneration of India and the world. Swami's idea was that women's monasticism in modern India would grow with Holy Mother as its center. Men's monasticism was already growing centered around Ramakrishna.

Interesting is the conversation Swami Vivekananda had, after returning to India, with one of his admirers, Saratchandra Chakravarty, who noted all that was said. Swami Vivekananda felt very free with him and vice versa. The place of their talks was Belur Math and the year, 1901. Swami Vivekananda: "... with Holy Mother as the centre of inspiration a Math is to be established on the eastern bank of the Ganges."[6]

Then he went on to say: "It is very difficult to understand why in this country so much difference is made between men and women whereas the Vedanta declares that one and the same conscious Self is present in all beings. You always criticize the women, but say, what have you done for their uplift? ... binding them by hard rules, the men have turned the women into mere manufacturing machines! If you do not raise the women who are the living embodiments of the Divine Mother, don't think you have any other way to rise."[7]

But the disciple had his doubts and his own opinions. It would seem as though women were a snare and a delusion.[8]

Swami Vivekananda, however, felt that women were competent for knowledge and devotion. His response was that women were denied access, in a period of degeneration, to the study of the Vedas. This was at a time when the priests considered some other castes incompetent for Vedic knowledge. In the Vedic or Upanishadic age only a few women like Maitreyi, Gargi and others took the places of rishis in discussing about Brahman with great skill and were revered. Vivekananda felt that if such ideal women were entitled to spiritual knowledge, why not the women of today. He also felt that where there was no regard, no appreciation of women, and where they lived in sadness, that family or country couldn't rise in the world. Women needed to be raised up first so therefore a convent or Math should be started for them, which would be ideal in every way.[9]

Finally, after further doubting, the disciple became curious about Vivekananda's plan.

His reply: "On the other side of the Ganges a big plot of land would be acquired, where unmarried girls or Brahmacharini widows will live; devout married ladies will also be allowed to stay now and then. Men will have no concern with this Math. The elderly Sadhus of the Math will manage the affairs of this Math from a distance." He continued to elaborate on different aspects of what the Math would be like, the training it would have for the inmates. "Spirituality, sacrifice, and self-control will be the motto of the pupils of this Math, and service... the vow of their life. In view of such ideal lives, who will not respect and have faith in them? ...To what straits the strictures of local usages have reduced the women of this country, rendering them lifeless and inert, you could only understand if you visited the Western countries. You alone are responsible for this miserable condition of the women, and it rests with you also to raise them again. Therefore, I say, get to work."[10]

What feeling Swami Vivekananda had for the condition of women in India. He knew a high ideal had to be established because in women as in men there is this longing for knowledge and devotion. Dedicated women would be educators, nurses, doctors, etc. and would serve their communities and other women wherever they could. But Swami Vivekananda's vision of a convent for women would have to wait.

In 1951 a move was started to realize it. While Swami Akhilananda was returning to the United States from India in early 1951, he stopped at Gretz, France to see his brother disciple, Swami Siddheswarananda. While there he received a letter from Swami Saswatananda of Belur Math about a piece of land that was for sale, "a nice garden house at Dakshineswar." The description of the land and buildings on it showed it to be ideal for a women's Math. As Swami Saswatananda wrote: "If you could see it, you would have given the advance money to purchasing (this land) without any hesitation while you were here. Please don't give the chance of giving it to other's hand. Whoever will see, he will tell the same thing.... It is a chance of a lifetime. ... Let our patrimony be blessed by trying to give status and responsibility and due share to mothers. Sri Sri Thakur (Ramakrishna), Ma and Swamiji by making you an instrument have created unimaginably the stone Temple at Belur Math. Similarly, this work also will be done through you."[11]

At the same time, in an addition to the letter, Swami Prabodhananda wrote to Swami Akhilananda: "This property is very inexpensive, we have to sign an agreement at once, we might lose it if we wait; please send the cable and reserve it. Me and Saswatananda have looked into all the details. My feeling is this - Thakur made you do the granite temple (at Belur) and he wants you to do the ideal Srimath (women's math) and he will. You are blessed - please do not delay for a day even; it can go to someone else. ... Thakur gave us exactly the place we wanted."[12]

Swami Akhilananda did not need to be coaxed. He himself was adamant about a math for the women. He wrote in a timely letter to Belur Math:

"We should certainly start to carry out the plan and wishes of Sri Sri Swamiji regarding women's institutions on the centenary of Sri Sri Holy Mother. The world very badly needs this work.

"Yes. Women's Math should be established as Sri Sri Swamiji wanted in his rules for the monks, as women will gain experience in spiritual life, karma yoga, and public relations. Although they need help from the senior leaders of the Math, the three important leaders should be solely responsible for their activities.

"The elderly ladies who are disciples of Sri Sri Mother should be given Sannyasa immediately by our revered President. Of course, if he kindly considers that it is better to do so as the time of the Centenary Celebration of the Mother, we must obey his wish and decision as to the matter of time, as he is our leader of the Order.

"Brahmacharya and Sannyasa should be given to the deserving trained women devotees who are living the dedicated life in our Mission institutions. I understand some of our Swamis feel that Sannyasa should not be given to women as Sankara did not give this to them. Is Sri Sri Swamiji inferior to Sankara? It seems to me some of our Swamis are audacious enough to think that we have to follow Sankara's tradition while Sri Swamiji explicitly wanted that women should be Brahmacharins and Sannyasins, as he wanted to start a women's Math parallel to the Belur Math for the monks....

"Sri Sri Swamiji explicitly wanted that the women should manage their own institutions. According to Swamiji, monks were asked to manage the women's institutions from a distance until they were in a position to handle their own affairs, I feel women are getting ready to take care of their own institutions. Sri Sri Swamiji could see far ahead of time so he advised the monks to allow the women to work for themselves."[13]

Swami Akhilananda made everything abundantly clear. He concluded his letter by saying Brahmacharya and Sannyasa had been given by Swami Vivekananda and Holy Mother to several women devotees. Would he have known of the following incident? There was a day in March, 1916 when a young girl came to Swami Brahmananda yearning to lead a spiritual life. He listened to her and then sent her to an ashrama. Swami Brahmananda at that time said to Swami Premananda: "Who can understand the divine play of Sri Ramakrishna? Swami

Vivekananda wanted to see a convent established for young women, and now I see that some day soon his desire will be fulfilled. Young women are becoming imbued with the ideal of renunciation as taught by our master."[14]

Many letters were written by the Treasurer at Belur, Swami Saswatananda, to Swami Akhilananda, requesting that he send money towards the purchase of this property for the monastic quarters for the women. Other legal questions had to be settled. In a letter of December 31, 1951, Saswatananda wrote: "Hope you are getting better by the grace of the Holy Mother. When you feel better and stronger, please engage yourself whole-heartedly for the responsibility you have undertaken for welfare of the women - this prayer is coming always from the heart of everyone of us. I'm very much relieved to know from the cable and letter that you are 'out of danger'. When you become active, please jump into the work taking the name of Sri Sri MA. I firmly believe that this work will be done by you."

Swami Akhilananda sent money from time to time. Swami Saswatananda wrote on December 26, 1952: "I was waiting for your check after I got your cable and the letter... It was great that you could send this money. No matter how anxious we are when the time comes things will happen smoothly and miraculously. Thakur earmarked you for this purpose. He arranged everything for His own huge temple, now how can He cause any problem during Mother's memorial? That will never happen."

From India, letter would follow letter. In one of October 29, 1953 Swami Saswatananda wrote: "I understand you are trying hard for the funds for the Women's Math... Pray the 'Four Forces' be on your side." The 'Four Forces' being Four-in-One (Sri Ramakrishna, Holy Mother, Swami Vivekananda, Swami Brahmananda). Again on the 18th of November, Swami Saswatananda was urging Swami Akhilananda to send money for the women's Math. On March 20, 1954 he sent another letter to Swami Akhilananda: "Please get involved a little more intensely now. ...We could not collect money in this country.. I do not think any Swami in America will be of any help." A letter of Swami Saswatananda to Swami Akhilananda, dated May 11, 1954 discloses: "At present that property is listed in your name, Satyan Maharaj's and Priya Maharaj's name.. If we cannot start women's Math this year at least by

December we would let go a unique historic occasion without being able to make a permanent memorial to Holy Mother.'"

On June 7, 1954 Saswatananda wrote: "Abani Maharaj (Swami Prabhavananda) told us that he will try to get some help for women's Math." At last on the 22nd of October, 1954, Saswatananda wrote to Swami Akhilananda: "...Finally with your great personal efforts 'Ladies' have a place of their own to stay. Sri Sri Thakur is doing his work through you." Swami Akhilananda was able to send forty thousand dollars ($40,000.00), the gift of Miss Esther Harrington of Providence, one of his devotees, for the women's Math.[15]

The consecration ceremony for the new monastic quarters for women was held on 2nd December, 1954.[16] Sarala Devi was the new head of this women's Math. She had served the Holy Mother. Her new name, would be Pravrajika Bharataprana. Swami Saswatananda wrote on the 21st of July, 1954: "Everybody likes this link of her with the Holy Mother." Many women celebrated the consecration. "About "three and one-half thousand women got prasad," wrote Swami Saswatananda. "The nuns arranged everything by themselves....At present ten of them are living there."

Those not familiar with Holy Mother may well ask who was this lady, the Holy Mother, for whom so much effort was expended? She was the virgin wife of Sri Ramakrishna to whom she was wed when she was very young. At about 17 years of age she left her country home and came to Calcutta to see him. One would think she was just a simple country girl, but, no, Sri Ramakrishna would never let anyone think so.

He saw that she was divine in nature. On an auspicious holy day in 1872, Ramakrishna worshipped her as an aspect of the Divine Mother. "After several hours Sri Ramakrishna came down again to the relative plane, sang a hymn to the Great Goddess."[17] He then offered at her feet his rosary, himself, and the results of his austerities. Universal motherhood became manifest in the Holy Mother and she became a partner in his dedicated life.

After Ramakrishna's death in 1886, she became a guru to hundreds if not thousands. Many Indians would walk hundreds of miles to receive her blessings, her teachings, her counsel. The disciples of Ramakrishna revered her as not different than him. "There is no difference between Sri Ramakrishna and the Mother,"[18] said Swami Brahmananda. "Mother assumed this human body," said Swami

184

Shivananda, "in order to awaken the entire womanhood of the world. Don't you see, after her advent, what amazing awakening has set forth among the women kind of the world? ...This is just the beginning."[19]

It seems as though it was her great heart which distinguishes Holy Mother. From the West came women to India to be with her and when they saw her they were captivated by her modest and loving nature. One of them, a young woman who became Sister Devamata wrote of their meeting: "...found Holy Mother alone in a room behind the Shrine and laid myself and my offerings at her feet. She repeated my name twice with tender surprise. Then she placed her hand in blessing on my head. At her touch a spring of new life seemed to bubble up from my innermost heart and flood my being.

"... A Sannyasini (woman medicant) came in and began to rub her body, a usual mode of loving service in India. As I watched her the question crossed my mind, would I ever be worthy to serve her thus. Scarcely had the thought been formed before she motioned me to take the Sannyasini's place. ... We had no common tongue, but when there was none to interpret for us, she spoke that deeper wordless language of the heart and we never failed to understand each other."[20]

That great Scotch-Irish lady, Margaret Noble, who met Swami Vivekananda in London, later with his encouragement went to India where she stayed, described in one of her letters the Holy Mother:

"... this woman, when you know her well, is said to be the very soul of practicality and common-sense, as she certainly gives every token of being, to those who know her slightly. Sri Ramakrishna always consulted her before undertaking anything and her advice is always acted upon by his disciples. She is the very soul of sweetness - so gentle and loving and as merry as a girl. You should have heard her laugh the other day when I insisted that the Swami must come up and see us at once, or we would go home. The monk who had brought the message that the Master would delay seeing us was quite alarmed at my moving towards my shoes, and departed post haste to bring him up, and then you should have heard Sarada's laughter! It just pealed out. And she is so tender - 'my daughter' she calls me. ...The best proof I can give you of her real greatness is that she is always attended when in Calcutta by 14 or 15 high caste ladies, who would be rebellious and quarrelsome and give infinite trouble to everyone if she by her wonderful tact and winsomeness did not keep perpetual peace. There is no foundation for this statement in the character of these ladies. It is only my inference about women in general."[21] So wrote Sister Nivedita.

Holy Mother wrote affectionate letters. To Sister Devamata: "My sweet daughter: My blessings be on your head....You are my daughter, you are also my mother because you have prayed for my welfare to the Lord. ...What grief I have suffered due to the passing out of Baburam (Swami Premananda) I cannot convey in a letter.....Write to me about your own welfare. Write me."[22]

When Sister Nivedita was traveling in the West in 1900, trying to raise money for her school in Calcutta, Holy Mother wrote to her. With what reverence she began her letter, first acknowledging Ramakrishna —

"My trust is in His sacred feet - May this letter carry all blessings! My dear love to you, Baby Daughter Nivedita! I am so glad to learn that you have prayed to the Lord for my eternal peace. You are a manifestation of the ever-blissful Mother. I look at your photograph which is with me, every now and then. And it seems as if you are present with me. I long for the day and the year when you shall return. May the prayers you have uttered for me from the heart of your pure virgin soul be answered!...

"He, the Breath of the Universe, is singing His Own praise, and you are hearing that Eternal song through things that will come to an end. The trees, the birds, the hills, and all are singing praise to the Lord. The Banyan of Dakshineswar sings of Kali to be sure, and blessed is he who has ears to hear it..."[23] Who can fail to hear the poetry that was in Holy Mother.

Once, on a bright moonlit night at Dakshineswar not far from where Holy Mother stayed, a young man, remorseful for his conduct, approached Ramakrishna. Sister Devamata writes: "Ramakrishna smiled at him and said: 'Of what use to go to Mother. She is not in this world just now. Her soul is far above it. Did you not see her, as you passed, sitting on the upper verandah rapt in deep meditation.'"[24] Her soul was drinking the nectar of the gods, infinite joy, infinite love.

If Holy Mother could be above the world, she was also in it, playing with her little 8 year old niece, Radhu, losing herself in fun and merriment. She would be amused over a jack-in-the-box which had been given to Radhu. Every time it jumped out with its familiar squeak, Holy Mother would repeat the sound with a good hearty laugh. Holy

Mother had a subdued but gentle cheerfulness, a lurking sense of humor which enabled anyone to approach her and talk to her of anything.[25]

Those who lived with Holy Mother could see that religion was sweet, joyous, and natural; that purity and holiness were tangible realities.[26] Had she been on earth, Holy Mother with her caring and affectionate nature, would have been overjoyed to see that her daughters, the nuns, now had a place of their own. Years before, when Swami Vivekananda had wanted to sell Belur Math in order to have funds for relief work, she had objected.[27] Holy Mother saw the future and the need for monasteries. Women as well as men would need a place that was theirs.

For the Sarada Math, another legal step was needed. Samvit, the semi-yearly publication of Sri Sarada Math, #19, March 1989 states: "In 1960 the Trustees of Sri Sarada Math founded the Ramakrishna Sarada Mission Association registered under Act XXI of I960, with headquarters at Dakshineswar. The General report of the Sarada Math and Mission states: 'The object of the Mission is to carry on educational, cultural, charitable and similar activities among women and children, irrespective of caste, creed, colour or nationality. Thereby, the Mission is trying to bring about a kind of harmonization between secular and spiritual development, specially among the women of India." The nuns of the Sarada Mission have expanded in India and abroad. They frequently conduct retreats in Europe and the U. S, where they at times lecture at different Centers.

The work done primarily by Swami Akhilananda and other Swamis in the West for the Sarada Math, is unknown. Swami Akhilananda's cousin, Shirish Chandra Sanyal in his reminiscences, wrote of him: "Sri Thakur and Swamiji accomplished many tasks through Akhilananda towards the growth and expansion of the Belur Math organization. Many of the facts remained unknown to the public. Indeed, Akhilananda never cared for name and fame. He loved to work outside of public view. He was truly detached with the fruits of his works.[28]" At the annual meeting of the Ramakrishna Vedanta Society in Boston in 1955 Swami Akhilananda only casually mentioned the efforts that he and others had made toward the establishment of the Sarada Math.

At times during his Sunday lectures Swami Akhilananda would speak of Holy Mother, whom he used to see frequently while going to college in Calcutta. He used to say that if there was anything good in him it `was due to those great personalities, Holy Mother, Swami Brahmananda, Swami Premananda, and others.

20

THE EXPANDING CIRCLE

At the end of May, 1953 Swami Akhilananda had a heart attack at 58 Deerfield Street, Boston. He was able to be taken care of at the Center with round-the-clock nursing. In early August he was well enough to give a Sunday lecture, but his activities were very much curtailed during the summer months. Perhaps he had been well enough to have lunch with Prof. Harlow Shapley on the 29th of May. Not until September did he resume his classes and lectures, his luncheons and dinners with friends. As Mrs. Worcester's granddaughter, Carole Moreau, writes: "He derived great pleasure preparing large dinners he would have occasionally at the Centers... His luncheons, lectures, and trips would take their toll, though, and he would become ill and need rest... The only thing that would irritate him was when he was rendered passive by illness."[1]

Swami Akhilananda's illness accented the need he had for an assistant. His workload had been very heavy for more than a decade, serving two Centers, Boston and Providence, writing books, having interviews, speaking engagements, traveling monthly as a rule to New York City and frequently Philadelphia, going out of state to lecture at colleges and universities, and let us not forget his luncheons and dinner engagements with his academic friends. He was doing ail this on four hours of sleep a night, at the utmost five.

In a letter of May 5, 1953, Swami Saswatananda wrote from Belur Math to Swami Akhilananda: "Everybody agrees that you should have an assistant in view of your work load", and then again on the 20th of March, 1954, the General Secretary Swami Madhavananda wrote to Swami Akhilananda: "For a long time we are trying to send you a suitable assistant..." At last the Trustees of the Ramakrishna Mission selected Swami Sarvagatananda, who arrived here in Boston on October 6, 1954. It was with great relief to Swami Akhilananda to have him as an assistant. The young Swami would be staying in Providence, coming occasionally to Boston to give a lecture or participate in a service.

But before his young assistant could arrive, Swami Akhilananda received a letter from India from his close brother monk, Omkarananda, chiding him for being too busy to write. "Man! nice work!", writes Swami Omkarananda, "showing the world how busy you are. Today in Boston with the devotees, tomorrow in New York sprinkling peace water to the yogis, or in Providence congregating with friends...! Hail to you! Only when it comes to write letters you are busy..."[2] Swami Akhilananda enjoyed it all with great good humor. He wrote to him.

Swami Akhilananda's association with the academic community was expanding. He was developing a connection with MIT, which had already begun unobtrusively. He noted in his diary of a meeting there for January 26, 1946 at 4 pm. On March 14, 1947 at 12:15 he had an appointment with Dean Everett M. Baker. We don't know the substance of these meetings. Following this he had an invitation for June 13, 1947 for 10 o'clock for some function and on July 1st for dinner at MIT at 7pm. In 1948 on the 15th of April he again saw Dean Baker at 12:30, perhaps for lunch, and met Dean Chalmer on June 11th.

The next contact with MIT was on August 6, 1949, Saturday, at 4pm when he was to go to Harvard and MIT. On October 21, 1949 at 3:30pm Prime Minister Jawaharlal Nehru of India was at MIT and at 5pm there was a reception for him which Swami Akhilananda attended. The personal diaries of the Swami for 1950--1952, being either lost or missing, it is not until April 14, 1953 that it is noted that Swami Akhilananda will give a lecture at 5pm at MIT on "Hindu View of Life" followed by a dinner there at 6:30. Swami Akhilananda was a guest at President James Killian's home on Sunday, May 3, 1953 at 4pm. Ostensibly for tea.

In the early 1950s MIT would start planning and building a chapel for its community. It would be a place of worship for all religions. This came about as an outgrowth of President Killian's interest in science and the humanities and what the humanities could do for the students. What President Killian didn't disclose in his autobiography is how he decided to include the humanities in the curriculum of MIT. It grew out of the atom bomb being dropped on Hiroshima. President Killian wondered what kind of human beings we were producing, especially in the fields of science and technology. Thus, for ten years he worked to introduce the humanities, art, philosophy and religion to the curriculum of MIT. President Killian disclosed all this to the Swamis Akhilananda and Sarvagatananda in conversation with them.[3]

190

President Killian's book, *THE EDUCATION OF A COLLEGE PRESIDENT*, an autobiography of an unusually gifted intuitive administrator, has a section on the affinities and intersections in science and the humanities. He felt that "the arts have impressively contributed to science and technology,"[4] and writes "The syncretic relations of science and the arts are coming to be more widely understood. In a very deep sense they are interdependent, and they spring from the same act of the imagination."[5] He then goes on to relate two fascinating incidents, which may seem unrelated to the field of religion, but show his appreciation of diverse intellectual cultures. He continues: "Dr. Wiesner is fond of quoting a comment made by the poet, Stanley Kunitz, at a meeting of the MIT Council for the Arts. 'There are many disciplines,' said Kunitz, 'but only one imagination…'

"In his posthumously published Pegram lectures, Andre Maurois recounts an anecdote told to him by the poet Saint-John Perse (Alexis Leger Leger). Once while he was living in Washington, Einstein called Perse from Princeton and asked him to come and see him. 'I have a question to ask you,' said Einstein. Saint John Perse did visit Einstein, and the great physicist put to him the question: 'How does the poet work? How does the idea of a poem come to him? How does this idea grow?' Saint-John Perse described the vast part played by intuition and the subconscious. Einstein seemed delighted. 'But it's the same thing for the man of science,' he said. 'The mechanics of discovery are neither logical nor intellectual. It is a sudden illumination, almost a rapture. Later, to be sure, intelligence, analysis, and experiments confirm (or invalidate) the intuition. But initially there is a great forward leap of the imagination.'"[6]

A related kind of illumination and rapture was experienced by Swami Vivekananda one day in India when he was a young monk in 1890. Let us tell the story of a discovery by him as passed on by Swami Akhilananda: "At one time Swami Akhandananda took Swami Vivekananda to the bank of a river, a tributary of the Ganges and they took a bath and sat down to meditate. After about six hours Swami Akhandananda opened his eyes and saw that Swami Vivekananda was still deeply absorbed in meditation. He waited a few hours but still Swami Vivekananda remained absorbed in meditation. It was quite some time before Swami Vivekananda opened his eyes. Then he said to Swami Akhandananda, 'Ah, brother, what a great favor you did for me today by bringing me here. Today I have realized that what is in the macro-cosm is in the microcosm"[7] Then Swami Akhilananda said: "You cannot comprehend the greatness of such a realization."[8]

For that whole day the Swami Vivekananda maintained a rapturous, high state of mind.[9] Swami Vivekananda noted at that time" "... The microcosm and the macrocosm are built on the same plan. Just as the individual soul is encased in a living body, so is the universal Soul in Nature... This dual aspect of the Universal Soul is eternal. So what we perceive or feel is this combination of the Eternally Formed and the Eternally Formless."[10] In New York City in January, 1896 he delivered two lectures on the Cosmos based on his experience.[11] He had looked into the basic pattern in nature, in the universe, and in all life. One could say that this was science -- a discovery by a spiritual man -- In 1988 the physicist-astronomer Stephen Hawking said: "To discover something new about the universe. That is a tremendous joy."[12]

In the building of the chapel as instigated by President Killian, the MIT Corporation engaged Eero Saarinen, who designed "a round chapel surrounded by a moat to reflect dancing sunshine onto its interior walls."[13] The round chapel was criticized for its design. Killian writes: "Those who had not experienced the reverential quality of the chapel's interior and its lovely altar and Bertoia screen crudely described it as a 'gas tank'. Today it is on the itinerary of sightseeing buses... In an article in <u>Time</u> magazine (May 7, 1984) architectural critic Wolf von Eckardt described Saarinen's chapel as 'one of 20th century architecture's greatest triumphs.'"[14] The whole intent of the design of the chapel was to avoid any bias; "the chapel itself should not express commitment to any particular tradition."[15] The chapel was dedicated on Sunday, May 8, 1955. Swami Akhilananda would be one of the chaplains.

It would appear from his engagement diaries that Swami Akhilan-anda started having student interviews at MIT in early January, 1955, and also services. Some would be scheduled at times for Monday, or Tuesday or Friday. Not until the fall of 1956 and the beginning of 1957 were his services and interviews on a Friday afternoon, the former at 5:15 pm and the latter at 2:30. During the year he would be at MIT for meetings, sometimes frequently, at other times on occasion, or attend a conference or luncheon meetings with the deans.

In addition to his expanding activities such as the chaplaincy at

MIT, Swami Akhilananda in the early 1950s belonged to several groups who had an interest in religion from a scientific point of view or in its practical application. One of these was the Institute of Religion in an Age of Science, which was founded by Prof. Ralph Wendell Burhoe, then Executive Officer of the American Academy of Arts and Sciences.[16] He wanted to bring together scientists and religious scholars, clergymen, and those with an interest for a more harmonious relationship between science and religion.

Prof. Burhoe recalls that he and Swami Akhilananda worked together in its development, "which was a group of a few hundred persons at most..."[17] Swami Akhilananda's contribution was important "because he was so familiar with two major religious cultures: the Christianity of the West and the Hinduism of the East. He seemed to have a natural and almost instinctive tendency to translate from one to the other, back and forth. But he was also especially concerned with the sciences and the implications of the sciences for religion. I found him interested in the whole range of the sciences from the physical to the psychosocial and their implications for human values and religion. ...He became with a few dozen others a member of the Advisory Board of IRAS, and a faithful participant in and contributor to its annual conferences during a midsummer week on Star Island (ten miles out in the Atlantic Ocean from Portsmouth, NH) as well as to its smaller occasional meetings in the neighborhood of Boston during the 1950s and until his death."[18]

In 1960 a book was published, *SCIENCE PONDERS RELIGION*, ed. by the astronomer Harlow Shapley. It was a collection of essays which he selected, written by the scientists who participated in the IRAS conferences at Star Island. Prof. Shapley introduces his book: "The Star Island group, consisting of laymen, clergy from various denominations, and scientists from several disciplines and from a score of universities and colleges, come together to inquire, discuss, answer - and some of them put their thoughts on paper."[19]

The book comprised their thoughts on the universe and ethics while asking such questions as "Is the administration of the universe purposeful?" and "Will it be possible to develop an ethical system more suited to our dramatic times than are the ethical systems of less sophisticated cultures?" or, "Will the now widely accepted hypothesis of highly developed sentient life throughout the stellar universe affect religious creeds?"[20] Prof. A. G. Huntsman of the University of Toronto would state: "In this life of change the eternal seems beyond comprehension."[21] - a challenge to a Swami or clergyman or even to a fellow scientist.

A group of scientists and the clergy would get together in the late evening for discussion and hilarious talk. It was called the Owl Session and would last until two in the morning. The group didn't realize that Swami Akhilananda would get up at four in the morning. He loved these occasions and the wit and banter that went with them. Swami must have enjoyed the following told by Prof. R. W. Gerard of the University of Michigan: "It is salutory to keep in mind the patient who came to a psychiatrist, continuously snapping his fingers. The psychiatrist, thinking this symptom a good starting point, asked about the snapping. 'That's to keep away the wild elephants,' 'Very interesting. Of course, you know that the nearest wild elephant is seven thousand miles away, don't you?' 'Certainly. Effective, ain't it!'"[22] Giving Swami a good chuckle.

At the Star Island conferences which Swami Akhilananda attended and participated in. Prof. Shrader wrote: "A session in which he presided was crowded."[23] Throughout the Western world this dialogue between men of science and men of religion would continue off-and-on throughout the 20th century. Beginning in the 1960s a rash of books on science, religion and the humanities would be published. *THE PHILOSOPHICAL IMPACT OF CONTEMPORARY PHYSICS*, by Capek; Heisenberg's *PHYSICS AND PHILOSOPHY; THE MEANING OF EVOLUTION*, by George Simpson, and later *THE TAO OF PHYSICS*, by Capra; *DIALOGUES WITH SCIENTISTS AND SAGES*, comp. by Renee Weber; and the magazines Main Currents in Modern Thought and Re-Vision.

Ralph Burhoe voices one of the concerns of thinking men and women: "This impact of science has led to the feeling that there is perhaps no existing religion - no socially transmitted set of ideas and ideals - adequate for a civilization confronted with the new circumstances, the new human environment, provided by science."[24]

Harlow Shapley, a dominant force in the Society, had become a good friend of Swami Akhilananda. On the 12th of November, 1947 at 1pm, presumably for lunch, the Swami and Shapley met at the Harvard Faculty Club. Swami gave a talk on Indian mysticism. On February 20, 1948 at 7pm Prof. and Mrs. Shapley were dinner guests of Swami

Akhilananda. In 1949 there were several times when they dined to-gether. This would be true, in the years following.

Swami Akhilananda in his lectures would speak of Shapley now and then. "The other day," he would say, "Prof. Shapley and I had lunch together. As soon as we came together we started talking of space. He asked, 'What is your definition of space?' and we spoke for 2-3 hours just on the 'space'. We ate but neither of us knows what we ate."[25] They would talk on the phone. Swami would relate: "Even the scientists say that nothing is lost - that the breath of Moses can be felt. Just think how many thousands of years ago Moses lived. Yet they say the breath of Moses can be felt. Prof Shapley and I have a joke between us. When he calls on the telephone, he asks if I can smell the smoke of a cigar. Since nothing is lost than the cigar smoke is not lost either."[26] (laughs)

Swami Akhilananda would be a guest, staying in a hotel at Shapley's summer place in Peterborough, NH on July 26 and 27, 1955. He had visited Peterborough on March 13, 1955. For the summer visit he had dinner with the Shapleys on July 26. He became friendly with the whole family. He recounts: "One of my friends, a very great scientist, jokes with me a lot. Both he and his wife are scientists... This scientist always says something to make me laugh, either when we speak on the telephone or in person. He has three sons and all are following in the parents' footsteps in science. One of the sons, the youngest son, is deeply interested in religion. This youngest son is also studying science and is a brilliant boy, but he is also deeply interested in religion. I joke with my friend sometimes and say, 'Well, what has happened here? You have produced a heretic.'"[27]

They had a long-lasting friendship and were in frequent contact for years. Harlow Shapley went to India in late 1960. He wrote a letter to Swami Akhilananda from Delhi, dated 12/18/60: "Dear Swami - Your friends are kindly and important in this town. Two of them met my plane. Two days later we had lunch at the Mission (we is Prof. Kushmaha), and just now (8pm) I have come from my lecture on <u>Religion in an Age of Science</u> for a packed house (at the Mission) of 1500 or 2000. They sat on the floors and stood around the edges, and around a loud-speaker in the court-yard. I hope I did some damage! But Swami Ranganathananda says that my phil-osophy is easy for them to accept. They made a recording, and

195

Swami R. was complimentary. With all their hospitals and schools they certainly are important saints. Swami R. says that *SCIENCE PONDERS RELIGION* is not yet here, but he plugged it and the forthcoming Hindi edition of *OF STARS AND MEN*. Thanks for your intercession and introductions.

"I trust you are pretty well - well enough to get some fun out of life and to eat a Happy New Year Goose or other fowl. Mrs. S. is in London. I go to Calcutta and Dacca and Chadigahr and Pooni for meetings, etc., and then Canberra, L. A. and home on 3/1/61.

"Be good! Harlow Shapley"

Years later in another context Swami Akhilananda wrote about Shapley whose lectures in different institutions and religious organizations "definitely indicate that he is going beyond the old materialistic attitude in trying to show the necessity of the religious attitude, based on reason and scientific validity."[28] Shapley was a great scientist and he brought his scientific attitude to bear on ESP, which he did not accept at that time without a thorough investigation into all its different aspects.[29] Harlow Shapley, a man of wit and wisdom.

Prof. Shapley gave his book *A TREASURY OF SCIENCE* to Swami Akhilananda with the inscription: To Swami Akhilananda with the high regards of Harlow Shapley, September, 1956. Swami would delightedly tell that Harlow Shapley would carry in the pocket of his jacket a copy of Swami Vivekananda's *JNANA YOGA*.[30]

One other group that had a scientific focus to which Swami Akhilananda belonged was the Society for the Scientific Study of Religion, which met on the top floor of Emerson at Harvard.[31] Walter Houston Clark recalls that he first met the Swami at one of the early meetings about 1951 or 1952.[32] Prof. Clark writes: "From that time on until his death he attended practically all of the meetings of the Society and made important contributions to its program. As one of the co-founders and officers of the new Society I much appreciated the positive support and encouragement the Swami gave."[33]

The meetings of the Society were infrequent. The first one that Swami went to was in November, 1953, perhaps at Harvard; in 1955 on November 5 there was another meeting at Harvard lasting from 9am to 10pm. In 1956 the Society met on April 21 from 8:30 to 9pm, again on September 10 and 14 at the Boston City Hospital. There was a meeting at Harvard University from 8:45am to 5pm on December 8. And this was followed by a dinner party at 6:30. In 1957 there was an all day meeting in New York City on April 13th. On April 12th 1958 there was an all day meeting in New York City at the Columbia University faculty Club. Another in 1959 on April 11 from 9am to 3pm in Chicago.

Betty Bogert, a Christian minister of Lisbon, NH met Swami Akhilananda once at one of these meetings. She writes: ..."I happened to sit beside him at a meeting of the Society for the Scientific Study of Religion in the early 1960s at Yale University."[34] She was impressed, and continues to write: "I knew almost nothing about him. He spoke little. Yet he radiated such unique and transforming power that this one encounter left an indelible impression. Were I to attempt to paint his portrait, his almost transparent body could not get in the way of his gentle and penetrating power. ...Were I asked the question, 'What influence persuaded you in the direction of seeking God along the personal path of spiritual enlightenment for yourself and others?' I would point to the mysterious power in the spirit of Swami Akhilananda, whose light shines eternally in the lives of many."[35]

Swami Akhilananda was to belong to the Research Society for Creative Altruism founded by Pitirim Sorokin, Professor of Sociology Emeritus of Harvard University. Before meeting Sorokin, in early 1945 Swami Akhilananda became acquainted with Professor of Psychology, Gordon Allport of Harvard. They had lunch at the Harvard Faculty Club on March 8 at 12:30. They were to be good friends over the years. Later in 1945 on October 29, Swami Akhilananda had a meeting with Professor Sorokin at the Harvard Faculty Club at 12:15. Both these men were supporters of Swami and his work. Their friendships lasted until his death.

Pitirim Sorokin, condemned to death by the Russian Communists during the Bolshevik Revolution, and expecting, for thirty days to be shot by a firing squad, but reprieved by Lenin, was exiled from Russia with his wife in 1922.[36] Before coming to Harvard in 1930, Dr. Sorokin had been teaching in Minnesota for six years. He was to become the foremost sociologist in the U.S. with an international reputation. He wrote many scholarly books; one of his best-known is *THE CRISIS OF OUR AGE*.

Having witnessed the Russian Revolution, the first and second World Wars and all their horrors, Dr. Sorokin writes: "The unprecedented destructiveness, bestiality, and moral insanity of these convulsions - and the millions victimized by them - led me, in February 1946, to the decision to devote my free time from then on to the study of unselfish, creative love, and of effective techniques for transforming the motivational systems of man and thus transforming his socio-cultural universe."[37]

His studies and research in this area led to the publication of several books; *RECONSTRUCTION OF HUMANITY,* and *WAYS AND POWER OF LOVE*, the latter being one of the outstanding books of 1955. Having started the Harvard Research Center in Creative Altruism, Sorokin wanted to establish "a national and even international research society in this field, which could be an independent institution and could do the research and educational work of the Center on a larger and deeper scale.

"In accordance with this idea, I organized a meeting on October 29, 1955 at Emerson Hall, Harvard University of an initiatory group for discussion of this problem. The group consisted of Melvin Arnold, Dean E. F. Bowditch, Dean Walter H. Clark, Senator Ralph E. Flanders, the Rev. Duncan Howlett, Dr. F. Kunz, Prof. H. Margenau, Chancellor Daniel Marsh, Professors A. Maslow, F.S.C. Northrop, J. H. Shrader, R. Ulich, Dr. I.I. Sikorsky, and Swami Akhilananda. After a careful discussion the group unanimously voted that the Research Society for Creative. Altruism should be established..."[38]

Swami Akhilananda took an active part in organizing the Society. Prof. James Houston Shrader of Eastern Nazarene College writes: "He and I were frequent visitors at the home of Professor Sorokin in Winchester, where we planned the Research Society in Creative Altruism... The Swami deeply deplored the failure, of this organization to function, and joined with Professor Walter H. Clark in urging me to reorganize and carry on the work."[39]

Dean Walter Clark writes in his memoir of Swami Akhilananda about the Society:

"With his pregnant intuitive insights concerning the nature of society and his enormous energies, Dr. Sorokin was a creative genius, though not strong in the patience and tact that such a collection of intellectuals required if the Society were to emerge as the viable and influential scholarly society that it deserved to be. Largely because of friction with the Administrative Director and some of the members of the Council, the Research Society foundered several years later after some achievements but with very little money raised. I can remember very vividly several of the stormy Council meetings that threatened the demise of the Society even earlier than it actually occurred. Those of us on the Council who were Christians required the calming and tolerant offices of the Hindu Swami to remind us that patience and a focus on our great goals were an essential if the Society were to achieve its purpose. This he did with patience and a wit that again and again served to pour oil on troubled waters."[40]

In October 1957 this Society held its first Conference: "New Knowledge in Human Values" at the Kresge Auditorium, MIT. A two day affair, the participants in the Conference included Paul Tillich, Erich Fromm, Gordon Allport, Abraham Maslow, D. T. Suzuki, Walter Weisskopf, Jacob Bronowski, Gyorgy Kepes, Pitirim Sorokin and several others. Swami Akhilananda, a member of the Program Committee, participated in the final afternoon session.

The Conference papers, under the same title, were published in book form in 1959. Dr. Maslow in his Preface states the raison d'etre: "This volume springs from the belief, first, that the ultimate disease of our time is valuelessness; second, that this state is more crucially dangerous than ever before in history; and, finally, that something can be done about it by man's own rational efforts."[41]

Dean Francis Bowditch of MIT was important in organizing the Conference. He and Swami Akhilananda became good friends, Swami being friendly with the whole family. In the mid 1950s there were many dinner engagements and luncheons together, with Swami staying with the Bowditches at Rye Beach, NH on August 4, 1955. He would take their son, Ben, to the Window Shop, a popular restaurant in Harvard Square, for several luncheons. Or visit Mrs. Bowditch when she was a patient at the N.E. Baptist Hospital.

Swami Akhilananda made many friends in the academic world. Nor were his friendships limited to this group. He had an empathy for struggling souls, whatever their struggle was. A concerned and conscientious shepherd to those who approached him for spiritual guidance, he would occasionally dine with some. He was always encouraging. Dean Walter Clark says it well: "Hospitable to all walks of people, he was nevertheless most at home with intellectuals like himself, students, scholars, and scientists, particularly those who shared his devotion to the religious quest, even though few had advanced along the path as far as he. Professors Pitirim Sorokin, Gordon W. Allport, Robert Ulich, and O. Hobart Mowrer, as well as Clarence Faust and Dean Walter G. Muelder, were examples of the type of person he sought out as friends. ... It was not in his nature to be authoritarian, narrow, or intolerant either in his teaching or his writing, and it was his humility that brought out the wisdom in others at the same time that it recommended his own."[42]

Robert Ulich, Professor of education at Harvard, supplements and, in some ways, differs from Dean Clark's perception. He writes:

"The Swami was a highly-gifted man of wide international knowledge, but he was not an 'intellectual'. Rather, he had achieved that inner depth and unity, or that wisdom, which merges the rational and the trans-rational as well as the single items of knowledge into a coherent whole. ...

"Thinking of Swami Akhilananda and his friends, I am reminded of an experience I often had at large conferences} I found there that a certain type of men discover each other in the crowd by an instinctive sensitiveness. At Harvard the Swami's friends became acquainted without formal introductions. Some of them did not fit into the departmental niches of 'experts'. They were esteemed scholars with a great respect for painstaking research...[43]

In a previous passage Dr. Ulich had written: "Religion was for him (Swami Akhilananda) the achievement of a sense of universal belonging and at the same time of inner freedom that did not demand the sacrifice of the intellect. His mysticism did not contradict but transcended the empirical urge in man."[44]

Dr. Amiya Chakravarty, who taught at Boston University, happily recollects those times and occasions spent with Swami Akhilananda and his friends. "Through the Swami, I met two great men, his friends in Cambridge, Profs. Pitirim Sorokin and Gordon Allport. ... Both these men accepted the Swami as a supreme spiritual leader."[45]

Swamis Pavitrananda, Satprakashananda, Akhilananda, Vividishananda
in the ashrama at Marshfield, 1953

Dr. Pitirim Sorokin of Harvard University

Dr. Harlow Shapley of Harvard

21

THE COLLEGE CIRCUIT

For those interested in developing their spiritual life, or, if a person was troubled with a problem, Swami Akhilananda would grant interviews. More than once a person would find that the conversation never got around to the individual's question. Rather the Swami and his presence would cause a change, the atmosphere would become light, all minor problems or vexations would be forgotten, and the devotee or counselee would leave full of joy. Many experienced this. Whatever the purpose of the visit, it was already buried in time.

As Swami Akhilananda in his cooking for Maharaj (Swami Brahmananda) was very delicate in his flavoring of the food, so was he in his interpersonal relationships. How delicate he was in his dealings with others! Soft-spoken, attentive, at times tender, perceptive, encouraging, sympathetic, merry and uplifting. Which leads us to say that Swami Akhilananda's work in pastoral care was unusual. He seemed to know intuitively just what was appropriate and necessary.

He belonged to the Institute of Pastoral Care, which would become a part in his expanding circle. He served as a board member and attended meetings as often as he could. Another society, which he at times would attend, was the Fellowship of Reconciliation. A Quaker organization, it held meetings at the Friends Meeting House in Cambridge. In 1953 it had a two day conference on September 25 and 26th, which was of interest to him.

Swami Akhilananda was to be sought by many groups. His friendliness, his merriment and wisdom were pervasive. One of such groups was the Philosophics Anonymous where he participated in "sophisticated philosophical discussions".[1] Dr. Janette Newhall of B. U. School of Theology describes it: "…monthly meetings of a small group of professors from Andover-Newton Theological Seminary, Boston University, Episcopal Theological School, Harvard, Tufts, and Wellesley.. Swami was a faithful attendant and took his turn at leading the discussions. His comments were always integrative rather than divisive. He had a great capacity to enter into the thought of another person and to feel kinship and sympathy."[2]

Following the 1956 Conference on Science, Philosophy and Religion, Swami Akhilananda went to Chicago on September 1st for another conference, the name of which is not known. From what is known, Swami Akhilananda saw Dr. O. Hobart Mowrer every day from September 1 thru 4. On September 3rd Swami Akhilananda had dinner and discussion with the group on the topic of "Religion and Psychology".

Swami Akhilananda, in addition to local speaking engagements such as the one he had in Braintree, MA Congregational church on the evenings of October 24 and November 7, 1955, or giving a lecture at the Roslindale, MA Unitarian church on March 27 at 7pm, plus a host of similar commitments, spoke and lectured at a number of colleges throughout the year. In 1955 there were 13 such occasions.

It was a natural for Swami to speak to college students. He caught their wave-length. He understood the times. Whenever he could, he would speak and inform the students. He would immediately put them at ease and answer all their questions. Vivekananda used to do the same.

In the spring of 1897 what did Swami Vivekananda say when he was on a visit to Calcutta? "Educate, educate, than this there is no other way,"[3] as he turned to a disciple. How true this was for the American people. How many knew of the Upanishads, the Bhagavad Gita, the universal sacred scriptures of the Vedic seers applicable to our modern problems, and even know today of Swami Akhilananda's recent book, *Hindu View of Christ*?

Everywhere there was a need for reliable knowledge. Would there be more mature young men and women who would dedicate themselves to whatever tasks lay ahead for a better humanity everywhere? Swami Vivekananda thundered against casteism, priestcraft, the tyranny over women. He wanted people to be free with a sense of responsibility. While in Calcutta in January 1898, Vivekananda had said: "We want that education by which character is formed, strength of mind is increased, the intellect is expanded, and by which one can stand on one's own feet."[4] This was Swami Akhilananda's aim also as he said on more than one occasion to his students. Counselling and writing his several books, it is said that Swami Akhilananda was a living example of what he taught. For him there would be many talks at different colleges in the years ahead.

He attended a dinner meeting at Chicago University on March 25th, 1955. This followed his two day visit to Toronto. The group that he addressed there were students from Victoria College planning to enter the ministry who "believe that your approach to Christianity would enhance our knowledge and stimulate our thinking."[5] Swami spoke to them on the subject of "Comparative Religions". The letter continues: "We understand that you will speak to us in Alumni Hall, Victoria College, University of Toronto... on Monday and Tuesday evenings, February fourteenth and fifteenth."[6] In addition to his lectures, Swami had lunches with the students, attended dinner and tea time. There were also trips to the city. One of his students, Isabel Beveridge, a blind social worker, told that the Jewish students thought he would make a wonderful rabbi, the Catholics voiced the same liking and admiration - if only he were a priest, and the Protestants felt he would make a great minister.[7] All these separate groups of people were enthusiastic.

Swami Akhilananda was to go to Pembroke College in Providence and also Brown University on February 22nd,1955 where he spoke with the students and had lunch and dinner at Brown University. He would be at Harvard University on February 23rd at 2pm, the reason for this unknown. On March 2nd he would be at Brown University again to speak on Hinduism. He was at Chicago University on May 6th when he participated in the chapel service and the dedication service at 8 in the evening. What was being dedicated was not mentioned. He met, however Prof. and Mrs. Paul Schilpp for dinner at 6pm. On Nov. 16 he was at Yale University Divinity School for a meeting lasting from 11:30am to 3pm. An hour Later he met with Prof. F.S.C. Northrop. On November 22nd he went to Philadelphia and then to Haverford College where he met Prof. Douglas Steere and attended a meeting until noon, having lunch at 12:30 and then a lecture at 1:30. The previous Sunday on the 20th, Wheaton College students attended a class at Providence Center in the evening. Not to be forgotten are Swami Akhilananda's meetings at Boston University School of Theology on October 28 and participating in chapel services there on November 15th and December 2nd. On November 12th he had been at the Tufts Theological School for a meeting with the Greater Boston Biblical Society.

Swami Akhilananda was to be in New York City in January, 1956. A psychologist there, Lee R. Steiner, a consultant in personal problems, invited Swami to appear on Psychologically Speaking - WEVD University of the Air. He was to talk on the topic "How to Cure Emotional Tension". The program would be recorded on January 27th and would be broadcast on February 16 from 9-9:30pm.[8] The university of the Air focused on human relations and invited authors of current books to be its guests.

Going out of New England on these trips, Swami Akhilananda traveled everywhere by train. He would reserve a sleeper so that at night he could get some rest and sleep, traveling between his appointments. He did not go by airplane, not even when he went to India. He had promised someone he would not fly. His travel by train gave him a chance to write letters, read, and have a little privacy.

On January 11, 1956 he was at Wellesley College from 10am to 1:30pm, but the reason is not clear. Perhaps a seminar and following which to have lunch with the students or faculty member. In the midst of February, the coldest month of the year, he went to Albion College, a liberal arts college in Michigan for February 16th where he participated in a chapel service, gave a lecture to a sociology class, had a lunch party, and then went to Chicago to the Vedanta Society.

The following day he went to Urbana, Illinois to the University, where he had lunch, met Dr. Hobart Mowrer, and was part of an afternoon chapel service. He then returned to Chicago. On the 18th he gave a lecture at the School of Theology, Chicago University in the morning at 9am and was there in the afternoon at 3, having had lunch with some of the professors. On the 19th he left Chicago again for Albion where he gave a lecture at the college at 6:30pm and was entertained by professors and friends from 8pm to 10pm. At Albion for the 20th he gave several lectures in the morning, the subject of which is not known; a lecture at 1pm on Hindu philosophy, another lecture at 2 with a lecture on religion in America at 3pm. In the evening he attended a dinner party. He gave two lectures on the 21st; one on sociology at 8am and one on modern religion at 9am. At 10:30 he left for Ann Arbor and the University of Michigan where he had lunch and a lecture from 12:15 - 2:30. At 4:15 he gave a lecture on Hindu psychology. He had dinner with one of the minister and his wife. He was at a lunch party at 12:30

the next day, February 22, with a religious group from University of Michigan. At 3:15 he traveled to Rochester, NY.

There, on February 23rd, he had a busy day. He saw several devotee friends, met Dr. David Rys Williams of the Unitarian Church and his wife, attended a ministers' meeting at 12:15, saw more friends for interviews in the afternoon, went to a dinner party at 6:30pm, gave a lecture at 8, more interviews followed, and caught the 11pm train for Boston.

He gave a lecture at Brown University on February 27th at 10am. We don't know the topic or the class or classes he gave it to. He was at Wheelock College on March 1st at 10:15 until 12:30 when he saw Professor Herrick of Andover Newton Theological School. On March 9th he was in St. Louis, Missouri, where he was feted by Swami Satprakashananda all day with lunch and dinner parties. On March 10th he was in Kansas City to lecture at Kansas State College, following which in the late afternoon he left for Pittsburg College where he spent the next two days in discussions and meetings. There was a lunch party with the students. On March 12, at 9am he was part of a convocation service, gave a lecture at 10 on The differences of Reality in contrast to his lecture at the convocation service: The Reality of differences. Then followed four lectures on psychology, adolescent psychology, a school lecture at 1pm, another lecture on psychology at 2, followed by a lecture; Do religious teachings conflict with societal justice? At 3:45pm he gave a talk at a faculty meeting on religion in education.

The indefatigable Swami then returned to Kansas. The next day he was in Chicago, spending the day with Swami Vishwananda, and leaving at 10pm for Boston by train. On March 22 he traveled to New York City and attended a two day meeting of the Metaphysical Society at Fordham University on March 23 and 24. While he was in New York, on March 26th, he was at the American Association for Advancement of Psychotherapy Graduate School on Monday morning at 11. At 1pm he attended a board meeting of the Parliament of Religions. Then to Philadelphia in the afternoon to meet with Dr. Rose and psychiatrists from 4-9pm. After which he traveled to New York and home to Boston. On April 5th at 5pm he gave a talk at MIT on mysticism in the student lounge. At the end of March on the 29th he was again in New York for the dinner of the Jewish Theological Seminary at the Waldorf Astoria.

For July 18 and 19, 1956 he was at the University of Vermont at Burlington and on October 24 he gave a talk on altruistic love at Yale University. He was present at B. U. School of Theology on November 5th for a function that lasted from 4:40 to 10:30pm. He met with Dr. Douglas Steere at Haverford College on November 13th and participated in a seminar on <u>Religion in Education</u> at the Harvard Graduate Center on November 16th and 17th sponsored by the Religious Education Association, Harvard. His last college talk for the year was on December 18th at Brown University where he gave a lecture in a meeting that lasted from 6 to 9:30pm.

In 1948 and also 1949, Swami Akhilananda's contact with colleges and universities was confined to New England; however, in less than 10 years his college circuit had expanded to include the mid-West. Over the years he maintained a relationship with N. E. colleges such as Boston University, Brown University, Harvard University and its Divinity School, and Andover-Newton Theological School, at which places he would be invited to speak or visit during he school year.

In 1957 he would be at the B.U. chapel on January 9th at 8:45 in the morning to conduct the chapel service. On the 11th he was at Wellesley College from 9:30-1:30. What the occasion was we do not know. He traveled to Hartford, Connecticut on January 29, 1957 to lecture at the Hartford Seminary and had lunch with Dean Walter Clark. His lecture topic was pastoral psychology. There was a dinner party at 6pm, followed by discussions with the deans and professors. The next day on January 30th there was a breakfast party and a talk by Swami Akhilananda on Hindu contribution followed by conversation with Dean Walter Clark. He would again be in Hartford on May 23 and 24 for the Hartford Seminary Conferences.

On February 2nd, 1957 Swami Akhilananda visited Wheaton College to see Dr. and Mrs. Albin Gilbert. He gave a lecture at Rochester University Divinity School on February 12th at 11 in the morning. There was another lecture at 7:30 in the evening, the location of which is unknown, whether at the Divinity School or at a group gathering. On February 13th he was at B. U. at 7pm for a program on Brotherhood and Peace. On Sunday February 17th he visited Colby College in Waterville, Maine. Rev. Clifford Osborne of Colby College's Inter-Faith Association wrote the Swami a letter On March 8th 1957: ..."Your visit to us was so rewarding, so stimulating, and various students are still talking and thinking about what you brought to them. It is a general regret that you could not stay longer...."

February 19th, 1957 finds Swami Akhilananda at Grinnell College in Grinnell, Iowa. The first evening he had dinner and a party at Dr. and Mrs. Winston King's home and saw them the next morning at 8 o'clock. Swami participated in a chapel service and gave a talk on "Hindu view of life". Interviews followed and at 11 he gave a talk on the "Religion of the Hindus". A lunch party followed and then at 1:30 Swami gave a talk on "Hindu view of ethics". At 3 o'clock he left for Chicago where he would be at Northwestern University and meet with Dr. Paul Schilpp, associate professor of philosophy. Later he went to Chicago University and gave a lecture at 8 at the School of Theology. The following day he traveled to Urbana, IL to Illinois University to meet with Dr. O. Hobart Mowrer and his family, which would be followed by another party at Rev. Hines. These get-togethers of lunch and dinner parties would continue to the next day with Swami Akhilananda leaving on the 23rd for Chicago at 4pm in order to see Mr. Bowditch in the evening. On February 24th he left for Albion College where on the morning of the 25th there was a 7:15am breakfast party. At 9 o'clock he gave a talk on <u>Hindu view of Christ</u>; at 10 Swami was part of a chapel service and gave a talk on test of religious experiences. Then followed a lunch party. In the afternoon he gave talks on <u>Vedanta movement in America</u>, the <u>Contribution of the Gita</u>, and <u>Schools of Vedanta, Swami Vivekananda and Radhakrishnan</u>. A dinner party in the evening.

His lectures the next day were on <u>Hindu conceptions of God</u>, <u>Hindu view of Jesus</u>, and at the Chapel service, <u>Different religious experiences and methods</u>. There were interviews and then a student's party. His three day visit concluded with talks and lectures on <u>the Hindu family</u>, <u>the goal of religion</u>, <u>Methods and purpose of religion</u>, <u>Sociology of religion</u>, <u>and History of Hinduism</u>. In the evening after the dinner party, he spoke on international affairs. Then he took the 11pm train to Ann Arbor, Michigan, and the University of Michigan.

In inviting Swami Akhilananda, the program director, Harold Duerksen, had written: "We are happy to know that you will be on campus for we have heard only good reports of your previous visit here. You will want to know that we have arranged for you to speak to a number of psychology classes."[9]... Swami Akhilananda spoke at the request of the professors on <u>Hindu conception of man</u>. The Swami was requested to stay for a coffee hour on March 1st to speak on <u>Hindu view of Christ</u>, but he left at 3:30 for Boston and Sri Ramakrishna's birthday on Sunday, March 3rd.

Again he resumed his lecturing, being at the B. U. School of Theology on April 24 at 9am, Brown University at 7pm and gave a lecture to the Harvard University School of Business at 4:15pm. In March on the 7th he had gone to the Milton Academy to give a lecture on <u>How to know God</u>. He was at Hartford on May 23 and 24 for the Hartford Seminary Conferences. Again he attended the Jewish Theological Seminary dinner in New York on May 26th.

There would be a break in his college trips, but not in his lecturing. On May 27 at 3pm Swami Akhilananda entrained for Chicago, left there on the 29th for Seattle, writing to Charlotte Morrison on June 5, 1957: "I am having a very nice time with Swami Vividishananda." Swami had gone to Portland, Oregon. "He came even here with me. Swami Aseshananda and his students are also very nice to me." He would be leaving for San Francisco that afternoon. His itinerary included a stay in San Francisco until June 9th when he would go to Lake Tahoe where he would lecture on the 9th and attend the Institute of Philosophy through June 28th. He would then return to San Francisco and give a Sunday lecture on June 30th following which he would go to Santa Barbara and give a lecture on July 1st.

While he was at Lake Tahoe in June, 1957, he was staying with Swami Ashokananda. Some other devotees were visiting in the evening. Gargi(Marie Louise Burke) relates what happened: "They laughed over stories that Swami Akhilananda told, such as the one about Saint Theresa when she came down from heaven to see how things were going with her convents. Saint Peter had asked her to phone him. She phoned him from New York and Chicago, each time saying, 'Saint Peter? This is Saint Theresa. I find things going very well!' Then she phoned him from Hollywood and said: 'Hi Pete, this is Tess.' The Swamis laughed uproariously."

The next day there was a dinner party at one of the cabins. Swami Akhilananda gave out complex Indian recipes and told of how he had been mistreated while being Swami Paramananda's assistant in 1927. But there were amends for this period of hardship.

"I am amazed at it," he said, his face wreathed in smiles. "Such grace! I have no qualifications at all, and yet I am asked to speak everywhere, everyone loves me." Said by him so ingenuously, so unself-consciously.

Swami Ashokananda was getting ready to leave. "Swami Akhilananda said to him, 'I can see how much these people love you, and I love you; so I want to do something for them.'

"Now?" they asked

"Yes, now." Swami Akhilananda said with an air of mystery. "I want to do something."

Swami Akhilananda always had a little black box with him, about the size of a small matchbox. He carried it in his vest pocket. It was very sacred for it contained relics of Ramakrishna, Holy Mother, and Swamis Vivekananda and Brahmananda. Swami Akhilananda gave Swami Ashokananda a small bottle of Ganges water, which he then sprinkled on himself and the four devotees, Gargi, Edith Soule, Josephine Stanbury, and Helen Sutherland, having washed their hands and rinsed their mouths. Swami Akhilananda gave the small box to Swami Ashokananda, who touched it to his head. Swami Akhilananda then touched the top of the heads of the others.[10] He had blessed them as he had others in Boston and Providence or elsewhere who were close and devoted.

Meanwhile he wrote to Charlotte Morrison from Lake Tahoe on June 19th. Evidently she was doing some work on a manuscript. Swami Akhilananda writes: "I do not know if I told you about a request Dr. Faust made to me. He asked me to write a book on spiritual practices. In fact he again reminded me when I met him on Sunday, May 26th. Well, let us see what can be done...You will be glad to know that I have been giving interviews between the lectures and classes."

Subsequent to Santa Barbara he went to Hollywood and Swami Prabhavananda, from there to its monastery at Trabuco, where he gave a lecture, and then to Chicago and Boston. Swami Akhilananda would continue to be a guest at B. U., being there on April 24 at 9am, ostensible for a chapel service, again on October 30 for a workshop at the School of Theology, and on December 5th and 6th, when on the latter date he gave a talk on Hinduism.

It is almost redundant to keep repeating year after year all the colleges that Swami Akhilananda lectured at. Suffice it to say that in 1958 he was invited to 16 different colleges, including Bowdoin College, Franklin College and Bradford Jr. College. While he was at Bowdoin, a student spoke to Swami Akhilananda saying:... "that his psychiatrist

212

told him that all mystical experiences are hallucination. The answer for the boy was in a form of a questions 'Is he not having hallucinations himself when he makes such a statement without authentic observation and experimentation?' He may be acquainted with a certain type of psychiatry, but this does not mean necessarily that he is aware of the total mind."[11]

After meeting Dr. and Mrs. Gordon Allport on December 16 at 6, he was at Harvard Divinity School at 8:15, the purpose of which we do not know.

What shouldn't be forgotten were his frequent trips to New York City where he met old friends like Dr. Allen Claxton and his wife, and made many new ones. Over the years beginning in the 1930s Swami Akhilananda had tried to establish Centers in Washington D.C. and Philadelphia. New York City was a stop on the way. While discontinuing his trips to Washington, he continued to go to New York City and Philadelphia many times a year. There he became well acquainted with intellectuals and others interested in philosophy and religion.

One of these was Dr. Ordway Tead, former chairman of the Board of Higher Education of New York City and vice-president of Harpers. He had many meetings with him as he did with his good friend Dr. Clarence Faust. Occasionally he would dine with Dr. Faust and his wife. Another close friend was Dr. Emil Gutheil of the Postgraduate Center for Psychotherapy. Mrs. Gutheil in a letter of January 31, 1963 wrote that Swami Akhilananda always came to visit Dr. Gutheil when he was in New York, "He was a wonderful and understanding man." Swami saw frequently Dr. Richard Evans of the Presbyterian Church and on occasion Dr. Fritz Kunz. Renee Weber writes about Dr. Kunz in her book DIALOGUES WITH SCIENTISTS AND SAGES: "He was the earliest pioneer of the current movement that tries to reconcile science and mysticism, and the first to call attention to what he felt were remarkable similarities between Western science and the wisdom traditions of India and Greece."[12]

Dr. Fritz Kunz, who became a good friend of Swami Akhilananda, founded the Center for Integrative Education in New York City, which drew many prominent scholars for lectures and seminars. In 1956 Swami Akhilananda spoke at the Buddha Jayanti which was held there, a series of three programs, the Swami speaking at the last session on May 20, 1956. Other speakers were Prof. Donald Tewksbury of Teach-

ers' College and the Grand Lama Dilowa Hutukhtu. They were followed by Swami Akhilananda. On this third program of the Buddha
Jayanti there was an overflow audience.

Swami Akhilananda would on occasion meet Father La Farge, Dr.
Douglas Steere, Dr. Anderson of the Academy of Religion and Mental
Health, and Dr. Ruth Anshen, who planned and edited a series of books
called World Perspectives. She writes that "the thesis of World Perspectives that man is in the process of developing a new consciousness,
which, in spite of his apparent spiritual and moral captivity, can eventually lift the human race above and beyond the fear, ignorance, and
isolation which beset it today."[13] His other friends in New York, Dr.
and Mrs. Grumble, Dr. and Mrs. Engle, Richard Adair, and numerous
devotee friends, who wanted interviews, kept Swami Akhilananda very
busy.

Swami Akhilananda's contacts and association with the contributors
to the Conferences on Science, Philosophy and Religion, his work with
the professors and deans in the Boston, Cambridge, and Providence ar-
eas, his lectures at various colleges and universities, through all of
these his name became known to many of the crème de la crème of
academic and intellectual life in the United States.

"His modesty was as great as his competence," wrote Dr. Dana
McLean Greeley, President of the Unitarian-Universalist Association,
"and he was at home among the intellectuals and the literati on the one
hand, and the meek and poor in spirit, on the other hand."[14]

22

WINDS OF CHANGE

At Thanksgiving time in 1958, Swami Akhilananda was stricken with a severe case of shingles on the left side of his chest, covering a large area with blisters. It curtailed his activities for several months. It was the first of several illnesses he would have in the following years. Dean Walter Muelder of B. U. School of Theology writes: "In the face of physical suffering he was a patient and courageous man. He experienced a great deal of pain in his later years. He tried not to let it interfere with his ministry in Boston and Providence."[1]

He went about with his appointments and interviews in early the 1959. He would still conduct the pujas, the special worship services. He would see friends: Dr. and Mrs. Amiya Chakravarty, Dr. Pitirim Sorokin, Dr. Harlow Shapley and attend a few meetings: American Academy of Arts and Sciences, the Philosophy Association, and he gave a talk at the Congregational church in Natick on Feb. 22nd. On Feb. 25th he had an appointment at Boston College, conducted the worship of Sri Ramakrishna on March 11th, and gave a wonderful talk on Good Friday, March 27th. On April 1st he took Dr. and Mrs. Robert Ulich to lunch at the Window Shop in Cambridge. He went to Rochester, MY on April 2nd and then on to Albion College, the University of Michigan at Ann Arbor, returning to Chicago and then on to Boston by mid-April. On the 19th he gave an evening talk on Hinduism at St. Paul's church, Boston. On the 21st he had lunch with Dr. and Mrs. Dana Farnsworth at the Window Shop. Then to New York City on the 24th for a meeting with his good friend the psychiatrist, Dr. Emil Gutheil, President of the American Association for the Advancement of Psychotherapy, and to attend a meeting of psychiatrists at 8pm. This would be followed the next day with another meeting with the psychiatrists from 9am to 2pm. On the 28th of April he left for Miami as the guest of Richard Adair. He would be vacationing there for two weeks. This had been the Swami's custom since 1955. Although he had lessened his activities, they were hardly out of sight.

It was going to be his last trip to California. 1959 was the year when Swami Ashokananda was dedicating his New Temple in San Francisco. The two Swamis had been invited, Akhilananda and Sarvagatananda, and they left Boston by train. Swamis Vividishananda, Aseshananda, Satprakashananda, Bhashyananda, Nikhilananda and Pavitrananda would also be present there. Swami Sarvagatananda has said that in traveling across the country with Swami Akhilananda "It was just heaven." Relaxing in their suite, they enjoyed each other's company. Swami Sarvagatananda was having his first glimpse of the American continent. Swami Akhilananda's shingles had improved just a little.

The dedication of the New Temple was at the autumnal festival for the Divine Mother. The entire program lasted several days. It was also a vacation time for the Swamis, being able to enjoy the company of Swami Ashokananda and each other's and to meet with the devotees, some of whom had traveled across the country for the dedication.

Swami Akhilananda was a guest at the ashrama, located on the northern side of Lake Tahoe in California. Others were there also. A novice, assigned to Swami Akhilananda, who would take care of his meals, do his errands, and drive him to wherever he wanted to go, recalls those precious days. He writes: "A devotee, having seen the warm, genial Swami Akhilananda interact with all sorts of people, remarked of him that 'he could melt anyone down', and so, in my opinion, he could; that summer I had ample occasion to see him melt people down by virtue of what he was - a holy man full of infectious joy, with a heart for all and sundry, who made people feel good about themselves without quite understanding why. Something of the bliss he was steeped in rubbed off on you."[2]

The novice, Vimukta Chaitanya, stayed with the Swami in his cabin. He recalls the beautiful setting, "the shadows lengthening at the close of a warm day", the mixed blue-green colors of the lake, as several people were seated on the porch in deck chairs, "in Swami Akhilananda's holy presence". All were waiting for the Swami's words as he recalled Maharaj, Swami Brahmananda. It seems that Akhilananda as a young devotee in his teens was seated with Swamis and novices in Swami Brahmananda's presence. Swami Akhilananda, called Nirode, was then recovering from tuberculosis. Solicitously, tenderly Swami Brahmananda inquired about his health. In a moment, without any hesitation a brahmachari burst out with "What love you have for us, Maharaj!" Swami Brahmananda looked across the Ganges to Dakshineswar and pointing his outstretched arm, he said, "What love we saw there!"[3]

Swami Akhilananda would often in his lectures in Boston tell of this occasion with Swami Brahmananda. Swami Akhilananda impressed on our minds the love that Maharaj had and the love that Ramakrishna gave.

Swami Akhilananda had been traveling around the country in the 1950s and in the 1940s, participating in conferences, going to different colleges, meeting and talking with diverse groups, picking up feedback from his friends and colleagues in such organizations as the Institute of Pastoral Care, from various clergymen and psychotherapists, and in doing so, what did he find? What were the times like?

After the second World War, there hovered over the country distrust between the U.S. and the USSR, the Cold War. Then there was the era of McCarthyism from 1950-1954 when Americans were falsely accused of spying for Russia or of being a Communist. In a lecture of April 3, 1950, Swami Akhilananda gave an indication of the political climate: "And Prof. Hocking is also called a Communist. I would like to see another man as Hocking in this country - as truthful, as good, as honest, as liberal and generous, of such sterling character. Such integrity; He is a good Christian and yet there are people who say he is a Communist..." Another witch hunt was in progress.

The many tests of atomic weapons and the building of bomb shelters brought apprehension and fear of an impending third World War. Even as early as the summer of 1948, Swami Akhilananda disclosed a little of his concern. "The Compton brothers (Compton, Arthur Holly, 1892-1962, Nobel prize winner in physics, and Karl Taylor Compton, 1887-1954, physicist and president of MIT, 1930-1948) and other such thinkers think calamity is just around the corner... They mean within the next ten years. Prof Cadbury – I don't know how many of you know him - he is now the leader of the Friends' organization - he said to me recently, 'You know, Swami, I am not so afraid of the Russians as I am of my own country.'"[4] Swami Akhilananda was uneasy as to whether peace would last with world conditions the way they were in the 1940s and 1950s. The troubled times were often on his mind. What might this country face in the future? "I would hate to tell you what I see for this country,[5] he said in February, 1949. With sadness he disclosed his thoughts and his ominous feelings about the America of tomorrow. Now with school children killing school children, the rising rate of homelessness, the possibility of only a two-class society, and other social problems, it seems he was foresighted. Discouraged, but at the same time hoping for the best, Swami Akhilananda remarked a year later: "This country is not yet mature. There is a tendency to be unstable as in children. But experience will teach... This country has the tendency to make experiments in new things. You have got youthful vigor and enthusiasm. Maybe this very thing will save."[6]

Although it may seem that the Swami was pessimistic in pointing out the inadequacies in our culture, his outlook was that this is a great time to be alive. No one came away from his lectures feeling discouraged. Or depressed. Rather encouraged and uplifted. "Wait and see," he would say. He knew there would be a change.

In the later years of his life in the summer of 1959 at the ashrama in Marshfield, MA., Swami Akhilananda told a group of his friends that he was writing four books. One of them turned out to be *MODERN PROBLEMS AND RELIGION* in which his concern for our civilization pulsates throughout. In his preface the Swami lists what he felt the contemporary world was facing: political, racial, international, family, labor-management, and educational problems. He mentions the names of many prominent thinkers and scholars who were trying to do something constructive about contemporary conflicts and tensions. "We are thoroughly convinced," writes the Swami, "that the contemporary problems cannot be solved unless we have basic understanding of religion and its application in life."[7] By basic understanding of religion, he did not mean only the observance of rituals and ceremonies or attendance at some institution, but the application of the basic principles as taught by Jesus, Buddha, Krishna, Lao-Tse, great Islamic leaders and great Jewish prophets.[8]

Considerable stress in the book is given to education in our schools and colleges. In 1948 Swami Akhilananda remarked in a lecture that he had been following the speeches made by the presidents of universities to see the trend of their thought. He had been doing this for about ten years.[9] Again, in *MODERN PROBLEMS AND RELIGION* he writes about university presidents: "They express their ideas in such a way that it seems they want to convert the universities and colleges into technological institutions... It may be said that some college presidents regret the trend in the educational system and still advocate general culture for the students... We often observe that the development and integration of the emotions are pitifully ignored by these systems; in fact, the growth and integration of personality is completely neglected... This trend certainly reflects the understanding of the culture itself by the educators."[10]

Joseph Campbell in *THE POWER OF MYTH* seems to concur with Swami Akhilananda: "What we're learning in our schools is not the wisdom of life. We're learning technologies, we're getting information. There's a curious reluctance on the part of faculties to indicate the life values of their subjects."[11] The emphasis on technology was leaving a vacuum in the educational system: spiritual values and cultural standards. Albert Einstein issued a warning: "It is essential that the student acquire an understanding of and a lively feeling for values. He must acquire a vivid sense of the beautiful and of the morally good. Otherwise he - with his specialized knowledge - more closely resembles a well-trained dog than a harmoniously developed person.[12]

Swami's concern was with the young people, the students. Committees were being formed to try to remedy their emotional problems. "We know how disorganized," the Swami writes, "the students are in the high schools, colleges, and universities. They do not seem to realize that they should be responsible for their own actions."[13] The emotional reactions of the students were in need of change, and, as Swami Akhilananda said, "emotional training."[14]

The Swami evaluated this need of students, when he wrote in his paper, "Religious Culture and Integration", presented by him at the 1947 Conference on Science, Philosophy, and Religion: "Unfortunately, the modern educational system does not furnish anyone the methods for emotional integration ... The modern educational system should take into consideration that basic religious ideals are to be inculcated in young scholars..."

With serious thinkers considering how the educational system could be improved, how the emotions could be integrated and personality growth developed, Swami Akhilananda suggested: "What can religion do for us?"[15] He felt that religion should be the nucleus of the educational system. Scientific, technical, academic courses and other such types of training would supplement it, be inspired by it. This far-reaching suggestion also carried with it the insistence that teachers should not attempt to convert students from one religion to another. Dogmatic religion was not the way. Students needed an ideal of their own choosing.[16]

Nor would only an intellectual conception of a religious ideal integrate the emotions. Students would need the utility of religious practices. "Historical evidences," writes the Swami, "prove that we need something more than mere intellectual conception to manifest the dynamics of religion in personality. Herein lies the utility of religious practices."[17] Where spiritual practices were concerned he suggested that students cultivate the spirit of service. By cultivating the thought that God's presence is the innermost being of people and by doing something kind and loving for our fellow being we gradually remove negative and disorganizing elements in our emotional system.[18] This would apply to teachers as well. Their responsibilities would be not to interfere with a student's religious belief and in a thoughtful way clearly present the philosophical background of religion.[19]

Swami's focus was not only on service, but prayer, meditation, and worship for the students' emotional integration. "... real development of personality and emotional integration can be achieved only through the practice of concentration and meditation," so writes Swami Akhilananda. "We may have exalted ideals, yet, if we do not have sufficient will power, our emotions distract us..."[20] The emotions the Swami was referring to were uncontrolled emotions, disturbed mental states. "All the great spiritual personalities belonging to the various religions of the world recognize them as disturbing and destructive states of mind,"[21] the Swami continues. Our inordinate tendencies can be controlled through the practice of concentration and meditation.

In addition to service, Swami Akhilananda felt that young people should be encouraged to turn their negative and destructive emotions such as jealousy, hatred, anger, etc. into positive and constructive thoughts and actions. He writes: "Patanjali, the father of Hindu psychology, emphasized that the disturbing emotions can be properly redirected by the cultivation of opposite tendencies."[22] Such as St. Francis, overcoming his distaste of lepers, by giving one of them a kiss.

Teachers should try to train the students with love and sympathy, not with rigid authority. Young students are intuitive and understand the nature and motives of teachers and leaders.[23] Teachers themselves must try to attain integration of their emotions so as to be fully effective. The implementation of such a program would require tact and wisdom. As Swami Akhilananda said: "We cannot force a person into spirituality. If we try to force him his progress may be hindered. We understand his spiritual manifestation according to our own ideas, not according to the person's spirituality."[24]

This was an audacious and far-reaching agenda some 50 years ago. Swami Akhilananda's suggestions were not meant to imply a church governed program sponsored by the state. Separation of church and state would remain. Each community would work out its own program. Whatever its format and whether it would be for a public or private institution, the program of services at MIT might be considered as a model. "It is worthwhile for scholars and educational leaders to note the program being introduced for the good of the students in the Massachusetts Institute of Technology," the Swami writes. "Our heartfelt thanks go to former President Killian and his colleagues and co-workers for dedicating a chapel...where Roman Catholics, Eastern Orthodox Catholics, Protestants of various denominations, Jews, Vedantists, and others may worship and conduct their individual services. This is indeed a great effort to offer individual methods of spiritual development according to the mental make-up of individuals."[25] In addition he was a firm believer in ethical and moral conduct as a prerequisite to religious life. Such conduct made the mind stable and fit for spiritual practices.

Some of Swami's students felt that he was like a mother. He cared for the students and the country's future. He quotes his good friend Dr. Robert Ulich, Professor Emeritus of Education, Harvard University: "An education, therefore, which believes it thrives better without deeper metaphysical interest may produce a materially informed and busy society, but it will be one without depth. Sooner or later even its efficiency will run dry for lack of inspiration. It may be remembered for its quantity, but not for its quality.

"Such a society will lack the great ethical impulse. For a while it may live prosperously on legality and convention, but neither of them will produce the creative individuals who are the leaven of civilization."[26]

Swami Akhilananda felt that education should be presented in such a way that students would understand the higher values of life - otherwise they would find life frustrating if only given science and technology. If the higher values were included and students were able to integrate their emotions, they would also be able to harmonize their lives and develop their personalities. "Education without these achievements becomes meaningless,"[27] concluded the Swami.

MODERN PROBLEMS AND RELIGION was not published until after his death in 1964. It is in its last chapter that we see, his views on mass movements. Even before the counter-culture of the 1960's, Swami Akhilananda emphasized that in trying to develop people's higher or spiritual nature, attempts must be made individually. Spiritual growth doesn't take place in a mass movement.[28] Before one can change others he has to change himself. Mass movements have failed for this very reason. What does religious history tell us? That it is only a person of God consciousness who can awaken the desire for spiritual growth.[29]

The Swami explains: "Did Jesus start a mass movement in a big way to rescue souls? No. He spoke on the shores of Galilee, on the street corners, in small houses or huts. He talked with individuals, a tax collector, a fisherman, or an agriculturist. He inspired, molded and transformed the lives of these individuals with the teachings from his own dynamic spiritual realizations and experiences... There was no fanfare, no excitement, nor any attempt to produce a new civilization in a mass movement, which is the trend today. Human life cannot be really changed in that way. There must be a personal touch in the transformation of the soul of man."[30]

Swami Akhilananda reiterates this observation in writing about the disciples of Ramakrishna, who were overwhelmed at seeing Ramakrishna intoxicated with the love of God, and they were so inspired that the realization of God became very meaningful to them. Ramakrishna lived in a temple compound and did not give lectures to large crowds. Neither did his disciples with the exception of Swami Vivekananda. "They treated us with such love and affection... Love affects the souls of men. The touch of loving souls transforms the personality,"[31] so wrote the Swami about Ramakrishna's disciples. Even a deplorable person could be blessed if he or she saw a great personality.[32]

If the educational system and the students could benefit by fostering spiritual values, Swami Akhilananda felt that the philosophy of life, which was at the time too materialistic, could profit from a shift of emphasis and bring about a better balanced outlook for living. As early as 1946 in his book, *HINDU PSYCHOLOGY, ITS MEANING FOR THE WEST*, the

Swami considers the hedonistic philosophy to be the cause of troubles, psychological and otherwise, in individual and collective life.[33] He carries this conclusion into his latest book, *MODERN PROBLEMS AND RELIGION* when he writes: "The Western sensate philosophy has undermined the spiritual values of life."[34] And what would be the sensate philosophy of life? Eat, drink, and be merry - as if there was nothing beyond that, that was the be and end of all. He felt that those religious leaders who promoted humanism and Marxism could not keep at bay the "perils of the modern Western outlook on life. Many psychiatrists and psychotherapists also seem to feel that they can remove frustrations and mental conflicts of their clients and patients by psychoanalysis, autognosis, and so on, while clinging to the old outlook on life, the pleasure principle... The solution of unhappiness does not lie in these methods."[35] Swami Akhilananda didn't mean to give the impression that pleasure was a sin, something evil. To make it the only thing in life was unwise.

This book reflects his intense thoughts on todays problems. He felt strongly that the words and ideals of Jesus were pragmatic. So was the spirit of service which Ramakrishna emphasized and which was not mere philanthropy; such service being based on awareness of the divinity within. Such service would help to provide in its quality of giving an inspiration that people would respond to. It would in time help to foster a new outlook on life.

Some may say that Swami Akhilananda was a spiritual idealist. He would say that what he envisioned was based on Truth. On the words of Ramakrishna, Jesus, Buddha and other great personalities.[36] It has been said that in his later years the Swami "expressed the faith that soon some great break-through in the religious development of mankind would take place."[37]

In manuscript form *MODERN PROBLEMS...* was read by his friends Dr. Ordway Tead, former chairman of the Board of Higher Education in New York City, Dr. Harlow Shapley, Professor Emeritus of Harvard University, Dean Walter Muelder, Dean of the School of Theology, Boston University, Dr. Dana Parnsworth of Harvard University, and several other well-known academic friends. With Swami Akhilananda associating so frequently with professors, great scientists, psychiatrists and other intellectuals, what was it like for the ordinary person to attend his services? At that time in the 1940s and 1950s those attending were Americans, maybe one or two Indians, and a professor or two. There was no music. Listening for the first, or even the second time to one of his sermons, was an experience of trying to digest and assimilate a wholly new thought on the spot, immediately! His thoughts were stimulating, his quotations from the Upanishads, the Gita, or any other scripture were brought into the context of our own times. All the great disciples of Ramakrishna became part of his lectures. He even spoke of Ghirish Ghosh in such a way that Swami's reverence and regard could not be concealed, including Latu, Swami Turiyananda, Swamis Premananda, Shivananda, Saradananda, Brahmananda and Vivekananda - all jewels in a crown. When he would give talks on the Gita for his evening classes, he would include this disciple or that one as an example of what the Gita taught. The same would be true if he read a passage from an Upanishad. Nor did he hesitate to include a personality from another religion. He would often speak of Jesus or Buddha. And, of course, Ramakrishna and Holy Mother. This was true throughout his ministry. Now and again amidst such spiritual references would be scattered the observations of some scientists and contemporary thinkers. His sermons and classes were never boring, but uplifting.

In his sermons, there were times when he would speak of the unusual, such as; "St. Teresa of Avila described a very high state when she said that compared to the Effulgence the sun and the moon are pale... When I read that I was thrilled... when you see it you forget the world - you are not conscious of the world so attractive it is... And yet there is even a higher state than the shining Effulgence and that is the benign Presence. The passage says (in the Upanishads) 'Oh remove Thy veil and reveal Thyself.' In other words remove the veil of the Effulgence, because even there there is duality. God and the devotee, lover and beloved, and reveal Thyself to me. You see (leans forward) even greater than that shining Effulgence is the Presence."[38]

Swami always held people's attention. "Once you have tasted love you never forget it... You can never say that the romance is gone. Once a man loves, he loves. There is no waning of his love... one thing that these people feel is not love. It is a kind of fascination."[39] Or on another occasion: "From the Absolute standpoint there is no motion. Motion implies that something is going somewhere. There can be no 'somewhere' in the Absolute. It is Existence Itself... Blissfulness is our real nature."[40]

224

He would tell us: "Om is the sound of all sounds... I cannot help thinking in this connection of the Gospel of St. John 'In the beginning was the Word', etc. In the beginning was the Absolute and the Absolute manifested itself until, it gradually manifested as this world. From subtle to gross. It is the Logos of the Greeks ... If you utter the word 'Om', you notice it includes the whole region from the throat to the lips. It takes in all the sounds."[41] Or he would clue us in: "Nowadays if a scientific man accepts a spiritual force in the world, then he is labeled a 'mystic'... There are some like Eddington, etc. who believe in a spiritual basis ... There is one scientist, however, who is still acknowledged as one of the greatest scientists and has not been labeled a mystic even though he said that monistic Vedanta is not only possible, it is acceptable to a scientific mind. That man is Schroedinger, a German scientist now living in Ireland."[42]

Or he would tease our curiosity when he said: "when we were in Europe years ago we had dinner at the home of a great scientist in Switzerland. He is a botanist. After dinner we were speaking of different things..."[43] Who was this botanist?

Then he would be encouraging: "The nucleus of our potentialities is in us... All things are possible with God... There was an actress who used to visit Holy Mother and Maharaj. They treated her just like she was their own daughter. In time she gave up everything and went away to practice spiritual disciplines... It's through the grace of God if we have the desire to be changed... Anything is possible with God."[44]

He told us what he had learned from Swami Brahmananda and Holy Mother: "The spiritual teacher is the mother of emotional integration."[45] Swami Akhilananda had a captive audience. His Sunday services and evening classes were well attended. Dr. Frederick Shepard who knew Swami Akhilananda in Boston during the late 1940s and early 1950s, remembers him well. He writes: "For me he encompassed all that God can be in human form. He enabled me to taste the sweetness of a 'baby step' on a spiritual path. The perfect teacher that he was, allowed me to go anywhere in the world and realize a 'presence' no less precious than that of sitting at his feet in Boston."[46] Dr. Shepard was not the only one who had that realization.

Swami touched each life in an authentic individual way. In Providence Elizabeth Littlefield, as a high school student, early on, began asking questions about life. Her cousin took her to see Swami Akhilan-anda. She writes:

"... I clutched my list of questions, thinking it would be an out and out confrontation to the end. But, halfway through I began to feel very safe, quite comfortable and also so relieved. Not only could I live and believe it the right thing to do but everyone in the world must do it too... The world door opened wide... I was to be responsible doer to myself and to my fellow beings. It was the most wonderful revelation. This smiling empathetic wise one had seemingly answered all the daunting questions. His understanding and perception of my true nature gave me the opportunity to grasp a value system and way of life that would be truly meaningful. And how simply he had made this all possible."[47]

Dr. John Parks of Lexington, Kentucky came to Swami Akhilananda in 1949 while a medical student at Harvard. Swami influenced him to become a psychiatrist. Dr. Parks writes: "...I received a glimpse of what spiritual realization was all about by Swami's discussing Swami Premananda, Brahmananda, and of course the stories of Rama-krishna... I saw in Swami that self-realization or enlightenment was a practical goal in life... Through Swami's service and counseling to others I saw 'love in action'... I saw that he meditated every morning for several hours, so the actual doing and carrying out of these qualities came through meditation."[48]

Some students intuitively felt that Swami Akhilananda was like a father to them. How could this all-knowing, all-loving person be anything but! One devotee's mental imagery would be that he floated his children on the palm of his hand, so supportive yet leaving them to fly free. That this is what a good father did. Dr. John Parks acknowledged that Swami Akhilananda was a father to him and his wife. Swami, in one of his last letters to Dr. Parks acknowledged the relationship. To many Swami Akhilananda was like a father.

In whatever he was doing, Swami Akhilananda was a giver of happiness. One would not think that in merely saying "hello" or, in greeting Swami, in shaking his hand, one would feel so happy, but one did. He radiated joy without being over-bearing. Helen Rubel, who was devoted to him and who helped him financially, wrote to him from Shillong, India, sending her Vijoya greetings of October 10, 1940: "The people must appreciate more and more, as they understand gradually, all that you are giving them and doing for them... I hope that all come to understand spirituality better and better and get the happiness which you want to give..." The happiness which you want to give; words showing a depth of perception that would not be caught by all. Sister Nivedita in her biography of Swami Vivekananda, THE MASTER AS I SAW HIM, quotes him, who, at the end of a lecture, which was delivered in London, November 23, 1895, answered a question with: "Art is the most unselfish form of happiness in the world."[49] Even those in the arts are givers of happiness, for, isn't that true of all spiritually inclined persons? And is not the giving of spirituality, its happiness, the greatest happiness and the most subtle and greatest art? It may come as a surprise to find that that is true. Swami Akhilananda wanted to give and share his happiness. Somewhere Vivekananda said that spirituality can be given from one person to another. Swami Akhilananda quotes Swami Turiyananda in one of his sermons: "Swami Turiyananda said that there comes a stage when a spiritual person has the urge to give. And it is true. He has the urge to give and he gives and gives."[50]

James Houston Shrader, Professor Emeritus of Chemistry, Eastern Nazarene College, recalls one such moment: "Once he took me upstairs and told me that he wanted to share an experience... I felt a strange uplifting stimulation that lasted for several days."[51] William Page, one of Swami Akhilananda's students, writes: "You might come to him with many problems, with your mind distraught and upset; but after sitting with him for a while all that would vanish, and you would feel irradiated by bliss. This feeling would last for hours after you left him - sometimes even a day or more."[52] Swami Akhilananda was generous to a fault. So Swami Sarvagatananda has said many times.

Working too hard and not feeling well, nevertheless, on February 20, 1961 Swami Akhilananda went to Rochester, NY by train to meet with friends there. He went out to dinner the following evening, returned to his hotel and in the early morning of February 22nd, he telephoned to devotee, whom he had seen in the evening, that he was sick. He was rushed to Rochester's Strong Memorial Hospital. He had had a heart attack. From Boston, Mrs. Anna Worcester and Swami Sarvagatananda drove with a devotee to Rochester. They stayed there until his doctors, finding him recovered, discharged Swami Akhilananda on March 6, 1961.

During the summer of '61 he cut back on his activities, but visited the ashrama in Marshfield and he took the Sunday services in Boston. At the end of August, preparing to go to New York City, Swami suddenly had a stroke. Swami Sarvagatananda was summoned from Providence. Swami Akhilananda remained at 58 Deerfield Street where he was given medical attention. Some friends never saw him again.

Swami Akhilananda in the 1950s

Swamis Vishwananda, Akhilananda, Sarvagatananda in Boston

23

HIS LAST YEAR

G radually toward the end of 1961, Swami Akhilananda was improving. The effects of the mild stroke had lessened. His speech was all right. He stayed in his room, upstairs on the second floor, in Boston. Swami Sarvagatananda was attending to the work of the services, including MIT lectures on Friday afternoon.

The days must have been long long days for Swami accustomed as he had been to almost ceaseless activity. How many times he would drive during the week between Providence and Boston, perhaps more than once on a single day, to keep his appointments for interviews or to attend meetings. Those several trips each month to New York City and Philadelphia were a thing of the past.

For a time he could not see anyone. There would be no long conversations with his friends Prof. Gordon Allport and Harlow Shapley. Walter Houston Clark, who was a visiting professor at Andover-Newton Theological School, visited him during this time, which turned out to be his final farewell.[1] There is no doubt that Swami's thoughts were full of Maharaj. So sensitive and intelligent as he was, he must have known that his work would now be curtailed. But he was not one to complain. He was the most accepting of men. Once, years before, a devotee was in a hospital with an unexplained fever and she spoke of her anxiety and tension to him over the phone. "Submit," he said.[2] And so it was now that he did the same.

In January 1962 his doctors in Providence diagnosed a fever and pain in the body as a kidney infection and he was hospitalized in the Rhode Island Hospital, in the Jane Brown section. His worn-out body found it difficult to fight off the infection, which lasted for several months. At one point in March his life was despaired of. It took several months more for his strength to return. During this period Swami Sarvagatananda supplemented his hospital food with a nourishing broth.

From the end of August or early September, he was no longer at the hospital, but he did not go to either the Providence or the Boston Center. Instead Mrs. Worcester took him to the Kenmore Hotel in

Boston. She did not inform anyone where she had taken the Swami except her close friends. Swami Sarvagatananda was mystified. He came to Boston to see what he could find out. Walking up and down in Kenmore Square, he noticed the number plates of their car. Watching when the car drove away, he went into the hotel for a visit with Swami Akhilananda, who was very glad to see him. He requested Swami Sarvagatananda to go and stay in San Francisco and told him that Sri Ramakrishna had marked him for work here in the New England area.

Swami Akhilananda was not to stay at the hotel for long. His infection returned and he was moved to a nursing home in Wellesley. But that was unsatisfactory and the doctors moved him to the Peter Bent Brigham hospital in Boston. With his usual composure he endured. From what he had said in a lecture in Providence in 1948, we can infer that he had suffered during his life. "The more you can make yourself endure, the more you can endure."[3] And in February, 1950: "Swami Brahmananda used to say we had to have endurance, endurance, endurance, endurance (very gently)."[4]

During this time, Dr. Arun Kumar Biswas, who was at the time a student at MIT and known to the Swami for two years, came to know of his illness on 16 of September. Devotees took him to the third floor of the Brigham Hospital. Dr. Biswas writes:

"Swami Akhilananda was very pleased seeing us. He took my chin and blessed me, inquired about the coming Durga Puja and requested me to send rupees fifteen to the Belur Math in his name. I sang many songs before him for seven days. ...Music seemed to partially relieve his intolerable pain. I visited him daily except 21 and 22 September. Luckily for me I had the privilege of meeting him alive on the 23rd September, the day he passed away. I wish I had seen Swami's face while I chanted and sang; but I had closed my eyes with deep concentration and feelings. On 19 September he called me repeatedly to hear more songs. ...Swami Satprakashananda came from St. Louis to see Swami. ...Swami Akhilananda told us that 'they came to see me.' We inquired whether it was Sri Thakur and others. He replied, 'Yes, all of them.'" (At this point a devotee remembers this incident as told in 1962 that one evening the nurse and others noticed Swami Akhilananda with a fixed gaze staring at a certain point. They were interested and he said: "Don't you see them? They are all there.")

232

Dr. Biswas writes: "Sep. 23 (Sunday) I reached the hospital at 11 am and heard that the Swami's condition was precarious last night. Mrs. W. was there. ...Very soon Swami called me and uttered 'Radhakrishna'. I sang some songs on Lord Krishna.

"I suggested to Mrs. W. to bring some statue of Lord Krishna. ...I entered the room at about 1:30 pm to chant and sing more. Mrs. W. came back at 2:30 and showed Swami a statue of Lord Krishna, which he repeatedly saluted, the picture of Lord Ramakrishna, Swamiji, etc. Ganges water was also given to him. ...Swami Akhilananda was very happy and touched the sacred relics with his forehead. Before Mrs. W arrived, I had gone to his bedside and asked if I should sing. I sang the last song for him 'Brajer Kanai Braje eso, Braje basi dake' – 'O Kanai, you come back to Braja or Vrindababa' - in the style of kirtana. Those were the last moments I saw him alive.[5]

"After 4 pm, none of us entered the room. Only a nurse was inside. At 4:55 pm the Swami had a heart attack. Immediately two other nurses and two doctors came and tried to cause artificial respiration. The Swami passed away at 5:15pm."

Although Dean Walter Muelder and his wife had arrived at 5 pm, neither they nor anyone else were allowed inside Swami's room. Dean Muelder assisted in the funeral arrangements for Waterman's Funeral Home in Kenmore Square. In the following days Swamis Vividishananda, Vishwananda, and Pavitrananda joined Swamis Satprakashananda and Nityaswarupananda.[6]

The funeral service was held on September 26 at 4 pm, conducted by Swami Vishwananda, who spoke with feeling about Swami and how he had worked himself to death. Swami Vividishananda recalled his association with Swami Akhilananda. The funeral parlor was packed with people, some standing inside and some outside. After the service the body was taken to Mt. Auburn Crematory. In 1971 Swami Sarvagatananda took the ashes to India for deposit in the Ganges at the site of Holy Mother's Temple.

In San Francisco Swami Ashokananda, a close brother monk, speaking at a Sunday service on September 30, 1962, recalled Swami Akhilananda's gentleness, his serenity, his luminosity. "Of all the disciples of Swami Brahmananda in this country," said Swami

Ashokananda,... "he (Swami Akhilananda) was the most beloved of him, he was closest of all, he was dearest to Swami Brahmananda."[7]

What was the meaning of Swami Akhilananda's life in the West? He was a pioneer in presenting the value of spiritual practices for mental health. He was a spiritual force inspiring and lifting the minds of numerous seekers. A bridge-builder between East and West. Swami Akhilananda was an exemplar of what one of the direct disciples of Ramakrishna, Swami Premananda, said to the monks at the monastery in India: "We need silent workers. We need preachers, who by the example of their lives, can silently transform the lives of others."[8]

He brought to all his experiences with the direct disciples of Ramakrishna. Swami Akhilananda shared his precious memories of Holy Mother, Brahmananda, Premananda, Shivananda, Akhandananda, and others. "Our lives are the Upanishads,"[9] Swami Shivananda once said. Talking about those disciples, Swami Akhilananda made religion real. So did he make the life of Ramakrishna and his words.

Ramakrishna's teachings are spreading throughout the world. Some years ago an article appeared in a magazine which said: "The story is told of a lady disciple of the Master, who saw him some years back in a vision, standing with legions of ochre-robed monks behind him. She inquired who they were and was told by the Master that they were his officers, a very significant expression."[10]

Swami Akhilananda was an instrument of Ramakrishna'a love and concern for humanity, and as Swami Sarvagatananda has often said, "a master mind". Swami Akhilananda felt he was a servant of the Order. He would be the last to lay claim that he was an officer. How else, however, can we explain his unusual presence? As one person, a physician, said about having an interview with him, "It was like talking with God".[11]

EPILOGUE

Carole Moreau, who was a young friend of Swami Akhilananda, recalls that he had a passion for peace. She writes: "I once asked him what he wanted most in the world. He replied: 'I would like world peace.'"[1]

His wish and his words for peace have gone round the globe. On the 26th of June 2001, an unusual event took place in Russia. In the Academy of Arts in Moscow on the second floor is a large Peace Table, fashioned by a master woodworker, George Nakashima from Pennsylvania. On that day in June about 150 people including Russian artists and intellectuals, others from Auroville, India; the United States, including representatives of four religious traditions, and various Indian ambassadors, joined hands around this Peace Table, consecrating it, breaking down barriers between different factions and groups, making it a holy Altar.

In that room there is something else of great interest. "On long, narrow scrolls that hang from the walls are words of peace from the scriptures or holy men of various traditions - Lao Tzu, the Seraphim of Sarov, Swami Akhilananda, the Dhammapada, Guru Arjan, St. Matthew, Martin Luther King - together with a Navaho chant and a Celtic prayer, among others."[2] Those words of peace from Swami Akhilananda were heard at the close of every prayer: "Peace, peace, peace." Those words would seem to have attached themselves to him - the children of his thoughts and prayers.

The idea for the Altar of Peace came to Nakashima, who was born in Seattle of Japanese parents, as a dream when he was recuperating from an operation in 1983.[3] He dreamt that there was to be a "shrine to peace, located someplace in the world which people from 'all over the world' might visit for prayer, meditation and contemplation... a shrine which would be part of nature."[4] He fashioned the Altar from an aged black walnut tree that grew in the U.S. The completed Altar is 10 ½ feet long and weighs 3/4 of a ton. There are three Altars for Peace: one in Moscow, one in Auroville, India, and one in the Cathedral of St. John in New York City.

GLOSSARY

arashana —experienced truth

ashrama — a place of retreat

avatar — Incarnation of God

brahmacharya — first monastic vows

Brahman — the Absolute

Divine Mother — feminine aspect of God

Durga puja — autumn worship of the Divine Mother

guru — spiritual teacher

initiation — ceremony for receiving a mantra

Kali puja — worship of the Divine Mother

karma yoga — work without attachment

mantra — a sacred word

math — monastery

Qm — the most sacred word of the Vedas, symbol of Brahman

payas — rice pudding

pranams — reverential greeting

prasad — food or drink offered to God

pravrajika — a nun

puja — ritualistic worship

rishi — a seer of Truth

sadhu — a holy man

sannyas — final monastic vows

tabla — a small drum

Thakur — master

NOTES

The Preface

1. By a disciple, Swami Gnaneswarananda. (Mallika Clare Gupta, 1972):98.
2. Lorraine Donati. In visiting her in Shelburne, Nova Scotia she told this to the author on August 20, 2003.
3. Shivananda, Swami, For seekers of God. 3d rev ed., (Calcutta, Advaita Ashrama), 1972.): 97
4. Sri Sarada Society Notes. Fall, 2004. vol.10, issue 2, p. 3.
5. Sudhansu Bikash Sanyal. Swami Akhilananda. Typed manuscript. 1995
6. Swami Sarvagatananda in conversation with the author in 2004.

Introduction

1. Marie L. Burke, Vivekananda in the West. 3rd ed., (Calcutta, Advaita Ashrama, 1985), 111:462.

2. Swami Ranganathananda, Universal message of the Bhagavad Gita, (Calcutta, Advaita Ashrama, 2000), I;9

3. Ibid., 10.

4. Joseph Campbell. The power of the myth, (New York. Doubleday, 1988), 5.

5. Swami Akhilananda, Spiritual practices, Memorial ed., (Cape Cod, Claude Stark, Inc., 1974), 183.

6. Providence Journal, October 6, 1929.

7. Swami Akhilananda, Spiritual practices. Memorial ed., 177-178.

8. Swami Akhilananda, Hindu psychology, its meaning for the West, (New York, Harper and Bros., 1946), x.

9. Swami Akhilananda, Hindu view of Christ, (New York, Philosophical Library, 1949), 6.

10. Lecture notes of an anonymous devotee, April 25, 1948.

11. Letter of John Parks to the author, dated August 3, 1980.

12. Swami Akhilananda, Mental health and Hindu psychology, (New York, Harper and Bros., 1951), 217.

13. Ibid., 220.

14. Lecture notes of an anonymous devotee, February 3. 1948.

15. Ibid., April 24, 1949.

16. Letter of Helen Rubel to Swami Akhilananda, October 10, 1940.

17. Interview with the author, December 5, 1953.

18. Swami Akhilananda, Spiritual practices, Memorial ed., l6l.

19. Ibid., 159.

20. Ibid., 197.

Childhood and Youth

1. Sudhansu Bikash Sanyal, Swami Akhilananda (unpublished, 1995).
2. Shirish Chandra Sanyal, Biography of Srimat Swami Akhilanandaji Maharaj, partially trans. by Sujit Purkayastha, (unpublished, 1999)
3. Jawaharlal Nehru, The discovery of India (Garden City, Doubleday Anchor books, 1959), 208.
4. Swami Vivekananda, Complete works, Mayavati memorial ed. (Calcutta, Advaita Ashrama, 1989) vol. 3, 318.
5. Eastern and Western disciples. The life of Swami Vivekananda 5ed. Calcutta, Advaita Ashrama, 1981) vol. 2, 228.
6. Ibid., vol. 2, 229-30.
7. Shirish Chandra Sanyal, Biography of Srimat Swami Akhilanandaji Mahraraj, trans. by Prithwish Basu (unpublished, 1998).
8. Sudhanso Bikash Sanyal, Swami Akhilananda (unpublished, 1995).
9. Shirish Chandra Sanyal, Biography of Srimat Swami Akhilanandaji Maharaj, trans. by Prithwish Basu...
10. Lecture notes of an anonymous devotee, June 6, 1948.
11. Shirish Chandra Sanyal, Biography Srimat Swami Akhilanandaji Maharaj, trans, by Prithwish Basu...
12. Sudhansu Bikash Sanyal, Swami Akhilananda (Unpublished, 1995).
13. Swami Akhilananda, Reminiscences of Swami Brahmananda (Unpublished, 1958).
14. Swami Akhilananda, Reminiscences of Swami Premananda (Unpublished version, 1958).
15. Swami Akhilananda, Reminiscences of Swami Brahmananda...
16. Ibid.
17. Ibid.
18. Shirish Chandra Sanyal, Biography of Srimat Swami Akhilanandaji Maharaj, trans. by Prithwish Basu...

19. Sudhansu Bikash Sanyal, Swami Akhilananda...
20. Shirish Chandra Sanyal, Biography of Srimat Swami Akhilanandaji Maharaj, trans. by Prithwish Basu...
21. Sudhansu Bikash Sanyal, Swami Akhilananda...

College Days

1. Shirish Chandra Sanyal, Biography of Srimat Swami Akhilanandaji Maharaj...

2. Ibid.

3. Lecture notes of an anonymous devotee, March 19, 1950.

4. Swami Akhilananda, Reminiscences of Swami Premananda, Vedanta Kesari (Madras) (July 1988): 247

5. Sudhansu Bikash Sanyal, Swami Akhilananda ...

6. Swami Akhilananda, Reminiscences of Swami Premananda (Unpublished version, 1958).

7. Swami Akhilananda, Reminiscences of Swami Brahmananda...

8. Swami Akhilananda, Reminiscences of Swami Premananda, Vedanta Kesari (Madras) (July 1988):250

9. Sudhansu Bikash Sanyal, Swami Akhilananda...

10. Shirish Chandra Sanyal, Biography of Srimat Swami Akhilanandaji Maharaj, trans. by Prithwish Basu...

11. Sudhansu Bikash Sanyal, Swami Akhilananda...

Brahmananda

1.   Swami Prabhavananda, Eternal companion 3rd ed. (Hollywood; Vedanta press, 1975), 14.

2.   Ibid., 14.

3.   Prabuddha Bharata (Calcutta) December, 1986: 505.

4.   Gospel of Sri Ramakrishna, Trans. by Swami Nikhilananda (New York, Ramakrishna-Vivekananda Center, 1942), 506.

5.   Swami Vivekananda, The complete works, Mayavati memorial ed.(Calcutta; Advaita Ashrama, 1989), VII:171.

6.   Prabuddha Bharata (Calcutta) December, 1986: 493.

7.   Swami Prabhavananda, Eternal companion 3rd ed. (Hollywood; Vedanta press, 1975), 104.

8.   The complete works of Swami Vivekananda, 7:4l4.

9.   Swami Chetanananda, Ramakrishna as we saw him (St. Louis, Vedanta Society of St. Louis, 1990), 345.

10. The Gospel of Sri Ramakrishna, Trans. by Swami Nikhilananda (New York; Ramakrishna-Vivekananda Center, 1942), 34.

11. The life of Swami Vivekananda by his Eastern and Western disciples, 4 ed., (Mayavati; Advaita Ashrama, 1949), 577.

12. Ibid., 598

13. Prabuddha Bharata (Calcutta) December, 1986:507.

14. Akshay Kumar Sen, A portrait of Sri Ramakrishna (Calcutta, Institute of Culture,. 1998),594.

15. Ibid., 581.

16. Swami Chetanananda, Ramakrishna as we saw him...16.

17. Swami Ashokananda, Swami Brahmananda (San Francisco: Vedanta Society of Northern California, 1970),36-37.

18. Swami Prabhavananda, Eternal companion 3rd ed, 50.

19. Ibid., l6l.

20. Ibid., 146-47.

21. Swami Ritajananda, Swami Turiyananda (Madras: Sri Ramakrishna Math, 1963), 33.

22. Swami Ashokananda, Swami Brahmananda, 32-33.

23. Swami Apurvananda, comp. Mahapurush Maharaj as we saw him (Hollywood: Vedanta Press, 1997), 173.

24. Vedanta Kesari (Madras) October, 2000:379.

25. Swami Akhilananda's Thursday evening lecture. Reminisce by the author. This statement was made following a question by Dr. John Parks, probably in 1955.

26. Reminisce by the author.

27. Swami Jnanatmananda, Invitation to holy company 2 ed (Madras, Sri Ramakrishna Math, 1980), 37

28. Ibid., 37.

29. Ibid., 37.

30. Swami Apurvananda, comp. Mahapurush as we saw him, 96.

31. Swami Akhilananda, Spiritual practices. Memorial ed. (Cape Cod, Claude Stark, Inc., 1974), 150-152.

Becoming a Monk

1. Swami Gambhirananda, History of the Ramakrishna Math and Mission, (Calcutta, Advaita Ashrama, 1957):242-243.
2. Swami Vividishananda, A Man of God (Madras, Sri Ramakrishna Math, 1957): 112-113.
3. Lecture notes of an anonymous devotee, June 6, 1948.
4. Ibid., October 9, 1949.
5. Ibid., November 10, 1949.
6. Swami Akhilananda, Reminiscences of Swami Brahmananda (unpublished, 1958).
7. Photocopy of bio-form from Belur Math archives.
8. Shirish Chandra Sanyal, Biography of Srimat Swami Akhilanandaji Maharaj, trans by Prithwish Basu, (unpublished, 1998).
9. Swami Akhilananda, Reminiscences of Swami Brahmananda, Unpublished, 1958).
10. Ibid.
    The reminiscences of Swami Brahmananda which follow in the rest of this chapter have not individually all been footnoted.
11. Sister Gargi, Swami Ashokananda's days at the Madras monastery, Vedanta Kesari (Madras) (December 1997):507.
12. Ramakrishna Cowsik, My gurukulavasa in Madras Math, Vedanta Kesari (Madras) (December 1997); 516.
13. Sister Gargi, Swami Ashokananda's days at the Madras monastery, Vedanta Kesari (Madras) (December 1997);509.
14. Ramakrishna Cowsik, My gurukulavasa in Madras Math, Vedanta Kesari (Madras) (December 1997): 518
15. Ibid., 522
16. Sudhansu Bikash Sanyal, Swami Akhilananda (Unpublished, 1995).
17. Swami Akhilananda, Memories of Maharaj in Madras, Vedanta Kesari (Madras) (December 1997):513.
18. Swami Prabhavananda, The eternal companion 3rd ed (Hollywood, Vedanta Press, 1975):51
19. Ibid.
20. Lecture notes of an anonymous devotee, October 12, 1948.

21. Swami Akhilananda, Reminiscences of Swami Brahmananda (Un-published, 1958).
22. Swami Akhilananda, Memories of Maharaj in Madras...
23. Swami Prabhavananda, The eternal companion...105.
24. Ibid., 106.
25. Swami Akhilananda, Spiritual practices, Memorial ed. (Cape Cod, Claude Stark, Inc., 1974) 194.
26. Portrait of Swami Akhilananda, Swami Pavitrananda and staff members of Sri Minakshi College, Home Chidambaram, Malayalee section, (1923-1924).
27. Ramakrishna Cowsik, My gurukulavasa in Madras Math...525
28. Swami Rudranananda's talk entitled "How I joined the Ramakrishna Order" at Sarada Ashrama, Marshfield, MA., July 19, 1973. Taped and typed.
29. Swami Akhilananda's conversation and talk with devotees at Sarada Ashrama, Marshfield, MA., August, 1957, Typed manuscript, unpublished.
30. Sister Gargi, A heart poured out (New York, Kalpa Tree Press, 2003) 94.
31. Sudhansu Bikash Sanyal, Swami Akhilananda...
32. Sister Gargi, Swami Ashokananda's stay at the Madras monastery...512.
33. Swami Akhilananda, Swami Akhandananda, Vedanta Kesari (Madras)(October 1988): 365-366.
34. Swami Akhilananda's conversation and talk with devotees at Sarada Ashrama, Marshfield, MA. in August, 1957• Typed manuscript, unpublished.
35. Sara Ann Levinsky, A bridge of dreams (West Stockbridge, MA Lindisfarne Press, 1984) 313.
36. Sudhansu Bikash Sanyal, Swami Akhilananda (unpublished, 1995).
37. Swami Akhilananda, Spiritual practices Memorial ed. (Cape Cod, Claude Stark. Inc., 1974) 6

America the Beautiful

1. Sara Ann Levinsky, A bridge of dreams (West Stockbridge, MA. Lindisfarne press, 1934), 273.
2. Calvin Coolidge in a speech before the Society of American newspaper editors, Washington, DC., January 17, 1925.
3. Sara Ann Levinsky. A bridge of dreams, 317.
4. Swami Akhilananda, Written lecture notes, (Unpublished).
5. Sara Ann Levinsky, A bridge of dreams, 324
6. Ibid., 255
7. Ibid., 333
8. Swami Akhilananda's talk to devotees at Sarada Ashrama, Marshfield, MA in August, 1957 typed manuscript, unpublished.
9. Swami Shivananda, Letter of 29/3/28 to Swami Akhilananda.
10. Helen Rubel, Letter to Bharat Maharaj, July 11, 1953.
11. Swami Shivananda, Letter of 29/3/28 to Swami Akhilananda.
12. Sara Ann Levinsky, A bridge of dreams, 341.
13. Ibid., 342
14. Swami Prabhavananda, Letter of July 20, 1928 to Swami Akhilananda.
15. Swami Akhilananda in conversation with the author, early spring, 1959.
16. Swami Akhilananda, Letter to Swami Vireswarananda, July 1, 1961
17. Swami Akhilananda, Spiritual practices. Memorial ed (Cape Cod, Claude Stark, Inc., 1974), 158-59.

Providence, Part One

1. Encyclopedia American International, (Grolier, 1999), XXVIII, 791.

2. Vedanta Kesari (Madras)(July, 1996), 265.

3. Carl T. Jackson, Vedanta for the West (Indiana University press, 1984), 35

4. Marie Louise Burke, Swami Vivekananda in the West, 3rd ed., (Calcutta: Advaita Ashrama, 1987): VI, 102.

5. Charlotte Morrison Pellini, Notes on history of Providence Vedanta Center, June, 1979. Typed manuscript.

6. Providence Journal, February 21, 1929.

7. Robert Louis letter to the author, August 11, 1991.

8. The Gospel of Ramakrishna, trans. by Swami Nikhilananda (New York, Ramakrishna Vivekananda Center, 1942), 405.

9. Charlotte Morrison Pellini, Notes on the history of the Providence Vedanta Center, June, 1979. Typed manuscript.

10. Swami Shivananda, Western Union, January 28, 1930.

11. Providence Vedanta Society annual report, 1931.

12. The Lamplighter; Swami Sarvagatananda in the West (Salem, NH. The Frugal printer, 1996), 9.

13. Charlotte Pellini, Notes on the history of Providence Vedanta Center, June, 1979. Typed manuscript.

14. Swami Akhilananda, Spiritual practices. Memorial ed (Cape Cod, Claude Stark, Inc., 1974), 200-201.

15. Helen Rubel letter of October 29. 1931 to her Zurich family.

16. Helen Rubel letter of October 4, 1930 to her Zurich family.

17. Swami Shivananda letter of 6 June 1930 to Mrs. Worcester.

18. Swami Shivananda letter of December 4, 1930 to Mrs. Worcester.

19. Helen Rubel letter of October 29, 1931 to her Zurich family.

20. Sister Gargi, A heart poured out (New York, Kalpa Tree press, 2003), 155.

21. Swami Gambhirananda, History of the Ramakrishna Math and Mission (Calcutta, Advaita Ashrama, 1959). 325.

22. Postal department envelope addressed to Swami Akhilananda.

23. Helen Rubel letter of June 14, 1933 to her Zurich family.

24. Swami Shivananda letter of 4 January to Mrs. Worcester.

25. Swami Akhilananda, Swami Akhandananda (Vedanta Kesari)(Madras) October, 1988: 366.

26. Swami Akhilananda letter to Belur Math, April 11, 1936.

Providence, Part Two

1. Marguerite Fleischman (Maitreyi) letter of March 18, 1994 to Swami Sarveshananda.

2. Swami Bodhananda letter of July 10, 1932 to Swami Akhilananda.

3. Swami Bodhananda letter of August 15, 1932 to Swami Akhilananda.

4. Swami Akhilananda, Swami Akhandananda, Vedanta Kesari (Madras) (October, 1988): 366.

5. Swami Akhilananda in conversation and talks with devotees at Sarada Ashrama, Marshfield, MA, August 5, 1958. Typed manuscript.

6. Bombay Chronicle, August 26, 1934.

7. Bombay Chronicle (?), August 27, 1934.

8. Swami Annadananda, Swami Akhandananda (Calcutta, Advaita Ashrama, 1993), 154.

9. Swami Sarvagatananda in conversation with the author, July 9, 1999

10. Swami Gambhirananda, History of the Ramakrishna Math and Mission (Calcutta, Advaita Ashrama, 1957): 122.

11. Swami Annadananda, Swami Akhandananda (Calcutta, Advaita Ashrama, 1993), 141

12. Ibid., 152

13. Swami Akhilananda, Swami Akhandananda Vedanta Kesari (Madras) (October 1988): 368

14. Ibid., 366-367

15. Ibid., 367

16. Ibid., 368

17. Ibid., 368

18. Helen Rubel letter to Swami Gnaneswarananda, January 20, 1935.

19. Sisumangal Pratishthen, Calcutta. First Biennial report, July 1932-June 1934, 11.

20. Shirish Chandra Sanyal, Biography of Srimat Swami Akhilanandaj Maharaj, trans. by Prithwish Basu, 1998. Typed manuscript.

21. Swami Akhilananda, Swami Akhandananda Vedanta Kesari (Madras) (October 1988): 368.

22. Shirish Ghandra Sanyal, Biography of Srimat Swami Akhilanandaj Maharaj, trans. by Prithwish Basu, 1998. Typed manuscript.

23. Swami Akhilananda, Swami Akhandananda Vedanta Kesari (Madras) (October 1988): 368.

24. Sudhansu Bikash Sanyal, Swami Akhilananda (unpublished, 1995).

Providence, Part Three

1. Swami Akhilananda, Spiritual practices. Memorial ed. (Cape Cod, Claude Stark, Inc., 1974), 8.

2. Lecture notes of an anonymous devotee, January 25, 1949.

3. Swami Akhilananda, Spiritual practices... 8.

4. Lecture notes of an anonymous devotee, January 16, 1949.

5. Providence newspaper, undated clipping,

6. Charlotte Morrison Pellini, Notes on the history of the Providence Vedanta Center, June, 1979. Typed manuscript.

7. Carl Jackson, Vedanta for the West (Indiana university press 1974), 119.

8. Charlotte Morrison Pellini, Notes on the history of the Providence Vedanta Center...

9. Swami Gambhirananda, History of the Ramakrishna Math and Mission (Calcutta, Advaita Ashrama, 1959), 358.

10. Providence newspaper, 1935 clipping.

11. Author's reminisce of Swami Akhilananda's comment.

12. Providence Journal newspaper clippings: June 29, 1935; July 6, 1935

13. Providence newspaper clipping, 1935.

14. Charlotte Morrison Pellini, Notes on the history of the Providence Vedanta Center...

15. Providence newspaper clipping, 1936.

16. Charlotte Morrison Pellini, Notes on the history of the Providence Vedanta Center...

17. Swami Akhilananda, Sri Ramakrishna and modern psychology Providence Vedanta Society, 1937), 13.

18. Ibid., 15-16.

19. Ibid., 7.

20. Ibid., 14.

21. Ibid., 15.

22. Ibid., 15.

23. Ibid., 18.

24. Ibid., 24.

25. Swami Vivekananda, Complete works, Mayavati ed. (Calcutta: Advaita Ashrama, 1989): I, 257.

26. Swami Akhilananda lectures, a reminisce of the author.

27. Sister Gargi, A heart poured out (New York: Kalpa Tree press , 2003), 217.

28. Charlotte Morrison Pellini, Notes on the history of the Providence Vedanta Center...

29. The Madras Mail, August 9, 1936.

The Temple

1. Swami Akhilananda, Swami Akhandananda, Vedanta Kesari (Madras) October 1988): 369

2. Ibid., 369

3. Shirish Chandra Sanyal, Biography of Srimat Swami Akhilanandaj Maharaj, Trans. by Prithwish Basu. Typed Manuscript. 1977.

4. Swami Akhilananda, Letter of April 11, 1936 to Belur Math.

5. Elva Nelson, Reminiscences of Swami Akhilananda at Sarada Ashrama, Marshfield, August 5, 1958. Typed manuscript.

6. Swami Akhilananda, Swami Akhandananda, Vedanta Kesari (Madras) (October 1988):369.

7. Charlotte Pellini in conversation with the author.

8. Swami Gambhirananda, History of the Ramakrishna Math and Mission (Calcutta: Advaita Ashrama, 1957), 346-347.

9. Linda Prugh, Josephine MacLeod and Vivekananda's mission (Chennai; Sri Ramakrishna Math, n.d,),439.

10. Ibid., 439.

11. Ibid., 440.

12. Swami Akhilananda, Swami Akhandananda, Vedanta Kesari (Madras) (October 1988): 369.

13. Ibid., 369.

14. Providence Journal, undated clipping, 1937.

15. Swami Akhilananda, Letter to Charlotte Morrison, September 22, 1937

16. Lecture notes of an anonymous devotee, November 2, 1948.

17. Swami Akhilananda, Spiritual practices. Memorial ed (Cape Cod, Claude Stark, Inc., 1974), 26.

18. Swami Gambhirananda, History of the Ramakrishna Math and Mission 3rd rev ed (Calcutta: Advaita Ashrama, 1983), 271

19. Swami Annadananda, Swami Akhandananda (Calcutta: Advaita Ashrama, 1993), 154-55.

20. Swami Gambhirananda, History of the Ramakrishna Math and Mission (Calcutta: Advaita Ashrama, 1957). 349

21. Ibid., 348-349

22. Shirish Chandra Sanyal, Biography of Srimat Swami Akhilanandaj Maharaj. by Prithwish Basu. Typed manuscript. 1977; 1998

23. Linda Prugh. Josephine MacLeod and Vivekananda's Mission. Chennai, Sri Ramakrishna Math, n.d., p. 440

24. Shirish Ghandra Sanyal. Biography of Srimat Swami Akhilanandaj Maharaj. Trans. by Prithwish Basu. Typed manuscript. 1-997, 1998. p. 8

25. ibid

26. ibid

27. M. Sivaramkrishna and Sumitra Roy, eds.. Perspectives on Ramakrishna Vivekananda Vedanta tradition. Sterling publications, 1991. p. 96

28. Sudhansu Bikash Sanyal. Swami Akhilananda. Typed manuscript. 1995.

The Return to Boston

1. Told to the author by Swami Sarvagatananda, who heard it from Swami Pavitrananda.
2. Lecture notes of an anonymous devotee. May 1, 1949.
3. Swami Akhilananda, Hindu psychology, its meaning for the West (New York, Harper and Bros., 1946), 166-167.
4. Swami Akhilananda, Hindu view of Christ (New York, Philosophical Library, 1949), 242.
5. Personal reminiscences of Swami Pavitrananda, Paragraph 64, unpublished manuscript.
6. Swami Akhilananda, Hindu psychology... ix.
7. Swami Akhilananda, Mental health and Hindu psychology, (New York, Harper and Bros., 1951) xiii.
8. Helen Rubel letter of Fenruary 19, 1938 from Allahabad to her uncle Eduard in Switzerland.
9. Carl Jackson, Vedanta for the West (Indiana university press, 1994), 114.
10. Sara Ann Levinsky, A bridge of dreams (West Stockbridge, MA Lindisfarne Press, 1984), 563
11. Ibid., 565
12. RCA radiogram February 17, 1941
13. Western Union cable, April 4, 1941
14. Swami Akhilananda, Hindu psychology...66-67.
15. Ibid., 66-68.
16. Mrs. Editha White, who knew Mrs. Abreu, told this to the author.
17. Swami Gambhirananda, History of the Ramakrishna Math and Mission (Calcutta, Advaita Ashrama, 1957), 367.
18. Edgar Brightman letter to Swami Akhilananda, March 28, 1942,
19. Western Union telegram, March 25-April 1, 1942
20. William Braude letter to Swami Akhilananda, no date
21. Allen Claxton letter to Swami Akhilananda, April2, 1942
22. Swami Akhilananda, Spiritual practices Memorial ed. (Cape Cod, Claude Stark Inc., 1974), 183-184

Boston the Brain of America

1. Told to the author by Swami Sarvagatananda.
2. Hindustan Times, September 12, 1934.
3. Reported to the author.
4. Swami Akhilananda letter to John Duane.
5. Ibid., March 16, 1943.
6. Ibid., February 11, 1943.
7. Ibid., September 15, 1943.
8. Ibid., October 5, 1943.
9. Lecture notes of an anonymous devotee, January 11, 1949.
10. Swami Akhilananda, Mental health and Hindu psychology (New York, Harper and Bros., 1951), 139.
11. Information about his engagements are from his yearly diaries.
12. Lecture notes of an anonymous devotee, January 31, 1950.
13. Ibid., January 25, 1949.
14. Ibid., January 25, 1949.
15. Swami Akhilananda, Spiritual practices. Memorial ed. (Cape Cod, Claude Stark, Inc., 1974), 183.
16. Ibid., 170-171.
17. Ibid., 194.
18. Ibid., 152-153.
19. Lecture notes of an anonymous devotee, January 22, 1950.
20. Swami Akhilananda, Spiritual practices...189.
21. Ibid., 189.
22. Ibid., 190.
23. Ibid., 190.
24. Ibid., 191.
25. Boston Globe photo available, no date.
26. Shirish Chandra Sanyal, Biography of Srimat Swami Akhilanandaji Maharaj, trans. by Prithwish Basu published, 1998).

Hindu Psychology, Its Meaning for the West

1. Christopher Isherwood, Letter to Swami Akhilananda
2. Swami Akhilananda, Hindu psychology, its meaning for the West (New York, Harper and Bros., 1946), xv
3. Ibid., x
4. Ibid., xii
5. Ibid., 18
6. Ibid., I7
7. Ibid., 18-19
8. Ibid., 105
9. Ibid., 113
10. Lecture notes of an anonymous devotee
11. Swami Akhilananda, Hindu psychology...102-103
12. Swami Akhilananda, Spiritual practices, Memorial ed., Cape Cod, Claude Stark, Inc., 1974) 98
13. Swami Akhilananda, Hindu psychology...51
14. Ibid., 207
15. New York Times advertisement, March 16, 1947, 37
16. Ibid.
17. Ibid.
18. Journal of Bible and religion, January, 1947, 6l
19. Swami Akhilananda, Spiritual practices... 167
20. Personal reminiscences of Swami Pavitrananda, Paragraph 64 Unpublished manuscript.

The Ashrama

1. Ilona Lesnyak's picture book of Marshfield photos.
2. Elva Nelson's typed class notes of Marshfield, a Friday, August 1957
3. Ibid., August 5, 1958
4. Ibid.
5. Elva Nelson's typed class notes, August, 1954.
6. Swami Akhilananda, Spiritual practices Memorial ed (Cape Cod, Claude Stark, Inc. 1974) 38.
7. Ibid., 39.
8. Ibid., 39.
9. Swami Akhilananda, Rules for the ashrama, 1947. Typed manuscript.

Time Goes By

1. Swami Akhilananda, Spiritual practices Memorial ed (Cape Cod, Claude Stark, Inc., 1974) 38

2. Ibid., 175

3. Ibid., 203

4. Ibid., 203

5. Ibid., 204

6. Claude Stark, God of all (Cape God, Claude Stark, Inc., 1974) 172

7. Pitirim Sorokin, A long journey (New Haven, College and university Press, 1963) 277

8. Lecture notes of an anonymous devotee, June 6, 1950.

9. Swami Jnanatmananda, Invitation to holy company 2 ed (Madras , Sri Ramakrishna Math, 1980) 4.

10. Ibid., 27

11. The Gospel of Sri Ramakrishna, trans. by Swami Nikhilananda (New York, Ramakrishna-Vivekananda Center, 1942) 34

Hindu View of Christ

1. Lecture notes of an anonymous devotee, December 20, 1949.
2. Swami Akhilananda, Spiritual practices. Memorial ed, (Cape Cod, Claude Stark, Inc., 1974), 7.
3. Swami Akhilananda, Hindu view of Christ (New York, Philosophical Library, 1949), 11.
4. Gospel of Sri Ramakrishna, trans, by Swami Nikhilananda (New York, Ramakrishna Vivekananda Center, 1944), 134.
5. Swami Gambhirananda, History of the Ramakrishna Math and Mission, (Calcutta, Advaita Ashrama, 1957), 95.
6. Sister Devamata, Days in an Indian monastery (La Croscenta, CA: Ananda Ashrama. 1927), 22.
7. Ibid., 160.
8. Ibid., 161.
9. Swami Akhilananda, Hindu view of Christ...194.
10. Lecture notes of an anonymous devotee, January 31: 1949.
11. Reminisce of the author.
12. Swami Akhilananda, Hindu view of Christ...13.
13. Ibid., 6.
14. Ibid., 38.
15. Ibid., 68.
16. Ibid., 72.
17. Ibid., 74.
18. Ibid., 95.
19. Ibid., 100.
20. Ibid., 107-108.
21. Ibid., 108.
22. Ibid., 123.
23. Ibid., 117.
24. Ibid., 167.
25. Ibid., 194.
26. Ibid., 179.
27. Ibid., 183.

28. Ibid., 184.
29. Ibid., 185.
30. Ibid., 217.
31. Lecture notes of an anonymous devotee, April 9, 1950.
32. Swami Akhilananda, Hindu view of Christ...222.
33. Ibid., 224
34. Ibid., 243
35. Ibid., 282.
36. Handwritten letter at the Ramakrishna Vedanta Society, Boston
37. Typed manuscript at the Ramakrishna Vedanta Society, Boston.
38. Swami Akhilananda, Spiritual practices.,.187.
39. Dr. Evans said this publicly at a Ramakrishna Banquet at the University Club, Boston, in 1956.
40. Swami Akhilananda, Spiritual practices..198.
41. Swami Ashokananda, The Origin of Swami Vivekananda's doctrine of service, Prabuddha Bharata (Calcutta) (February, 1928):66.
42. Editorial; what Sri Ramakrishna has done for the world, Prabuddha Bharata (Calcutta)(December, 1986):495
43. Heinrich Baralge, SVD., Christ, Saviour of mankind (St. Augustin West Germany, 1977): 11
44. Ibid., 255.
45. Swami Vivekananda, The complete works Mayvati memorial ed., (Calcutta: Advaita Ashrama, 1989), IV, 120.

Conference on Science, Philosophy and Religion

1.   Swami Akhilananda, Conference on Science, Philosophy, Religion. 1952. Typed manuscript

2.   Swami Akhilananda, Spiritual practices. Memorial edition Cape Cod, Claude Stark Inc., l974) 176-177.

3.   Swami Akhilananda, Conference on Science, Philosophy, Religion 1946. Typed manuscript.

4.   Ibid.

5.   Swami Akhilananda, Conference on Science, Philosophy. Religion 1947. Typed manuscript.

6.   Ibid.

7.   Conference on Science, Philosophy, Religion, Learning and World peace (New York, Harper and Bros., 1948) 115

8.   Ibid, 496

9.   Ibid., 497

10.   Ibid., 497

11.   Swami Akhilananda, Conference on. Science, Philosophy, Religion 1948. Typed manuscript.

12.   Ibid.

13.   Lecture notes of an anonymous devotee, October 3. 1948.

14.   Swami Akhilananda, Conference on Science, Philosophy, Religion 1949. Typed manuscript.

15.   Ibid.

16.   Ibid.

17.   Swami Akhilananda, Spiritual practices... 177.

18.   Ibid., 178

19.   Swami Akhilananda, Conference on Science, Philosophy, Religion 1954. Typed manuscript.

20.   Swami Akhilananda, Conference on Science, Philosophy, Religion 1951. Typed manuscript.

Mental Health and Hindu Psychology

1. Told to the author by Mrs. Anna Worcester.
2. Lecture notes of an anonymous devotee, March 4, 1951.
3. Ibid.
4. Harold A. Abramson, ed. Problems of consciousness (New York: Josiah Macy Jr. Foundation, 1951), 170.
5. Lecture notes of an anonymous devotee, April 3, 1951*
6. Swami Akhilananda, Hindu psychology, its meaning for the West (New York: Harper and Bros.. 1946), 133.
7. Lecture notes of an anonymous devotee, October 5, 1948.
8. Swami Akhilananda's standard diaries for 1947, 1955.
9. Herbert Benson, The relaxation response (Wings Books, 1992), 83.
10. Swami Akhilananda, Hindu psychology... 71-72.
11. Swami Akhilananda, Mental health and Hindu psychology (New York: Harper and Bros., 1951), 2.
12. Ibid., 3
13. Ibid., 36
14. Swami Akhilananda, Spiritual practices. Memorial ed., (Cape Cod: Claude Stark,.Inc., 1974), 95.
15. Swami Akhilananda, Mental health... xvii.
16. Swami Akhilananda, Sri Ramakrishna and modern psychology (Providences Vedanta Society, 1937), 24.
17. Jean Hardy, A psychology with a soul (London; Woodgrange press, 1996), 21.
18. Ibid., 74.
19. Ibid., 87.
20. Ibid., 117.
21. Roger Walsh, The transpersonal movement; a history and state of the art. Revision (Washington, DC) (Winter, 1994): 115.
22. Swami Akhilananda, Mental health... 186.
23. Swami Akhilananda, Sri Ramakrishna and modern psychology... 18
24. Roger Walsh, The transpersonal movement; a history and state of the art... 115.
25. Remembrance of the author.

26. Roger Walsh, The transpersonal movement; a history and state of the art... ll5.
27. Ibid., 115.
28. Journal of transpersonal psychology, vol. 1, no. 1, 16.
29. Journal of transpersonal psychology, vol 24. no. 1, 81.
30. Ibid., 82.
31. Ibid., 85.
32. Journal of transpersonal psychology, vol. 28, no. 1, 34.
33. Journal of transpersonal psychology, vol. 29, no. 1, 1
34. Viktor Frankl, The doctor and the soul (New York, Knopf, 1955) xi.
35. Ibid., xi.
36. Viktor Frankly Man's search for meaning, rev. ed. (Boston, Beacon Press, 1962) 113
37. Viktor Franki, The doctor and the soul... xxi
38. Ibid., xix.
39. Told in conversation with the author by Swami Sarvagatananda.
40. Viktor Franki, The doctor and the soul...xx
41. Swami Akhilananda standard diary of engagements, 1957.
42. Abraham Maslow, Religions, values, and peak experiences (Columbus, OH: Ohio State University Press, 1964, 20.
43. Jorge Ferrer, New horizons in contemporary spirituality, Revision (Washington, DC) (Fall, 2001): 3.
44. The Gospel of Sri Ramakrishna (New York, Ramakrishna Vivekananda Vedanta Society, 1942), 477.
45. Thich Nhat Hanh (Boston Globe, May 18, 2001) 37.
46. Ramakrishna as we saw Him (Vedanta Society of St. Louis, 1990) 10.
47. His Eastern and Western Disciples, Life of Swami Vivekananda 4th ed. (Calcutta: Advaita Ashrama, 1949) 750.
48. Swami Akhilananda, Spiritual practices. Memorial ed.. 165.
49. Swami Sarveshananda in conversation with the author.
50. John Parks, M.D. in a letter to the author, August 3, 1980

Swami as Guru

1. Sister Nivedita, The web of Indian life (New York: Henry Holt, 1904), 2.
2. Vincent Sheehan, The indigo bunting (New York; Harper and Brothers, 1951), 27.
3. Ibid., 48-49
4. Swami Chetanananda, Ramakrishna as we saw him (St. Louis: Vedanta Society of St. Louis, 1990), 1.
5. A Historical Record, from conversation with Swami Prabhavananda. Privately printed, n.d., 144
6. Swami Chetanananda, Ramakrishna as we saw him (St. Louis: Vedanta Society of St, Louis, 1990), 47.
7. Ibid., 48.
8. Spiritual talks (by the first disciples of Sri Ramakrishna), (Mayavati; Advaita Ashrama,1936), 311.
9. Ibid.,282-283
10. Swami Akhilananda, selections from Lecture notes of an anonymous devotee, mostly from 1949 and 1950.
11. Swami Ritajananda, Swami Turiyananda (Madras; Sri Ramakrishna Math, 1963), 73.
12. Swami Akhilananda, Spiritual practices (Cape Cod, Claude Stark, Inc.. 1974) 39-40.

The Convent, Sarada Math

1. Swami Vivekananda, Complete works Mayavati memorial ed. (Calcutta: Advaita Ashrama, 1989), VI. 272.
2. Ibid., 272.
3. Ibid., 272.
4. Ibid., 274.
5. Ibid., vii:484.
6. Talks with Swami Vivekananda, 2 ed. (Mayavati: Advaita Ashrama 1946), 256.
7. Ibid., 257
8. Ibid., 257.
9. Ibid., 258.
10. Ibid., 261-262.
11. Swami Saswatananda letter to Swami Akhilananda, 13/2/51.
12. Ibid.
13. Undated timely letter of Swami Akhilananda to Belur Math.
14. Swami Brahamananda, the eternal companion, 3rd rev and enl. (Vedanta press, 1970), 91
15. Told by Swami Sarvagatananda to the author.
16. Swami Saswatananda letter to Swami Akhilananda, Nov. 22, 1954
17. Gospel of Sri Ramakrishna, trans. by Swami Nikhilananda, (New York, Raraakrishna Vivekananda Center, 1942), 37.
18. Sri Sarada Devi, the great wonder (New Delhi, Ramakrishna Mission, 1984), 18.
19. Ibid.,19.
20. Sister Devamata, Days in an Indian monastery (La Crescenta, CA Ananda Ashrama, 1927), 213-214.
21. Sister Nivedita, Letters of Sister Nivedita ed by Sankari Prasad Basu, (Calcutta: Nababharat publishers, 1982), I, 10.
22. Sister Devamata, Days in an Indian monastery.,.228.
23. Sister Nivedita, Letters of Sister Nivedita...I, 412.
24. Sister Devamata, Days in an Indian monastery...224.

25. Ibid., 227.

26. Ibid., 228.

27. Swami Arupananda, comp. Mahapurush as we knew him (Hollywood, Vedanta press, 1997): 6.

28. Shirish Chandra Sanyal, Biography of Srimat Swami Akhilanandaji Mahara, trans. by Prithwish Basu (unpublished, 1998)

The Expanding Circle

1. Swami Akhilananda, Spiritual practices. Memorial ed (Cape Cod, Claude Stark, Inc., 1974), 187.
2. Swami Omkarananda letter of July 28, 1954 to Swami Akhilananda.
3. Disclosed to the author more than once by Swami Sarvagatananda.
4. James Killian, The education of a college president (MIT press. 1985), 230.
5. Ibid., 232.
6. Ibid., 232.
7. Lecture notes of an anonymous devotee, 4/25/48.
8. Ibid., 4/25/48.
9. His Eastern and Western disciples. The life of Swami Vivekananda Calcutta, Advaita Ashrama, 1979), I. 250.
10. Ibid., 250.
11. Swami Vivekananda, Complete works, Mayavati ed (Calcutta, Advaita Ashrama, 1989), II. 203.
12. Swami Ranganathananda, Human being in depth, (SUNY, 1991), 75.
13. James Killian, The education to a college president... 238.
14. Ibid., 238.
15. Ibid., 239.
16. Swami Akhilananda, Spiritual practices... 164.
17. Ibid., 159.
18. Ibid., 159-160.
19. Harlow Shapley, ed. Science ponders religion (Appleton, 1960) vi.
20. Ibid., vii.
21. Ibid., 183.
22. Ibid., 96.
23. Swami Akhilananda, Spiritual practices... 198.
24. Harlow Shapley, ed. Science ponders religion...76.
25. Lecture notes of an anonymous devotee, November 29, 1949.
26. Ibid., December 4, 1949.

27. Ibid., January 31, 1950.
28. Swami Akhilananda, Modern problems and religion (Boston, Bruce Humphries, 1964), 66-67.
29. Ibid., 70.
30. Reminiscences of Kinley Herboldsheimer and the author.
31. Swami Akhilananda, Spiritual practices...197.
32. Ibid., 163.
33. Ibid., 164.
34. Ibid., 154.
35. Ibid., 154.
36. See his autobiography, A Long Journey (College and University press), 1948.
37. Abraham Maslow, ed, New knowledge in human values (New York Harper and Bros., 1959), xii.
38. Ibid., xiii.
39. Swami Akhilananda, Spiritual practices...197.
40. Ibid., 164.
41. Abraham Maslow, ed. New knowledge in human values...vii.
42. Swami Akhilananda, Spiritual practices...167.
43. Ibid., 199.
44. Ibid., 201.
45. Ibid., 162-63.

The College Circuit

1. Swami Akhilananda, Spiritual practices, Memorial ed (Cape Cod, Claude Stark, Inc., 1974). 184.
2. Ibid., 191-192.
3. Swami Vivekananda, Complete Works, Mayavati memorial ed. (Calcutta, Advaita Ashrama, 1989), vol. 6, 494
4. Ibid., vol. 5, 3425
5. Kenneth R. Alien letter to Swami Akhilananda, January 20, 1935.
6. Ibid.
7. Isabel Beveridge in conversation with the author.
8. Lee R. Steiner printed invitation to Swami Akhilananda, January 6, 1956.
9. Harold K. Duerksen letter to Swami Akhilananda, February 6, 1957
10. Sister Gargi, A disciple's journal (New York, Kalpa Tree press, 33), 165-166.
11. Swami Akhilananda, Spiritual practices Memorial ed (Cape Cod, Claude Stark, Inc.. 1974), 100-101.
12. Renee Weber, Dialogues with scientists and sages (New York, Routledge and Kegan Paul, 1986-87), ix.
13. Swami Nikhilananda, Hinduism, its meaning for the liberation of the spirit (New York, Harper and Bros., 1958), ix.
14. Swami Akhilananda, Spiritual practices... 179.

Winds of Change

1. Swami Akhilananda, Spiritual practices. Memorial ed (Cape Cod, Claude Stark, Inc., 1974), 191.
2. Recollection of Brahmachari Vimukta Chaitanya through the courtesy of James Chadwick of Mill Valley, CA.
3. Ibid., with additional material by the author, who heard Swami Akhilananda speak of this occasion many times.
4. Lecture notes of an anonymous devotee, June 6, 1948.
5. Ibid., February 15, 1949.
6. Ibid., January 10, 1950.
7. Swami Akhilananda, Modern problems and religion (Boston, Bruce Humphries, 1964), 13.
8. Ibid., 14.
9. Lecture notes of an anonymous devotee. May 23, 1948.
10. Swami Akhilananda, Modern problems and religion...138.
11. Joseph Campbell, The power of myth (New York, Double Day, 1988), 9
12. Bhavan's Journal, 46, 1. August 15, 1999. 161.
13. Swami Akhilananda, Modern problems and religion...88.
14. Ibid., 88.
15. Ibid., 94.
16. Ibid., 94-95
17. Ibid., 85.
18. Ibid., 85.
19. Ibid., 95.
20. Ibid., 98-99.
21. Ibid., 99.
22. Ibid., 97.
23. Ibid., 99.
24. Lecture notes of an anonymous devotee, November 14, 1948.
25. Swami Akhilananda, Modern problems and religion. 86.
26. Ibid., 93.
27. Ibid., 74.
28. Ibid., 141.
29. Ibid., 141.
30. Ibid., 142.

31. Ibid., 142.
32. Ibid., 143.
33. Swami Akhilananda. Hindu psychology, its meaning for the West (New York, Harper and Bros., 1946), 214.
34. Swami Akhilananda, Modern problems and religion...143,
35. Ibid., 144.
36. Ibid., 132.
37. Swami Akhilananda, Spiritual practices...191.
38. Lecture notes of an anonymous devotee. May 5, 1949.
39. Ibid., April 24, 1949.
40. Ibid., November 29, 1949.
41. Ibid., November 17. 1949.
42. Ibid., October 10, 1948.
43. Ibid., May 29, 1949.
44. Ibid., May 8, 1949.
45. Ibid., February 19, 1950.
46. Frederick Shepard, MD in a letter to the author, March 5, 1998
47. Elizabeth Minefield in a letter to the author, June 2, 1997
48. John Parks, MD in a letter to the author, August 3, 1980.
49. Sister Nivedota, The Master as I saw him (Calcutta, Udbodhan Office, 1948), 6th ed., xii.
50. Lecture notes of an anonymous devotee, February 20, 1949.
51. Swami Akhilananda, Spiritual practices...197.
52. William Page in a letter to the author, September 21, 1991.

His Last Year

1. Swami Akhilananda, Spiritual practices, memorial edition (Cape Cod, Claude Stark» Inc., 1974) 166.
2. Known to the author.
3. Lecture notes of an anonymous devotee, November 2, 1948.
4. Ibid., February 7, 1950.
5. Dr. Arun Biswas, Notes, October 24, 1962 and February 17, 1953
6. Ibid.
7. Swami Ashokananda, Cassette tape, September 30, 1962.
8. Swami Premananda, Memories of a loving soul, ed. by Swami Prabhavananda (Calcutta, Advaita Ashrama, 1968) 123.
9. Swami Shivananda, For seekers of God, 3rd ed. rev. & enl., (Calcutta, Advaita Ashrama, 1972) 145.
10. Prabuddha Bharata (Calcutta) February, 1928; 62.
11. A Winchester, MA physician. Dr. Brock Lynch, known to the author.

Epilogue

1. Swami Akhilananda, Spiritual practices Memorial ed (Cape Cod, Claude Stark, Inc., 1974.) 187.
2. Peace Table. Webmaster @ auroville.org.
3. The Chico Enterprise Record, March 27, 1985.
4. New Hope Gazette, February 9, 1984.

PERMISSIONS

Grateful acknowledgement is being given to the following for permission to reprint previously published material:

Kalpa Tree Press, from A HEART POURED OUT: the story of Swami Ashokananda; by Sister Gargi (Marie Louise Burke). Copyright by Sister Gargi.

Vedanta Society of Northern California, from SWAMI BRAHMANANDA, by Swami Ashokananda. Copyright 1970 by Vedanta Society of Northern California.

MIT Press, from EDUCATION OF A COLLEGE PRESIDENT, by James R. Killian Jr. Copyright 1985 by Massachusetts Institute of Technology.

Steyler Verlag, from CHRIST, SAVIOUR OF MANKIND, by Father Heinrich Barlage. Copyright, 1977.

Josiah Macy Jr. Foundation, from PROBLEMS OF CONSCIOUSNESS, 1951.

Advaita Ashrama, from COMPLETE WORKS OF SWAMI VIVEKANANDA, various vols. and publication dates; and THE LIFE OF SWAMI VIVEKANANDA, 5th ed., by His Eastern and Western disciples, vol. 2. 1981.

Linda Prugh, JOSEPHINE MACLEOD AND VIVEKANANDA'S MISSION, Sri Ramakrishna Math, Chennai, India, 1999.

BOOKS AND ARTICLES BY SWAMI AKHILANANDA

Sri Ramakrishna and modern psychology (Providence Vedanta Society), 1937.

Hindu psychology, its meaning for the West (New York: Harper and Bros.,), 1946.

Hindu view of Christ (New York: Philosophical Society), 1949. Mental health and Hindu psychology (New York: Harper and Bros.,), 1951.

Modern problems and religion (Boston: Bruce Humphries),1964. Spiritual practices. Memorial edition (Cape Cod: Claude Stark, Inc) 1974.

ARTICLES

Mysticism and Altruism in Journal of Bible and Religion, #6, 1948.

Existentialism in Journal of Bible and Religion, #17, 1949.

Time and Eternity in Journal of Bible and Religion, #27, 1959.

On Swami Akhandananda Vedanta Kesari (Madras) (October 1988)

On Swami Premananda Vedanta Kesari (Madras) (July 1988)

On Swami Brahmananda Vedanta Kesari (Madras) (July 1989)

Memories of Maharaj in Madras Vedanta Kesari (Madras) (December 1997)

Mysticism and Altruism <u>Vedanta Kesari</u> (Madras) (May, 1997) Religious culture and integration <u>Vedanta Kesari</u> (Madras) (Aug. 1997)

Values of Life in <u>Vedanta for modern man.,</u> ed. by Christopher Isherwood (New York: Harper and Bros.,) 1951.

Extra-Sensory and Superconscious experiences in <u>The Cultural </u>Heritage of India. (Calcutta: RK Mission Institute of Culture). III, 1969.

BOOKS AND ARTICLES ON SWAMI AKHILANANDA

Heinrich Barlage, Christ, Saviour of Mankind: a Christian appreciation of Swami Akhilananda (West Germany: Steyler Verlag), 1977.

Claude A. Stark, God of All (Claude A, Stark, Inc.,). 1974:
Chap. XII. Swami Akhilananda: a practical application of Sri Rama-krishna's approach.

S. J. Samartha, The Hindu response to the Unbound Christ (Madras), 1974. Chap. Ill: Swami Akhilananda. 61-72.

Claude A. Stark, Swami Akhilananda and William James in The Journal of Religious Studies, V (Spring-Autumn. 1974). nos. I and II. 54-82.

APPENDIX A CENTENARY

The Providence birthday celebration of Sri Ramakrishna opened early on Friday, February 21st, 1936 at 7:30 am when Swami Akhilananda, speaking for the Ministers' Morning Devotions, gave a talk over the radio on the spiritual experiences of Sri Ramakrishna. That afternoon at 3, the Swami, speaking over a different radio station, read to the invisible public the message of Swami Vivekananda on Sri Ramakrishna and spoke on Sri Ramakrishna and future civilization.

A Committee called the American Centenary Celebration of Sri Ramakrishna had been formed during the winter. It comprised, besides the American Swamis, such outstanding figures as Professor William E. Hocking of Harvard University, Rev. Ivan Lee Holt President of the Federation of Churches of Christ, Rev. Frederick B. Fisher, President of the Council of Free Churches of America, Rev. Jabex Sunderland, Professor Franklin Edgerton, Head of the American Oriental Society, Professor Millar Burrows, President of the American School of Oriental Research, Rabbi Israel Lazaron and others. The chairman of this publicity committee, Rev. Frederick A. Wilmot, Universalist minister and religious editor of the Providence Journal, wrote three appreciative articles on Sri Ramakrishna portraying him vividly to the Western mind. These articles along with picture and cuts illustrating every article were sent successively during and after the celebration to the leading newspapers all over the United States.

On Sunday, February 23rd, a large gathering of about 300 came together at the Plantations Club, a big auditorium in the center of Providence, to hear ministers of different religions speak on mysticism. An unusual spirit of harmony and good-will toward one another and toward Sri Ramakrishna could be noticed among the ministers. After a short violin recital by the expert technician, Professor Henri J. Faucher accompanied by Mme. Marie B. Faucher, Swami Akhilananda opened the meeting by reading to all the message of good cheer from Swami Akhandanandaji. A Catholic monk, Father Chandler, struck a high spiritual note by his beautiful exposition of the stages of divine love as portrayed in the life of St. Thomas Aquinas showing the attainment of God to be the highest goal. This was followed by a very interesting account by Rabbi Braude of the charitable life of Rabbi Israel, the Master of Good Name. Rev. Ralph Harpole depicted practical mysticism in the Protestant Church from the life of Horace Bushnell. An entertaining note was then brought in by Rev. Frederick A. Wilmot's definition of mysticism, which he followed by a talk on Sri Ramakrishna stressing the fact that man must experience or realize God before he can become truly religious. The subject was drawn to a fitting close by Dr, Joachim Wach, formerly of Leipzig University and now Professor of Comparative Religions at Brown University, speaking on the Unity of Eastern and Western mysticism when he re marked that "mysticism denoted the harmony of man above his national and social barriers".

The glorious birthday on Monday dawned fair and bright although the previous weeks had been nothing but rain. Four Swamis, Swami Akhilananda, Swami Vividishananda, Swami Gnaneswarananda and Swami Paramananda, were able to be together on this day. The morning was spent in worship with Hindu rights and Horn ceremony. The shrine room and pictures were beautifully decorated with flowers given by different friends and a garland for Sri Ramakrishna. The Swamis and a few intimate friends present very much enjoyed the worship which seemed to leave an effect over all. During the afternoon Swami Akhilananda cooked for Sri Ramakrishna and this was offered. A few more friends were present at the arati service where the Swamis chanted, and the chamar, recently arrived from India, was used for the first time. When the small company sat down to dinner the conversation was all about Sri Ramakrishna. It was late before this enjoyable party thought to break up.

The following day, the message of Swami Akhandanandaji was broadcasted by the press on the radio over the whole of the United States. This day was spent in busy preparation by a number of the friends while Swami Akhilananda cooked a dinner for 100 on the large new stove recently installed for the purpose. Although the number of guests, ministers, Rabbis, professors and friends taxed the capacity of the house for dining according to Western fashion, and late applications had to be rejected, the dinner was nevertheless held in Sri Ramakrishna's place. The Hindu curries, new to many, were greatly relished. Then followed music and brief addresses on various phases of the life

284

of Sri Ramakrishna by the five Swamis present and a few prominent American friends. Swami Akhilananda opened by giving the early life and spiritual background of Sri Ramakrishna. Swami Paramananda continued by telling of the Master and other religions. Here Rev. Frederick A. Wilmot spoke a few words on Sri Ramakrishna's influence on the West, which was followed by a discussion of his practical teachings by Swami Vividishananda. The points of Sri Ramakrishna's contribution to the Christian world were noted by Rev. Allen E. Claxton, Methodist Minister, in a very clear, deep talk showing much careful thought and was appreciated by all. Swami Nikhilananda told in an interesting way about the "Master and his Disciples." This was followed with a few brief words by Professor Robert Casey, Professor of Comparative Religions at Brown University, on eclecticism and exclusiveness in mysticism and a word of appreciation of the philosophy of Sri Ramakrishna by Professor Arthur Murphy, Professor of comparative philosophy at Brown University. Swami Gnaneswarananda ended with a quick, lively little story bringing out the different temperaments of religious aspirants East and West and left with the company a thought tersely and strikingly expressed: that, "Sri Ramakrishna is Power", and "It Works" - that this power works for us in every phase of life; after which he gave a little Hindu Music.

Wednesday was spent quietly. Swami Akhilananda again read the message of Swami Akhandanandaji over the radio and gave a talk on Sri Ramakrishna. In the evening a gathering of friends enjoyed more music by Swami Gnaneswarananda interspersed with informal discussion and refreshments.

"Harmony of Religions" was the topic of Swami Akhilananda over the radio on Friday, February 28th. In the evening there was another large public meeting at the Plantations Club. This time, four Swamis delivered lectures on Sri Ramakrishna and his influence which did much to spread acquaintance among the public. After' Swami Akhilananda opened the meeting, Swami Paramananda, speaking first, told about Sri Ramakrishna, the Great Master of India. Swami Vividishananda stressed the harmony of religions as shown by the life of Sri Ramakrishna. That a combination of mysticism and practical qualities is not only possible but admirable was brought out interestingly and clearly by Swami Gnaneswarananda. While, by Swami Akhilananda, Western psychology and mystic experiences were set over against each other and given their relative values illustrated from the sublime life of Sri Ramakrishna.

The week of celebration proper ended on Sunday, March 1st. At a meeting in the evening, after a little violin music again by Professor Henri J. Faucher accompanied by Mme. Marie D. Faucher and vocal music by Miss Ruth Jobber accompanied by Mrs. Curry, Swami Akhilananda gave a lecture on "India and Her Master" illustrated by slides that made the members of the audience desire immediately to leave for India with the Swami in a large party.

The two regular lecture nights of the following week were devoted to questions on Sri Ramakrishna which brought out many interesting points and angles of vision new to the West. Then, on Sunday, Swami Akhilananda lectured on "Sri Ramakrishna and Modern Problems".

The Celebration was thereafter carried to Philadelphia and to St. Louis by Swami Akhilananda where, in both places, he delivered a number of special lectures on Sri Ramakrishna which interested and drew many people.

The immediately noticeable result of the Celebration was a greater number of letters from unknown people to the Swami, and an increased demand for the Swami as a speaker to various religious societies and gatherings of various kinds - of ministers, of men's and women's' church clubs, including a Jewish women's group, of young people's church societies, of Y.M.C.A. boys groups and of religious conferences of all ages.

APPENDIX B DEDICATION

THE DEDICATION OF THE NEW CHAPEL
of the RAMAKRISHNA-VEDANTA SOCIETY
in Boston, April 1st, 1942

The dedication of the new Chapel for the Ramakrishna-Vedanta Society in Boston, April 1st, 1942, was an occasion of deep spiritual significance. The beauty and dignity of the services can never be forgotten by those who were privileged to attend them. The new home of the Society, a residence admirably suited to become a temple, is located in an ideal spot for quietness, yet it is not far from the heart of the city. It overlooks the Charles River, as the Monastery in India overlooks the Ganges, and its atmosphere already seems to hold something of mystic beauty and peace. The many friends and visitors who thronged the spacious rooms were delighted, especially by the Chapel and the library. It was felt that such a place could not fail to be a powerful influence for the teaching of Truth.

Swami Akhilananda, the beloved teacher and friend whose untiring efforts and unselfish devotion have been instrumental in causing this new Centre to be opened, conducted the dedication services, with the assistance of two of his brother Swamis, Swami Bodhananda of New York and Swami Vishwananda of Chicago. In the morning, an elaborate form of worship, with all the beauty of Hindu ceremony and ritual, was performed by the three Swamis. At this time, in the presence of only a few very earnest devotees, the Temple was made sacred for the worship of the Divine Being. Then, in the evening, a public dedication service was held, and the place was thronged with the many friends, visitors, and distinguished guests who had come from far and near to be present on this great occasion.

The evening program began with several musical selections, beautifully rendered; then when the large audience had settled into quietness, the Swamis, who had taken their places on the platform, rose and intoned some ancient Vedic prayers, prayers whose mystic power could

287

be foil -- sacred prayers that seemed to hallow the Chapel and blessed the hearts of the listeners.

Following this, Swami Vishwananda of Chicago read a cable from the President of the Ramakrishna Order in India, as well as massages from other Swamis in this country, and from many devoted friends who were unable to come. All expressed their good wishes and prayers for the new work that has been started. Dr. Allen E. Claxton of New York City, who was present in the morning, and who was to have spoken in the evening, unfortunately had to leave earlier;, but he and another friend of Swami Akhilananda, Rev. Frederick A. Wilmot of Providence, both sent their sincere regrets and loving prayers for the new Centre.

Swami Akhilananda, the master of ceremonies on this solemn occasion, graciously welcomed the audience to the new home of the Ramakrishna-Vedanta Society, and, in the following words, he proceeded to deliver the opening address;

Swami Akhilananda

My Friends: Sri Ramakrishna's illustrious disciple, Swami Vivekananda, came to this country in 1893 to represent Hinduism at the Parliament of Religions. As I believe you all know, Sri Ramakrishna lived a life of God-consciousness, realizing Him continuously at every moment; that is to say, most of his life was spent in samadhi, or in the super-conscious state. Being inspired by Sri Ramakrishna, Swami Vivekananda came not merely to represent Hinduism, but also to spread his Master's message of harmony and of synthesis - His message of love. Swami Vivekananda himself was a man who lived that life - who experienced God-consciousness in samadhi, yet, impelled by the urge to do work that was greatly needed in the world, also because he felt that he had a message of vital importance to give, he came to this country, bringing divine light and blessings to many persons.

It was no accident that the Parliament of Religions had been organized. In fact, before he left India, Swami Vivekananda told one of his brother Swamis: "The Parliament of Religions is being prepared for me. It is meant for the message of Sri Ramakrishna."

It may interest you to know that some famous people, professors of Harvard, like William James and other men of high Intellectual attainments, recognized the abilities of the illustrious Swami Vivekananda, even before he spoke at the Parliament of Religions. These intellectual giants, as well as some other outstanding leaders in Boston, appreciated the Swami's greatness first, so we feel that Boston has a special claim to a share in our work. We think that it is only right that Boston should have a Centre for the Ramakrishna Mission. In fact, Swami Vivekananda really began his work here in 1893, - work that has been carried on successfully in America by some other great disciples of Sri Ramakrishna, - Swamis Saradananda, Turiyananda, Ahbedananda, Trigunatitananda, followed by other Swamia of the Order.

Last year, our President commanded us to start a Ramakrishna-Vedanta Society here. The Society was organized about a year ago. Through Divine Grace, we had the privilege of opening a Centre in the Name of the Universal Spirit, - in the Name of Sri Ramakrishna. We are dedicating this Chapel tonight in His Name, and in the memory of Swami Vivekananda and Swami Brahmananda, the two great personalities, the very bed-rock upon which the Ramakrishna Mission has been founded. We invoke the blessing of Sri Ramakrishna and of Holy Mother, as well as the blessings of Swami Vivekananda and Swami Brahmananda upon this new Chapel.

Sir Ramakrishna was the embodiment of all religious ideas and Ideals, so we are establishing a Chapel in His Name to express the harmony of all religions. Today we have a great need of such a place where we can worship God in His various aspects, where we can try to realize Him according to our individual requirements and possibilities. May the devotees belonging to different religious groups following different religious practices find here the highest expression of their particular Ideal. Our prayer is that this may be the purpose of this Temple, and this its use. As we dedicate this little Temple tonight, we pray that you all may have here the fullest expression and experience of God in your life, and we also pray that those who come here may grow in the knowledge of God and of Truth.

It is now my privilege to introduce to you our beloved and revered Swami from New York, Swami Bodhananda. It is fitting that he, a disciple of the great Swami Vivekananda, should be present on this significant occasion, and that he should speak to you of Sri Ramakrishna, in whose Name we are all here.

Swami Bodhananda

After paying tribute to the unselfish labors of Swami Akhilananda, whose love and generous efforts have made possible the opening of this now Centre, Swami Bodhananda spoke very feelingly of the wonderful life and teachings of Sri Ramakrishna. He told of Sri Ramakrishna's sincerity, of His burning passion to know God, and His rejection of everything that could not lead to a direct knowledge of Truth. Even when He was a small boy, Sri Ramakrishna questioned the value of any education that could only teach a man to earn his bread, but could not help him to find the Divine Being. He asked many questions about God, and was told that God is all-pervading, omniscient, the Creator of the universe, the preserver and lover of mankind. Sri Ramakrishna was greatly puzzled. "If God is so important, if He is really all that you have claimed for Him, why should I waste my time with an education that is meant only to teach me to earn a living, but cannot show me how to find Him?" Such an intense spiritual Personality could never be satisfied with secondhand experience, or indirect knowledge of Truth. He wanted to experience God at first hand, and thought that the only goal of life was to devote it wholly to that end. He Himself undertook intense spiritual practices, and in His passionate desire for God-realization, He was known sometimes to cry out, "Oh, Mother, another day has gone by and I have not seen Thee!" Nor could He be contented until He had made the Divine experience His own.

This great Personality, living a quiet life away from the materialistic world, could look deep into the heart of the troubles that beset mankind, and without any so-called scientific knowledge, could see the very roots of the cause of all suffering. He found that it is man's attachment to sense objects, and to the pleasures of this world that stands between him and true freedom, which is the realization of God. Not until man has freed himself from bondage to sense pleasures can he hope to discover the spiritual joys that lie beyond the sense plane. Those who would know the Divine Being must seek Him through renunciation of all things that do not lead to Him; they must seek Truth by lifting themselves above the desires that belong to the sense plane.

But the most astounding feature of Sri Ramakrishna's message was His contribution to the universal understanding of religion. To Him, religion was not merely the revelation of one personality or of one path. He saw the religious experiences of different persons, and the teachings of different faiths as the different paths to the same Truth. This wonderful power of integration, of harmonizing the various religions and philosophies that have been bewildering the world was His unique contribution to humanity. He proved conclusively, by actually practising different methods Himself, that all paths do really lead to one Goal, and that all Names that arc used for God are for the same Reality. This great Master, by synthesizing His own religious experiences, found that the One behind the many is the same, and so He taught reverence for all religions, as the various ways by which the One Truth may be reached.

Swami Akhilananda then introduced the next speaker, Swami Vishwananda, a very dearly beloved brother who shared with him their early days at the Monastery, and who sat at the feet of the same great Master, Swami Brahmananda. Swami Vishwananda has been well known in India as the head of the Ramakrishna Mission in Bombay. Now he is in charge of the Vedanta Society in Chicago.

Swami Vishwananda then gave one of the most brilliant and inspiring addresses of the evening. He called his topic, "Vedanta and the West," for it was not only a survey of the religious history of India and the deep spiritual achievements that are the flower of Indian culture, but he also showed how these great spiritual teachings of the East are needed to enlighten the materialistic darkness of the West. Although the western world can be justly proud of its scientific achievements, it has been given to India as her divine heritage to lead the way in matters relating to spiritual progress.

Swami Vishwananda

India is an ancient land. Her history goes back thousands of years into remote epochs of time, beyond the earliest records that man has kept. But all through her history, down through the ages, in every epoch, in every time, there have been men and women filled with the longing to seek for Truth, an intense desire to realize God. There have always been people in India who separated themselves from others, who sought lonely caves in the Himalayas, or lived in the forests or deserts in order that they might find God through renunciation and prayer. The great religious books, the Vedas, the great epics and the Upanishads, are the records of these deep longings and of the spiritual unfoldment of the race. Out of a remote period of antiquity even down to the present day, the search for God is the keynote of Indian development; it is the one theme that occurs over and over again, -~ the basic element of Indian culture. Hinduism itself is not the revealed truth about God as experienced by one person or group, but it is the

291

cumulated experience of all the great sages, teachers, and Divine Incarnations of the past.

The earliest sages, or seekers after Truth were known as Rishis. They were holy men and women who devoted themselves to spiritual practices and taught the knowledge of God to their disciples. The great epics, the Ramayana, the Mahabharata, the Bhagavad Gita, the Upanishads, show the deep influence that spirituality had upon the Hindus, even in the earliest times; that they had already found God in Rama, in Krishna, and in other great incarnations. Those who found Him were filled with longing to share their intoxicating experience. Says a great Rishi, "Listen, ye children of Immortal bliss. I have realized that Effulgent Being. By realizing Him alone one can attain to immortality and bliss." Again, in the Bhagavad Gita, the teachings of the great Incarnation, Krishna, we find the highest philosophical truth; the blossoming of the Divine Ideal in the person of the glorious Krishna. It is He who has declared that one can realize God not only by meditation and prayer, but also by performing duties in the spirit of service. The teachings of Krishna represent the highest and broadest type of religious unfoldment in India.

Buddha, that great Incarnation whose influence changed the destiny of the world, was a Hindu prince who donned the saffron robe and lived a life of intense renunciation, that he might save men from suffering. It is He who has given to the world that marvelous message, "Hatred cannot be conquered by hatred, but by Love alone."

One of India's greatest saints, Ashoka, was also a great king, who ruled during the golden age of Indian culture, when the arts -- literature, sculpture, architecture -- flourished, and when India was outstanding among the civilized nations of the earth.

There have been darker periods; there have been many changes, with now and then another great spiritual leader emerging, but through all her history, India's path to greatness has been along the road of spiritual development.

And now, coming close to our own time, in the early part of the Nineteenth Century, the Divine Light has come again to this ancient land, with the birth of Sri Ramakrishna, the God-man, who lived a simple life by the shores of the Ganges and taught truths that will illumine mankind. At the time of His coming, India, as well as the rest of the world, was facing serious problems. Contact was being rapidly established with the Western world, which had made great strides in the realm of science. But the West, though it could be justly proud of amazing scientific achievements, was, nevertheless, in the grip of materialism and doubt. There was danger that India, too, might be confused by the influx of new ideas and new ways of life. A new Saviour was needed, and so this Divine Teacher came, living His quiet life of God-consciousness and renunciation, giving to India and to the West the messages they so much needed. To India, He brought restoration of faith in her own great sages and teachers of the past, that she might not lose the spiritual blessings that have always been her birthright. To the West, He brought a message of hope that, if followed, could save it from spiritual destruction.

We have sat at the feet of some of the great Masters, the direct disciples of this Divine Incarnation, and we have seen the wonderful blessings that they have bestowed upon mankind. The great meaning of the Vedanta movement, the great teaching of Sri Ramakrishna that we bring to you tonight is that all men are one. All the differences that we see between men and women, between races, between nations, are only apparent and temporary. Behind them all is the One Reality, The One in the many, the Truth behind all forms. All those forms are but bubbles in an infinite ocean, and the wise man, when he looks at them will sec but the One. To those who find Him, all superficial differences will disappear, hatreds and prejudices must die, and they will live in peace and harmonious understanding of their fellow-men. When men can grasp this truth, all races will be able to meet upon a common ground, and all religions will be recognized as but the various paths to the One Goal. This is the great contribution that the teaching of Vedanta can bring to the West.

Swami Vishwananda then brought his eloquent address to a close with a prayer to the Divine Being — that He may enlighten our souls, and that we may learn to really love one another.

Swami Akhilananda then introduced the next speaker, Professor Walter Clarke, of Harvard University, saying that Professor Clarke is one of the outstanding scholars of Indian language and philosophy. He has visited India and has a profound appreciation of Indian culture. It is fitting that Professor Clarke should be present and should speak on such a great occasion.

Professor Walter E. Clarke

"Every civilization, every religious institution builds up around itself certain myths, or perhaps it might be better to say certain axioms of thought which are accepted on faith without much effort to criticize them and to prove them objectively -- they are based on the subjective experience of the nation or group, an attitude of mind towards the universe and human life.

"I am frequently told that my Indian studies are impractical, unnecessary, and useless. To this I always reply by comparing Indian and Chinese studies to the study of astronomy. If we leave out the calendar and navigation, the rest of astronomy serves only to develop an intellectual curiosity. This intellectual curiosity of astronomy has raised one point of view from a geocentric one to a heliocentric one and we are now going on to a concept of the Sun as part of a galaxy and even to the still larger concept of other galaxies.

"It is just as important to expand our point of view about human life on the Earth from a narrow provincial point of view concerning life in a particular village town, county, state, or nation to an intellectual curiosity about human life in other countries, in other continents, and on the whole earth.

"The population of India is nearly a fourth of the population of the world. Surely it is important to know about its experience with life and its attitude towards the universe.

"The people of India have developed certain axioms of thought which differ widely from those which we in the West have been born with and have come to consider to be the only logical and possible ones.

"The West has tended more and more to consider things to be more important than thoughts, to make ideas correspond to things, and to define religion in terms of social ethics, so much so that salvation often seems to be a, by-product of practical activity rather than the chief goal of life. India has always tended to insist that ideas are more important than things, that things must yield to ideas, and to define religion in terms of personal experience rather than in terms of active social services. As a result in the West there has been greater experimentation with things and with social life. Changes in social life have been rapid but the West has tended to be intolerant in the matter of creed and dogma and to carry them on traditionally and mechanically.

"On the other hand India has been over comprehensive and very tolerant in the matter of dogma -- in the matter of various views about the world, but has tended to be intolerant socially -- to keep social life going on in a traditional, mechanical, unchanging way. Life in the world is regarded as relatively unimportant -- the important thing is self-realization -- the perfecting of oneself while performing one's necessary social duties in a traditional way but emphasizing contemplation and ultimate extrication of oneself from the bonds of transmigration and karma. Social life is kept going not for an immediate but for an unseen result for the individual rather than for improving and perfecting human society on earth.

"India has always Insisted that the Kingdom of Heaven is within you and that it is not the function of religion to bring about a Kingdom of God on earth -- there can be no such thing since the goal of religion is other-worldly. This is much nearer to early Christianity than it is to modern forms of Christianity.

"Indian thought is so much interested in the goal that it tends to neglect the pathway leading to that goal and spends too little effort on the world which it must pass through. On the other hand the West tends to forget the goal and to spend too much of its energies on little practical activities without caring about their meaning.

"The West tends to put an over-emphasis on one necessary aspect of life but India tends to put an over-emphasis on another necessary aspect of life. The mutual influence of one on the other may lead to a more harmonious adjustment of the otherworldly religious attitude of mind and the worldly attitude of mind which would make human life on earth as comfortable and as happy as possible.

"To many in the West who are bewildered by a multiplicity of little activities, the Indian insistence' on the necessity of always keeping an ultimate goal in view comes as a helpful corrective'.

"The ideal life, according to all Indian teachers, is one which devotes some time to study, some time to the maintenance of the traditional duties of social life, but then devotes much time to contemplation with the aim of a personal realization of God. The West needs to spend more time in contemplation -- India needs to spend more energy on the forms of social life. We need a balanced effort without over emphasis on either factor."

Swami Akhilananda described the next speaker. Dr. Earle Marlatt, Dean of the School of Theology, Boston University, as one whom he has known for some time, and whose friendship is dear to him. Dr. Marlatt is not only a teacher of theology and philosophy, but he is also a poet and a mystic. Swami said that it gave him great happiness to have Dr. Marlatt for one of the speakers on this special occasion.

Dr. Earle Murlatt

"Swami Akhilananda, distinguished guests, members of the Vedanta Society, and friends;

"It is a double pleasure I have in greeting you tonight and congratulating you on the dedication of your so beautiful new house of prayer and meditation; first of all I am happy to do anything I can to advance the work of Swami Akhilananda; he is a scholar and a gentleman, whose friendship I treasure; after that, I find that this speech is, curiously or miraculously, the end of a long, long journey begun a quarter of a century ago. This is admittedly a dark saying which will require more than a little explanation.

"In 1916, while I was still a teacher of English Literature in an Indiana High School I came across a strangely impressive poem in Edgar Lee Masters*s Spoon River Anthology. It was called ironically "The Village Atheist" and it read:

"Ye young debater's over the doctrine
Of the soul's immortality,
I who lie here was the village atheist,
Talkative, contentious, versed in the arguments
Of the infidels.
But through a long sickness
Coughing myself to death
I read the Upanishads and the poetry of Jesus,
And they lighted a torch of hope and intuition
And desire which the Shadow,
Leading me swiftly through the caverns of darkness,
Could not extinguish.
Listen to me, ye who live in the senses
And think through the senses only:
Immortality is not a gift,
Immortality is an achievement;

296

And only those who strive mightily
Shall possess it."

"That poem was my first intimation of an affinity between the Vedas and the Christian Scriptures. Apparently each of them had the same regard for spirit-motivations in experience and spirit-realizations which give all life its light, music, and everlivingness.

"My more recent conversations with Swami Akhilananda have confirmed my earlier regard for the Vedas and their search for spiritual truth. Obviously he believes, as I and all sincere Christians do, that there is a thing-world of the senses, color, fragrance, light, and sound; and behind and beyond that thing-world is a thought-world of words, ideas and purposes; and behind and beyond both of those worlds is the power-world of spirit, giving all worlds their lustor, life and fruitfulness. Jeremiah saw it and heard it in an almond branch of which the All-Pervading Spirit seemed to say: "Behold I bloom through my word to perform it." The author of the Fourth Gospel saw it and heard it in "a light shining in darkness and the darkness comprehendeth it not, the darkness overcometh it not," and in a voice which said: "I am the vine; ye are the branches; abide in me and I in you; as the branch cannot bear fruit of itself except it abide in the vine, no more can ye except ye abide In me." And that same Light and that same Voice eventually "planted a tree by the river of life, whose leaves shall be for the healing of the nations."

"That, it seems to me, is what Swami Akhilananda did and what he meant to say when he placed the picture of our great teacher, Jesus, beside the picture of your great teacher, Ramakrishna. Both of them sought to know the truth, which alone can make men free. Both of them followed that light even unto the end of the world of things and the world of thoughts into the world of spirit where all differences of belief must finally be reconciled and all tragedies of life redeemed.

"Thank you for giving me this opportunity to confess our common faith in the highest things we know. These will eventually bring, I am sure, even in times like ours, a brave new world of freedom, appreciative understanding, and good will. This is, indeed, the tree of life whose leaves are for the healing of the nations."

At the conclusion of Dr. Marlatt's speech, Swami Akhilananda expressed his gratitude and appreciation to the students and friends who had contributed in many ways to the acquiring of this new home for the Society. He also thanked the speakers and all those present for coming to share in the joy of the dedication. Swami then gave his best wishes to all, and with a final prayer of benediction, the evening service was brought to a close.

Simple refreshments were served, and everyone had an opportunity of greeting the Swamis, and of expressing happiness at the opening of the new Centre. Indeed, those who witnessed these beautiful services can never forget them, but will always cherish the memory of this day in their hearts.

INDEX

Printed in the United States
203220BV00001B/5/A